POW on the Sumatra Railway

This book is dedicated, not only to my dad, John Geoffrey Lee, but to all the brave people who endured capture and slavery by the Japanese in the Far East during the Second World War.

To those brave souls who never returned home and were cruelly treated by their captors and died of horrific injuries or diseases.

To those brave souls, like my dad, who returned home, were cruelly treated, suffered many diseases and had to live with their demons and illnesses for the rest of their lives.

At the going down of the sun, and in the morning
We will remember them.

('For the Fallen', Laurence Binyon)

POW on the Sumatra Railway

JOHN GEOFFREY LEE

EDITED BY CHRISTINE AND EDDIE BRIDGES

Pen & Sword
MILITARY

AN IMPRINT OF PEN & SWORD BOOKS LTD.
YORKSHIRE – PHILADELPHIA

First published in Great Britain in 2022 by
PEN AND SWORD MILITARY
An imprint of
Pen & Sword Books Limited
Yorkshire – Philadelphia

ISBN 978 1 39901 525 7

Typeset in Times New Roman 11.5/14 by
SJmagic DESIGN SERVICES, India.
Printed and bound in the UK by CPI Group (UK) Ltd.

Pen & Sword Books Limited incorporates the imprints of Atlas, Archaeology,
Aviation, Discovery, Family History, Fiction, History, Maritime, Military, Military
Classics, Politics, Select, Transport, True Crime, Air World, Frontline Publishing,
Leo Cooper, Remember When, Seaforth Publishing, The Praetorian Press,
Wharncliffe Local History, Wharncliffe Transport, Wharncliffe True Crime and
White Owl.

For a complete list of Pen & Sword titles please contact
PEN & SWORD BOOKS LIMITED
47 Church Street, Barnsley, South Yorkshire S70 2AS, United Kingdom
E-mail: enquiries@pen-and-sword.co.uk
Website: www.pen-and-sword.co.uk

Or
PEN AND SWORD BOOKS
1950 Lawrence Rd, Havertown, PA 19083, USA
E-mail: Uspen-and-sword@casematepublishers.com
Website: www.penandswordbooks.com

Contents

PART TWO

Foreword

by Christine Bridges

My dad was John Geoffrey Lee, born on 26 June 1921 in a cottage in Clifton village in Nottingham. He was the youngest son of Adolphus and Annie Lee and had a sister Norah and two brothers, James and Albert. Dad, always known as Geoff, had lost both of his parents in 1937. He joined the RAF on his birthday in 1941, aged 20. Growing up, I knew he had been a prisoner of war, but he never spoke about this until I was older. I think this was partly due to a 'stiff upper lip' and 'just get on with life' attitude, but eventually he needed to find out the truth about his time as a Far Eastern prisoner of war. It became his life's mission.

This is entirely his story – the result of years of his research, of travelling around the world and contacting other survivors and their families, collating the details about what he discovered, and writing to get this book finished and the truth finally told. He became an avid researcher and was doing in the 1980s and 1990s what online associations, such as the Far Eastern Prisoners of War Association (FEPOW), the Children of Far Eastern Prisoners of War (COFEPOW) and the Java 42 Club, are doing now; he'd be answering up to fifty letters a day while his phone was constantly ringing. There are numerous people around the world who are grateful to him for informing them of the fate or otherwise of loved ones and comrades. Many relatives of those servicemen only ever received an official 'Killed in Action' or 'Missing in Action' 'somewhere in South East Asia' at the time. My dad compiled lists of where people had died and where they were buried, and made sure people knew about his findings.

His book was first written with two fingers on a typewriter, long before word processors and computers were thought of, and it took him five years to write. Sadly, he could not find a publisher and he passed away on 22 June 2002, just before his eighty-first birthday, without seeing his work published. In bringing his book to publication, I have tried to change as little as possible so as to retain his original 'voice', although the text has been sensitively edited for purposes of clarity and consistency. Now having the benefit of the internet and therefore much easier and quicker access to information and sources than he had, in checking his facts I have found the occasional anomaly, such as in exact details and their timings, or the spellings of place names. Where necessary I have added notes to amend or clarify the details. For the most part, the text remains much as my dad wrote it, in a narrative style that he felt would bring the historical events to life, and I hope he would be proud that, at last, his story is being shared as he always intended.

Glossary

Acker/s	Forces slang for money
Chunkel	A large hoe or Malayan shovel
COFEPOW	Children of Far Eastern Prisoners of War
Copra	Coconut kernels
CWGC	Commonwealth War Graves Commission
FEPOW	Far Eastern Prisoners of War
Fishplate	A flat piece of metal used to connect adjacent rails in a railway track
FO	Flying officer
Godowns	Warehouses
Hara-kiri/harakiri	A form of Japanese ritual suicide by disembowelment, using a short blade to cut the belly from left to right
IWM	Imperial War Museum
Kampong	A Malayan enclosure or village
MO	Medical officer
MOD	Ministry of Defence
NAAFI	Navy, Army and Air Force Institutes
NMA	National Memorial Arboretum (Alrewas, Staffordshire)
Parang	A Malayan machete
PT	Physical training
Romusha	Japanese word for labourer, or 'forced labourer' when referring to those made to work in the Dutch East Indies under Japanese occupation during the Second World War
RSA club	Royal New Zealand Returned Services Association club
Trishaw	A three-wheeled cycle carriage
WAAF	Women's Auxiliary Air Force

ix

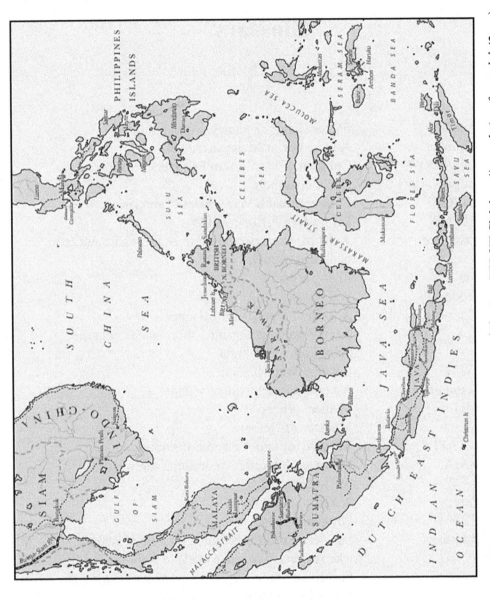

Map of Asia 1942. (*By Brian J. Green, courtesy of The Java FEPOW Club http://www.thejavafepowclub42.org*)

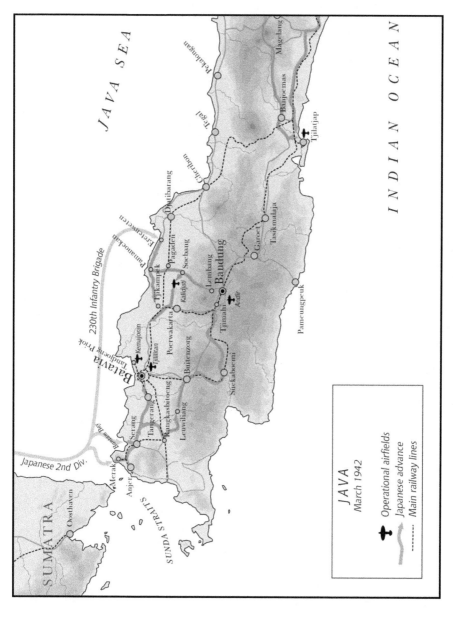

Map of Java 1942. (*By Brian J. Green, courtesy of The Java FEPOW Club http://www.thejavafepowclub42.org*)

PART ONE

Chapter 1

Farewell England

In 1976, neither the Imperial War Museum nor the Commonwealth War Graves Commission would believe me. Oh, they certainly knew all about the infamous Second World War Burma Railway and the terrible treatment meted out to the prisoners of the Japanese during the building of it, but nothing about the Sumatra Railway. Was I supposed to have made it all up? I had retained my released prisoner's pay book, which shows my date of release as 20 September 1945, at Logas, Pakenbaru,[1] Sumatra. I *had* helped to build a railway.

I knew what I had to do. I had to go back to Sumatra and take photographs. If the war historians needed proof, I'd supply it. This was my life's mission; this was my big challenge, and I had to succeed.

The date was 3 February 1980. My flight on Concorde was booked. I was due to leave Heathrow for Singapore at 2.30 pm, via Bahrain, but my destination was Sumatra. This was where I had spent the last twelve months of my three and a half years as a prisoner of war of the Japanese, building that railway. It began in 1941. I was 20 years old, an airman with 84 Squadron RAF, weighing 10 stone, and I ended up a 6-stone skeleton.

Over the tannoy came: 'Fasten your seat belts.' We were off, the ground receding beneath the birdlike plane. I was going back. Was I crazy? Who in his right mind would want to return to those hellish, endless days and years in Japanese prisoner of war camps? But of course, I would not be going back to those times, just to the places where I had been incarcerated and forced to work. I intended to visit as many locations as possible. My camera was a good one and I had plenty of film. The flight was to be a long one, so I settled back and closed my eyes.

That other journey had begun thirty-nine years ago – in a ship, not a plane. The date was 11 November 1941, two years after the start of the Second World War. At exactly thirty minutes before midnight I was boarding a large liner. Her name was the *Empress of Asia*.

Initially there was confusion regarding the allocation of bunks. Things soon settled down enough to enable me to snatch a few hours' much-needed sleep. With the coming of dawn, the engines started and we began moving away from Liverpool, not knowing for where we were bound, but not unduly worried. I was determined to enjoy this new experience to the full.

Walking on the deck as the mist cleared, I thought I heard my name called. Yes, there it was again – 'Geoff' – but it must be for someone else, I thought. I had been put on the draft as a reserve after spending just a couple of days at Kirby transit camp.[2] Again, 'Geoff, Geoff, it's me, Cyril.' Then I saw him coming towards me – Cyril Whitehead. We had been pals for years; we'd joined up at the same time, he in the army and I in the RAF. We had spent our embarkation leave together in Nottingham. His parents had seen us both off from the Midland Station just two weeks before.

My parents had died when I was 16. My sister Norah, to whom I was very close, was living in Colwyn Bay, and a letter I had received a few days ago told of the sad death of her husband. She would be moving to an address in Hope Drive, Nottingham. My brother Jim was also overseas with the army. Cyril and I had a lot to talk about.

'Do you remember the School of Dancing above Burtons in Hockley?' he asked.

'Oh yes, I'd two left feet. You were much better than me,' was my reply.

Then he mentioned Bill and Sis Wilford, and their three daughters, Joan, Doreen and Betty. Bill was the landlord of the King of the French public house on Woolpack Lane, Nottingham. We talked about the long hours we'd spent firewatching on top of the Tudor cinema. We could have gone on reminiscing, but duty called; guard duty and lectures on board were compulsory.

The *Empress* had joined a large convoy, which was escorted by many destroyers steaming south in the Atlantic. The convoy was called Winston's Specials, code-named WS 12Z. Three days out from Liverpool, passing through the Bay of Biscay, I saw for the first time the fury of a storm at sea. I was young and fit and liked nothing better than standing in the bow of the liner watching the gigantic waves tossing the ships about like corks. The liner *Arundel Castle* was ahead of us. It rose way above us, and then plunged back between the waves. All around were men heaving over the

4

side with seasickness. Cyril could not eat for days, even after the storm subsided. I couldn't resist offering to get him some greasy bacon and fried bread. Due to the conflict of our duties we had little time to meet, but on one rare occasion he was writing a letter home and I asked him to send my regards to his parents and thank them for all the hospitality they had shown me on the many visits to their home over the years.

I became aware that we were no longer travelling south. Then, in the distance, there was the sound of explosions and I could see one ship was on fire, sinking within minutes. This caused a feeling of apprehension in all of us. Was this an accidental fire and explosion? Or was there a German submarine out there? Several destroyers passed us at full speed, their klaxon horns blaring, then the sound of another explosion, and another, then several more ... but these were different. A plume of water rose into the air after each detonation, which indicated that depth charges were being dropped. This was confirmed by an announcement over the tannoy: 'A German U-boat has been destroyed, but one of our supply ships has been sunk. The crew were saved.'

With the temperature rising, we now wore tropical kit as we sailed south, without further incident, soon coming within sight of land on our port side. As we entered a harbour, another tannoy announcement told us this was Freetown, Sierra Leone, known as the White Man's Grave,[3] and there would be no shore leave while the ships refuelled. We could buy fruit from the native boats, providing it was well washed before being eaten.

With the coal barges moored on the port side, the natives' boats jostled for position on the starboard side, the occupants eager to sell their fruit. We lowered baskets, with money inside, from the deck. With luck they would be filled with fruit to the value of the money enclosed. Often the money was taken, with the boatmen rowing away without leaving any fruit, no doubt laughing their heads off. For my shilling I was fortunate to receive six bananas and two oranges, while Cyril was one of the many who got nothing. Three bananas and an orange each was something we had not seen in England in a long time.

Sailing out of the harbour, away from the sticky equatorial heat and into the cooling breezes of the open sea, the convoy reformed and continued its journey south, remaining in sight of land. On 9 December an announcement was made informing us that the Japanese, without warning, had attacked the US naval base at Pearl Harbor in the Pacific,

5

doing considerable damage to the fleet and installations. The American reaction was to declare war on Japan, Germany and Italy. England declared war on Japan.

The days passed pleasantly in the company of my new-found friends: Reg Webster, who lived on Huntingdon Street in Nottingham, Ginger Collins, from Middlesbrough, Bill Woodhouse, the eldest of the group and the only one married, who lived in Darnell, Sheffield, and the tall Scotsman, Jock McLeod, whose broad accent was difficult to understand at first. On deck one morning, the four came over to me. Bill was carrying a mug of water and said, 'The committee has decided that Geoffrey is too formal. From now on your name will be Taz.' He poured the water over my head.

We had turned east and could see the unmistakable outline of Table Mountain, at Cape Town. A few days later we arrived at Durban. The date was 23 December 1941. An incredible sight greeted us as we docked. A band played and hundreds of people, with dozens of cars alongside the dock, were ready to take us to their homes. By sheer luck, Cyril and I were taken to the same house. We had to return to the *Empress of Asia* by midnight, but our hosts were waiting for us at eight o'clock the next morning, displaying the names of their guests on placards. They took us on sightseeing tours of the city and treated us to super meals. With the temperature in the eighties, Christmas dinner was served on the veranda of their home. The four days passed all too quickly and our thanks seemed so inadequate to repay those wonderful people for their time, trouble, expense and hospitality. Then, sadly, came the goodbyes before we returned to the ship.

At dawn on 27 December we were ordered to parade on the dockside with all our kit. After the roll call, we were marched along the dock to where a small coaster was berthed. This was to be our next transport for the continuance of the journey. We still had no idea as to the ultimate destination. There were no bunks on this boat, so we had to collect a palliasse each, with instructions to find a space either on or below deck. Our group was together again, after being with different families ashore, and we chose to sleep on the open deck under an awning. The boat was somewhat overcrowded, with 600 RAF men and a small contingent of army personnel, and, wonder of wonders, Cyril was there again. The direction the boat would take after leaving Durban would give some indication as to our next port of call: north would take us to Egypt;

north-east to Ceylon. But as the sun sank behind the land mass, we were still heading east. With the dawn, Egypt became the most likely destination as we were then travelling due north.

There were no lectures to attend, just PT before breakfast, leaving plenty of time to talk about the four days in Durban. We had all been taken to different places, but possibly the most striking sights were the city lights at night – street lights, shop windows ablaze, fountains illuminated in various colours, and tall, floodlit buildings – such a contrast to the dark, blacked-out cities we had left behind in England. As we sailed through the calm waters of the Indian Ocean, dolphins were swimming alongside the boat, with flying fish leaping from the water as we crossed the Equator. Soon land could be seen on either side of us, which must mean we had entered the Red Sea, heading towards the Suez Canal. Four days after leaving Durban we docked at Port Teufiq, Egypt.[4]

Disembarking, I spotted Cyril just as we were ordered to fall in on parade. All I could do was shout, 'Cheerio, Cyril, see you back in Nottingham.'

He waved and called back: 'Good luck, Geoff, look after yourself.' Then we had to go our separate ways. Trucks were waiting to transport us to the RAF station at Heliopolis, near Cairo. This was an aerodrome with a variety of aircraft, including Spitfires and Hurricanes, while on the far side could be seen Blenheim bombers. Our first stop was the parade ground in front of the permanent buildings.

After the roll call a flight sergeant addressed us: 'You are here to join two bomber squadrons, both flying Blenheims. The names called out will move to the left to join 84 Squadron, the remainder will join 211 Squadron.' As the names were called, we were hoping that our five would not be split up. Bill was the first to be named, Jock the next, then Reg and me, and finally, Ginger. We could stay together.

Near the Blenheims was a tented area, which was to be our accommodation. Our first task was to arrange a round-the-clock guard against opportunist thieves who might attempt to remove equipment from the aircraft. As soon as darkness fell, we realised that Egypt was subject to immense changes in temperature – sweltering heat during the day but freezing at night under the clear sky, causing us to change from tropical kit to blue uniform with greatcoats. On the first pay parade we each received a 100-acker note. Those who were not on a guard detail were given permission to visit Cairo, with the proviso that we return to camp before six o'clock in the evening. On board the tram, the conductor went berserk when we each offered our 100-acker note for a three-pound ride.

There were about 100 airmen on this outing. We had been told that the NAAFI was on the right, along the street, opposite the tram terminus. Bill and I kept close to the main bunch, having no desire to get lost in a strange city. What we saw of Cairo was a complete contrast to the clean, airy city of Durban. Here the narrow, dirty streets were teeming with poorly dressed people, children begging and old women offering an assortment of goods from baskets on the pavements. There were few motor vehicles apart from British service trucks. Most shops were dull and uninteresting, apart from those selling the hand-crafted filigree silver bangles and necklaces for a few pounds each, which I thought would make a nice present for Norah. Bill wanted to buy a set for his wife. We each offered our acker note, which the shopkeeper was unable to change. I then saw an attractive enamelled cigarette case – black background with a Japanese motif and a picture of a volcano on the front. The vendor could now change one note for the two sets and the cigarette case. Quite a nice souvenir of Egypt, I thought. Then I looked on the back. It was clearly marked: 'Made in Birmingham'.

Reaching the NAAFI, it was time to eat. By paying five ackers each we could have as much food as we could eat. Sitting at our table was a soldier from a British Army camp,[5] the same unit as my brother Jim, whom I had not heard from for some time before leaving England. Perhaps a silly question, but I asked him: 'Do you happen to know Jim Lee, my brother?'

He replied, 'Yes, he comes from Nottingham, he's in the same camp as myself, Gizeh,[6] just outside Cairo.'

We all had the right change for the return journey to Heliopolis. Bill and I were due for guard duty at eight o'clock until midnight, guarding the aircraft. We were dressed as if for an English winter's day and armed with a Lee Enfield rifle. Our orders were to fire into the air should intruders be spotted. Luckily my watch passed without incident.

After the morning parade, I asked permission to visit the army camp in the hope of seeing my brother. Permission was granted. I could travel on the truck that was due to leave for Gizeh. The return journey would not be a problem as vehicles going to Cairo had to pass Heliopolis. We passed the pyramids and the Sphinx as we neared the army camp. When I arrived there, I was very disappointed to learn that Jim had been posted to a new camp that morning.

Chapter 2

Where Now?

It was the middle of January 1942, and for the last few days Heliopolis had been buzzing with activity as the Blenheims were prepared for take-off to an undisclosed destination. The news from the Far East was far from good. Japanese troops had landed in northern Malaya and were moving south against limited resistance. Rumours abounded that our departure was imminent. Would we be going to the Far East? Ordered to parade with full kit, we then boarded the waiting trucks to be driven back to Port Teufiq. From there we embarked on the SS *Yoma*, an old cargo ship that was ill-equipped to transport 600 airmen and the ground crew of 84 and 211 squadrons.

Sailing south through the mirror-like Red Sea, we were plagued by cockroaches. They were everywhere – in the bread, the soup, and crawling over the bunks at night; no matter how many we killed, their numbers didn't seem to decrease. It was driving us all insane. Three days later we arrived at Aden, at the southern end of the Red Sea, where we were allowed to go ashore to the town of Crater – a very apt name as it was in the hollow of an extinct volcano. A more desolate, dusty, hot and plantless place I had never seen. Walking out of the small town, gazing down from the barren hills overlooking Aden harbour, the white sails of the fishermen's boats against the azure sea was a pleasant sight.

Back on board the *Yoma* we were soon under way, sailing south-east through the Arabian Sea, into the Indian Ocean. We had the opportunity to meet new acquaintances, knowing them only by their nicknames and where they came from. There was a small lad, Ginger, from Glasgow, Taffy from Cardiff, Spud from Lincoln, and many more. If any of my mates heard me introduce myself as Geoff, they would chime in with, 'This is Taz, short for Tazreal from Shakespeare.' So, I would stay Taz.

The next port we called at was Colombo, Ceylon (now Sri Lanka). It was obvious now that our final destination was intended to be Singapore.

The news came through that the Japanese had occupied Hong Kong. They had also landed troops near Bangkok, Thailand, while Singapore had suffered its first air raid. Sea battles were raging around the Philippines and the Marshall and Gilbert islands in the Pacific.

There was a pay parade, this time in rupees, before we disembarked from the *Yoma*. Orders were given that we could go ashore each day while the ship was in port but must return by 8.00 pm in the evening. Walking from the dockside into the town proper, it was busy and bustling. The local inhabitants were moving with purpose. Most of the men wore dark-coloured sarongs, while the womenfolk were dressed in colourful silk saris. Bicycles were the commonest form of transport, with tricycles for carrying passengers. As Reg pointed out, most were made by Raleigh of Nottingham. Some shops were well stocked with fruit and vegetables, many of which we could not put a name to, while others displayed clothing, jewellery and carved ivory trinkets.

Jock, who had stopped to read a poster, called to us: 'Taz, Bill, this sounds nice. How about going there?' It was an invitation to visit the beautiful resort of Trincomalee, on the east coast, a three-hour bus ride through the Ceylonese countryside. There was not enough time to go that day but we made enquiries for a trip the following day. After eating a meal of highly spiced local food at the NAAFI, we wandered around Colombo looking at the fine buildings, including white mosques with slender minarets, some in reddish sandstone, with intricate carvings. By six o'clock it was time to think about returning to the *Yoma*, but which way? No one could be sure. The only answer was to go by tricycle.

The next morning, breakfast over and with the parade on the dockside dismissed, our party and several other chaps who had decided to go with us were eager to set off on the trip to Trincomalee. We boarded the Bedford bus, with all thirty seats occupied, and we were soon on our way, passing through avenues of flowering trees and tall coconut palms and catching an occasional glimpse of exotic birds. Reaching the hills, the views were magnificent, with people working in tiered paddy fields that reached down to the valley, where groups of houses could be seen nestling in groves of palm trees. We crossed bridges that spanned tumbling white water in deep gorges before leaving the hills as we neared the coast. Yes, the poster in Colombo was correct: Trincomalee was beautiful, the blue sea lapping gently onto a white sandy beach stretching either way as far as the eye could see. But there was something missing. Where were the people? There was no happy atmosphere one would expect at such a holiday resort. Most of the high-class hotels were closed, or occupied by service personnel, and only a few shops were open for business. It dawned on us that this must have been a stopover calling place for wealthy Europeans on sea cruises before the war. Those days had now gone. We had just a few hours to enjoy ourselves, in the sea and on the beach, and going for a meal at a nearby café. We had no option but to eat the local food, which I was beginning to enjoy, but Bill and Reg were not too keen. 'Too blooming hot,' was their verdict. The bus left at three o'clock for the return journey, after checking that all thirty chaps were on board. Apart from a short hold-up due to elephants being used to drag tree trunks across the road from the woods, it was free of incident.

The following morning we were given the order not to go out of Colombo and to be back on board by two o'clock. So this was to be the last time ashore, possibly for some time. But where would we land next? We all plumped for Singapore, having little knowledge of the Far East. At the NAAFI for our midday meal, Ginger said, 'Thank God for some decent food,' and this was echoed by the other three as they tucked into a large plate of fish and chips while I ate curry and rice. During the afternoon it was necessary to launder our clothing, which soon dried in the heat of the sun. Although there were no facilities to press our tropical tunics and shorts, the ship's crew were willing to do this for us in exchange for cigarettes.

I was awakened by the sound of the ship's engines as it moved out of the harbour. It was a dark, moonless night and myriads of stars appeared to hang like jewels from the cloudless sky, while in the east, the first glimmer of dawn reflected from the calm sea. Studying Bill's atlas, we decided the more direct route to Singapore would be north-east, through the Indian Ocean and into the Malacca Straits, north of Sumatra. At sunset it was clear that our course was south-east, which would take us across the Equator, heading for Java or Sumatra in the Dutch East Indies. The slight hum from the tannoy indicated that an announcement was imminent: 'Good morning, this is Squadron Leader Taylor. I know some of you have been plotting our passage; well, we have just crossed the Equator. Our aircraft have flown from Malaya to P2, an airfield at Palembang, Sumatra, hence the change of plan.'

Just after midday, land could be seen on the port bow. Drawing closer we could make out a small island with a larger mass beyond. Was this

Sumatra? The answer came the following morning when we docked at Oosthaven, the southernmost point of the large island of Sumatra. The date was Friday, 13 February 1942.

As only one in five men of the ground crew had a rifle, only they disembarked. This included me – the only one in our small group who had a rifle. Our kitbags were to stay on the *Yoma*. We took side packs containing eating and toilet needs. With no transport available we set off on foot towards Palembang. The oppressive heat and sudden downpours of torrential rain made the going extremely difficult along what could only be called a jungle track. As darkness fell, we came to a rope factory. This was to be our shelter for the night. After a meal of bully beef and biscuits it was hard to find a resting place for the 130 in the party. Although we were tired, sleep was impossible. Dozens of rats were running everywhere and there were strange sounds of animals and birds, and sometimes the noise of something moving through the undergrowth. Was it man or beast? We did not go to see, but just stayed quiet and showed no lights.

At dawn we resumed our journey, soon coming to a native kampong. Having no back-up supplies, food was our main concern. Without Dutch currency, barter with cigarettes and chocolate was the only means of obtaining cooked rice, bananas and green coconuts. We preferred to drink coconut milk rather than the available water. Nearby was a fast-flowing river, spanned by a stone bridge. Unlike the track we had come by, here was a main road, with army trucks driving past. A sergeant called us together, and then an officer addressed us:

'This is as far as we go. The Blenheims have left Palembang and have gone to an airfield in Java. We are to stay here to guard this bridge until the British, Australian and Dutch convoys have gone by. An explosive charge is to be placed under the bridge, and no one must cross to the other side. A twenty-four-hour rota of guard duties will be drawn up. Our accommodation is some empty native huts close by, but first trenches must be dug along the riverbank. That is all for now, apart from the news that the Fleet flagship, HMS *Prince of Wales*, and HMS *Repulse* have been sunk by torpedo bombers, off the east coast of Malaya.'

Heck! What is happening out there? Was there no way of stopping the Japanese? Perhaps they were already on the far side of this bridge. I'd rather face the cockroaches on *Yoma*! In the huts we were all disconsolate, the question, to which we had no answer: 'Why hadn't the army taken over from us?' They had better equipment. Our place was with the aircraft.

On my first duty that evening I was given instructions to fire at any movement on the far bank. Soon a flying officer approached me, saying, 'Keep a close watch on the branches floating down the river. It is known the Japanese use this method to cross rivers.' Dutifully, I concentrated on the debris – mostly small, with little foliage, presenting no threat. But I did not see the officer leave the bridge. Turning my attention to the far side of the river, it gave me a shock when I saw a quick glimmer of light, like someone lighting a cigarette. I fired my rifle. A figure emerged, shouting: 'Don't shoot. It's only me!'

The flying officer came back across the bridge. The whole unit turned out on hearing my shot. Red-faced, he explained, 'I only wanted to see if the guard was alert.'

Our senior officer told him: 'Don't ever do such a stupid stunt again! Anyone else crossing the bridge will be put on a charge. Understand?'

I needed no rocking to sleep after finishing my guard duty. With lack of sleep the previous night, even the sounds of the fauna did not disturb me. With the morning a supply truck arrived bringing a welcome issue of food. Now we could have something other than bully beef and biscuits. A consignment of Tommy guns had also been brought, together with an explosive charge with which to destroy the bridge. The guns were something new to us. After reading the enclosed instructions, we were able to assemble them.

News came through that Singapore had been taken by the Japanese. At the same time, Jap paratroopers had landed on P1 and P2 airfields at Palembang, just a few miles from us. The next two days passed without incident. No trucks had gone by for a while and it was with relief that we heard that transport was coming to take us back to Oosthaven. With the sound of the explosion as the bridge blew up ringing in our ears, I had no regrets at leaving this wet, dank and mosquito-ridden place.

A scene of utter devastation greeted us on our arrival at Oosthaven. All around buildings were burning and explosions could be heard, although it wasn't an air raid as we first thought, but the results of a scorched-earth policy. Anything that couldn't be moved was being destroyed: oil storage tanks ablaze, shuddering explosions as dockside godowns collapsed and cranes toppled into the water. There was no sign of the *Yoma*. We would be leaving Sumatra on a former pleasure steamer, which appeared to be overcrowded as we boarded for the short journey to Java. An English-speaking Dutchman pointed to the jagged rocks we were passing, explaining: 'That is what is left of the volcano Krakotao,[1] which erupted in 1883, causing the biggest bang ever recorded. Tidal waves destroyed many towns and villages on the coast of Sumatra and Java, even reaching the Indian coast. The dust created was said to have circled the Earth many times.'

We reached Batavia (now Jakarta) amid the shriek and thump of falling bombs. The only opposition to the Jap bombers seemed to come from HMAS *Sydney* and HMAS *Perth* anchored in the harbour. They had some success: one plane crashed on our port side. On disembarking, Dutch troops took away our firearms. Batavia was to be declared an open city. During a lull in the bombing, which was for the most part confined to the docks area, I went to the open godowns to find some food. There was a lot of activity, as the *Sydney* and *Perth* and HMS *Ajax* had docked to load supplies.

Nearby, the *Yoma* was berthed. I had the idea I might be able to get my kitbag as I needed to get a change of clothing. I had been wearing what I had on since arriving in Sumatra. My tunic and shorts were mud and sweat-stained, my socks hard, after being wet and drying on my feet many times. No one challenged me as I went up the gangway onto the deck. The first hold was empty, with the lower holds closed, as was the next. It dawned on me that I was on a fool's errand. If I found the kitbags, how could I identify my own? While looking in the next hold, which contained some crates but nothing else, a naval officer approached me. 'What are you looking for?' he asked. I explained, and he replied: 'You can't get at them; they're in the lower hold. Go and find something useful to do.' I went ashore. (Why hadn't I the gift of foresight? It would have saved me years of agony and starvation.)

Back at a damaged building, still burning at one end, I found a broken crate containing blankets. A label stated: 'Made in USA. Guaranteed proof against bugs, lice and fleas for two years.' One would not be missed. Nearby was another crate containing small portable radios, again made in the USA. There was room for one in my side pack. Then I saw a quantity of torpedoes at the far end. Hardly the place to be should the bombers return, so I hurried away. Walking away from the docks, along a road flanked by flowering trees, I saw a group of airmen ahead of me. As I drew closer, I recognised the tall figure of Jock. 'Jock, wait for me,' I shouted.

He turned. 'Taz, it's good to see you,' came the reply.

I could see Bill, Reg and little Ginger were also there. From the greeting one would think I'd been away for months rather than days. The questions came thick and fast: 'What have you been doing?' 'When did you arrive?' 'You look as if you've been pulled through a hedge backwards.' Bill cut the questions short: 'We'll have to get a move on. There's a pay parade at a Dutch barracks in half an hour.' That was welcome news. As I lined up for my pay, I was taken aside for being improperly dressed. My reasons were accepted.

We each received sixteen guilders (about £4 then)[2] and were told we would be paid an extra guilder a day by the Dutch government during our stay in the Dutch East Indies. After the pay parade a meal was provided at the barracks. It consisted of fried rice, meat, vegetables and fish, with garlic and chilli. This they called Nasi goreng. (I thought they said Nazi Goring!)

The sudden influx of Allied troops from Singapore and Sumatra had caused an accommodation problem. Bill and the others had already been billeted with Dutch families. Thankfully, the lady of the house I was taken to could speak a little English, as I, like the rest, couldn't speak Dutch. Her husband had been called into the army. The two sons moved into one bedroom, leaving me the back room in this pleasant, air-conditioned house. Answering my knock at the door, the lady asked: 'You haven't any other clothes?'

'No. My kit-bag is still on the ship,' I replied.

'Then wear these while I wash yours; they belong to my husband.'

After a much-needed bath I put on the clothes. He must be a very large man, I thought. Two fellows my size could almost have got into his shirts and shorts, but it was nice to feel clean again. After another meal of Nasi goreng, which was much better than the army version, I was then to bed.

The weariness of the previous day disappeared after a good night's sleep on a soft bed. Soon the lady brought my clean socks and underwear, with my tropical uniform neatly pressed. After a quick breakfast, I had to hurry for the 9.00 am parade at the barracks. 'You certainly look more human,' remarked Ginger as I joined my mates.

Flight Sergeant Brown addressed us: 'You can spend the day in town but keep away from the docks.' We really didn't need to be told that; we could hear the bombs from here. He continued: 'Tomorrow morning you will parade with full kit. You will be going to an airfield in central Java.'

We spent a pleasant day in Batavia, a clean city with wide roads and well-stocked shops. Tall municipal buildings stood alongside European-style churches and ornate mosques. The most outstanding among the people were the Eurasian girls – tall, dark-haired, slim, with slightly tanned skins and fine features. Later, in the evening, I set up my radio and after a time I tuned in to an English news programme. Then I wished I hadn't. In a cultured voice the announcer gave the bad news: 'Allied forces have been forced back to the Egyptian border. The Japanese have overrun a number of islands in the Pacific and bombing is reported from several coastal towns in Java. The warships *Sydney*, *Perth* and *Ajax* have been sunk in the Java Sea.'[3] I switched off. A deep feeling of foreboding came over me.

Chapter 3

Java Journey

On the morning parade I told my mates what I had heard on the radio. They were also apprehensive: 'It doesn't sound too blooming good but at least our kites are still flying.' Our own drivers were to drive the Dutch trucks that were lined up ready to transport us to the airfield. Soon we were aboard and on our way, leaving Batavia in a southerly direction on a deserted, gently rising road. We passed through avenues of trees until we reached the open countryside. The views were breathtaking. If only I had my camera!

After about an hour, our truck, the fourth in the convoy, came to a halt. All the others stopped. 'What is wrong?' enquired an officer.

'The clutch has gone, sir,' The driver replied.

'All of you find room on the other trucks. Driver, you stay here, I'll send help as soon as I can,' said the officer. Turning to me, being the last to get off the truck, he said: 'You stay with him.'

Tommo, a cockney, and I sat by the roadside for a while talking about home and what we thought would be the outcome of this episode. 'It'll all come out in the wash,' he joked.

It was peaceful and quiet, and it was hard to realise that only a few miles away guns were roaring and bombs falling. The scenery around us was magnificent. On one side paddy fields rose in tiers to distant mountains, hazy blue in the midday heat. One of the highest had a plume of smoke emitting from its peak. Groves of coconut palms must have been the sites of native villages, the homes of those who could be seen working in the fields.

Looking down the other side, where the ground fell away, still in tiers, the topmost fields were devoid of vegetation, while the lower ones ranged in colour from the gold of the ripe crop, to various shades of green. In the valley was a large river with buildings on either side. Several hours passed.

'I wish they would hurry up,' remarked Tommo, 'I'm hungry.'

'So am I. A nice thick steak with fried onions, washed down with a cool pint of beer would do nicely.'

The need for food and water was now urgent as we hadn't eaten since dawn.

'Tommo, you wait here while I go down there to buy some food. I've got some money,' I said.

There was no direct route to the valley because the paddy fields were staggered and I had to walk between two, turn left or right on reaching the next field, then step down about 18 inches to the next path. It was a pleasant walk, passing people busy in the fields who gave me a quick glance and carried on working. The inhabitants of the village greeted me in a friendly manner and with sign language they understood my needs. I bought some native food wrapped in banana leaves, filled my water bottle, drank some coconut milk, and then set off on the return journey.

Soon darkness came with the suddenness typical of the tropics. Unable to see the pathway ahead, I wandered aimlessly, stepping up in the wrong places, and without any landmark became disorientated. After what seemed like hours I was pleased to see the moon rising above the hills. I thought of Tommo; he must be blooming hungry by now. I had eaten my portion and was hungry again. In the bright moonlight I reached the road, but, within the limit of my vision, there was no sign of the truck. Having no idea which way to go I lay down and went to sleep.

As the morning grew lighter, there was still no sign of the truck. The only landmark to determine my position was the smoking mountain, which had stood out clearly from where the truck had stopped; now it was partly concealed by another mountain. From this I deduced I was too far north. For an hour I walked south, with the sun getting higher in the sky on my left. Still no truck, only a patch of oil on the road where it must have been. The view of the mountain and the clumps of trees were as I recalled seeing them the previous day. But now where to? I had not been told which airfield we were making for. Tommo knew, but he had gone.

I carried on walking until I came to a village, where some Dutch soldiers took me to their barracks. They were unable to tell me where I should go and I gladly accepted their offer of a meal, which they called ristaffel, a variety of dishes from which you help yourself.

For two days I stayed with them, until a convoy of trucks arrived with airmen of 211 and 84 squadrons on board, including my four mates. We were glad to be together again. They told me what had happened at Kalidjati airfield,[1] from where the planes had been making short hop raids, bombing Jap landings on the south coast. A number of planes had been lost. At dawn that morning, Japanese tanks were reported advancing up the runway. After the remaining aircraft had been destroyed on the ground, a rapid evacuation was ordered. There were some casualties. An officer told us the good news: 'Our orders now are to go to Tjilatjap, a port on the south coast, where a ship is waiting to take us to Ceylon.'

'About time somebody got their finger out,' said Reg, giving voice to our thoughts and a sense of relief that there was still a chance of getting off this island. We were all eager to set off for Tjilatjap as soon as possible, but no, we must stay with the Dutch for the night.

I took the opportunity to set up my radio once more, receiving a broadcast from Kandy, Ceylon, after painstaking tuning. A small group of fellows collected to hear the English-speaking announcer: 'The Japanese land forces, supported by superior air cover, are advancing into Burma. Borneo and Celebes have been overrun. Landings by paratroopers and landing craft have been reported from New Guinea and Java.'

'Switch it off, Taz, that's enough,' said Ginger.

A voice from the back interjected: 'Can't anybody stop these Japanese devils?' to which was added a selection of profanities.

With high expectations and in good spirits, we got under way at dawn. The journey of several hours, through lovely Javanese countryside, passed without incident. Tjilatjap was a small town at the mouth of a wide river and we could see the white ship, our passport to Ceylon, as we got down from the trucks. Soon aircraft could be heard approaching. Certain they could not be our planes, we rushed for cover in a nearby coconut grove. The absence of local inhabitants seemed rather strange. They must have left town before our arrival, as if they had had a prior warning, we thought. As the bombs began to fall, directed mainly at the docks, the single Bofors anti-aircraft gun on the dockside was kept firing by the brave gunners, but it was inevitable that it would soon be put out of action. A direct hit and it was gone, along with the poor devils who manned it.

With the Bofors disposed of, the planes flew in lower, hitting the oil storage tanks. The burning oil flowed into the river, engulfing our ship, which had already received a direct hit. One bomb fell on the edge of the grove, felling several trees.

'Phew! That was close. Another on that line would have been curtains for us,' somebody remarked.

'All right, we know. We'd been dreading the next one,' Bill replied.

Thankfully, not one of our chaps was injured. The raid had lasted just over half an hour and now the only sound was the roar and crackle of the burning buildings. We emerged from the trees. One thing was certain: our ship would never be sailing from here; it was ablaze from bow to stern and listing heavily to port. Our thoughts turned to the crew. We had no way of knowing if they had managed to escape, but there was no sign of anyone else in town.

The blazing oil had flowed over the spot where the Bofors had been, leaving no trace of the gun crew. Two of our trucks had been badly damaged, and a car, which had been carrying Dutch guilder notes, had been blown apart, the money blowing about the road.

'Do you want some money?' asked Bill.

'Shouldn't think it'll be any use if the Japs take over, which seems extremely likely.'

An officer called us together: 'You all realise that this was probably our last chance to get away. You must make your own way to Bandoeng,[2] in Central Java. The trucks will leave every fifteen minutes, so as not to attract too much attention. Climb aboard and good luck.'

I asked, 'Is there any reason why we shouldn't take that small truck abandoned down the road?'

'No! It's a good idea. Do you want a driver?'

'Yes.'

As Bill and the other three loaded their kit onto the truck, we were joined by the driver and his mate, also with their kit. There wasn't room for anyone else.

Without any knowledge of the route to Bandoeng, we got under way, soon coming to a fork in the road. Right or left? We didn't know. We went right. After a few miles we were stopped by Dutch soldiers who told us: 'The bridge ahead has been blown up. You'll have to take the other road.'

It wasn't long before the driver stopped. Ahead could be seen Jap paratroopers landing, so we turned to find another route. One Jap pilot dived low over us for a spot of gunnery practice but missed. Fearing he might make another run, we left the truck and dived for cover down a bank. Thankfully, the plane did not return. On the move again, we turned right to try another way, but soon, with a phut, phut, phut … the engine stopped.

'We're out of petrol,' yelled the driver.

Blimey, what now? Walk? But how far? With the other six carrying full kit, the going would be tough.

'Maybe one of the other trucks will come along,' someone suggested.

'Not much chance of that, we haven't seen any of them since leaving Tjilatjap.'

With the sun setting we would have the cool of the night and cover of darkness for the journey. Having no kit myself, I took turns carrying the others' kitbags.

By now we were hungry, and were thankful when we reached a native village after about an hour. At first the natives seemed reluctant to sell us food, but when they saw Dutch money, they relented.

Dawn was breaking when we heard a very British challenge: 'Halt! Who goes there?'

'Is this Bandoeng?' I asked.

'No, it's Poerbolingo,'[3] was the reply.

'There are two trains waiting at the station. Turn down the first road on the left.'

Dutch ladies were serving welcome tea and sandwiches on the station platform. As we boarded the second train, we were each given a tin of bully beef, with the instructions to open one tin at a time and share with three others.

It was dark when I awoke as the train started to move, having slept through the day. There were no lights, but I soon found Bill and the others close by. They had also slept through the day. Our spirits were low, and we spoke in muted voices. Reg didn't exactly cheer us up when he remarked: 'We need boats to leave this island and there won't be any at Bandoeng, if that's where we're going.'

We fell silent, looking into the blackness of the moonless night. As the train went along, showers of red sparks flew past the windows from the wood-burning locomotive. I must have dozed off again, and awoke with a start as a voice from further along the carriage shouted: 'Put that light out!' as someone lit a cigarette. This seemed somewhat illogical. If the Japs were close, they must have been aware the trains were coming by the sound and sparks.

21

Reg broke the silence. 'Back home the daffodils will be blooming, the nights getting shorter and the days getting warmer. Birds are building their nests, while the buds on the trees are bursting into leaf.'

Jock joined in. 'There's still snow on the mountains in Scotland.'

Ginger remarked, 'Yes, in England one can tell which month of the year it is. Here each month is like another. Each day ...' His words were cut short by the noise and shuddering as the brakes were violently applied. Even above that noise the rattle of rifle and machine-gun fire could be heard, punctuated by the thud of mortar fire.

As the train came to a halt we came under fire from the left. Bullets ripped through the carriage sides. A voice from the darkness shouted: 'Keep down and make for the door.'

Ginger let out a yell: 'I've been hit in the arm.'

I reached him and helped him from the carriage, feeling blood as I touched his right arm. The train had stopped on a high embankment covered in shrubs and bracken, making it difficult to negotiate in the darkness, but I managed to get Ginger to the bottom and to safety. 'You stay put, I'll go to find Bill and the others,' I told him.

A crescent moon was rising as I scrambled back to the train. Bullets, fairly high up, were still whistling past. Suddenly I was gripped by sheer panic. Must I go back in there? I'd escaped once, why take the risk? Cries of pain came from inside; maybe my other three mates had been injured. Pull yourself together, Geoff! You know you must help. Calmer now, I crawled into the carriage and called out: 'Bill, Reg, Jock, where are you?'

Bill answered from nearby: 'Give me a hand with this chap, Taz, he's been hit in the leg. Reg and Jock have taken another man out. They think he's dead.'

Others were assisting the wounded, and soon the carriage was clear. Moving forward, in the shelter of the embankment, we saw our engine had stopped just a couple of feet from the first train, which had been derailed but remained upright. It had received severe damage, being nearer to the ambush, and therefore there were more casualties. It was maddening to think that a small group of Japs, possibly fewer than twenty, had been able to ambush two trains carrying some 2,000 men without a rifle between them.

Almost half an hour after leaving the trains, the sound of gunfire having faded away, Dutch soldiers stopped us as we neared a large bridge and told us, 'Charges are set to blow up this bridge in fifteen minutes, at midnight. Your trains were due to arrive more than an hour ago.'

Those assisting the more severely wounded were told to take them to a nearby building where they could receive first aid. Ginger would not go for treatment: 'I'm alright, the bleeding has stopped.'

The rush was now on to get as many as possible across before the deadline. Suddenly there was a terrific explosion behind us, throwing us into a heap. Quickly scrambling to our feet we ran forward, fearing there would be further explosions, but none came. Looking back, we could see that only one of the river spans had been blown up. A Dutch soldier later explained that the fuses had hurriedly been removed from the four spans but it was too late with the fifth. A soldier had died in the attempt. There was no way of knowing how many had died as that section blew up. Anyone falling into the fast-flowing river would have had little chance of survival.

There were still a large number of men on the far bank. Ropes were brought by boat and fixed to the exposed steelwork to enable the men to cross the open space – a tricky job in the pale moonlight. A few rowing boats carried some wounded across the river. There was renewed urgency, with the coming of dawn, to get the remainder to the safe side before the expected attack by the Japs. A new danger could be from the air as the crowded bridge presented an ideal target. An officer shouted an order: 'Clear the bridge as quickly as possible, and scatter among the trees.' We didn't need to be told twice.

The five of us shared a tin of bully beef in silence, not wishing to express our fears for the future. Ginger's injury was not too serious, although he had received another knock when we were blown over, but I soon patched him up with a bandage from my side pack. An officer came over to us as gunfire could be heard from across the bridge and told us, 'There's not much point in hanging around here. I doubt if the Dutch can stop the Japs, who will be eager to take the bridge before it is further damaged, and we're not much use without rifles.'

As we prepared to move away there were four explosions, BOOM-BOOM-BOOM-BOOM! in quick succession, almost as one. The ground shook and the trees swayed from the blast, and debris fell around us without causing any injuries. With the bridge gone the Jap advance would be held up, but recalling the warning I had received at the bridge in Sumatra, it was more than likely they would soon cross the river.

We followed the crowd, having no idea where we were heading for. Late in the afternoon we arrived at a Dutch airfield, Tasikmalaya. There were thousands of British, Dutch and Australian troops gathered there, having come from all directions.

The realisation that our worst fears of the last few days had come about did nothing to raise our flagging spirits. Reg tried to be optimistic, commenting, 'It'll be all over by Christmas; the Yanks will soon drive them back to Japan.' Thankfully, the cookhouse was in operation for the first decent meal in days, which cheered us up to some extent. Maybe things wouldn't be too bad. There was no accommodation available, so we had no option but to sleep under the trees. No great hardship in the tropical heat. The date was Friday, 13 March 1942.[4]

Chapter 4

In the Bag

Several days passed without sight of the Japs, apart from aircraft flying over and some tanks near the perimeter of the airfield. A Glenn Martin bomber of the Dutch Air Force was hidden among the trees and was thought to be airworthy. An attempt to fly it to Australia was envisaged by the squadron leader. Under cover of darkness some of us were detailed to fill in the trenches, which had been dug across the runway to prevent Jap aircraft landing, to give the bomber a clear run. Mechanics checked both engines, but dared not test them, and reported that as far as could be seen they were in good order. The fuel tanks were full, but there was no ammunition for the guns. None of the pilots had flown Glenn Martins before and therefore had no idea of its range. Could it fly the estimated 1,500 miles without refuelling? There were doubts!

The names of twenty aircrew were put into a hat. Only six could go, which must include at least two pilots and two navigators, plus a senior officer and flight mechanic. The proceedings were interrupted by the first instructions from the Japs, via a loudhailer. The unseen Jap spoke in poor English: 'Everyone you place guns where tanks he stand. For each who runs away ten mens shoot. Any aircrafts going hundred mens shoot.'

This message was repeated several times from various positions beyond the perimeter. Not having any firearms to deposit, our meeting was resumed. Would the announcement put paid to the plan? The officer addressed us: 'Nothing has changed, we will go ahead. Those chosen will not be told until departure time, which will be five o'clock in the morning. No kit can be taken. Your help will be needed to manoeuvre the plane to the runway. Don't mention it to anyone outside this group.'

At my suggestion, after the group broke up the five of us went across to the main buildings to try to get some news from my radio. The first building was occupied by Dutch soldiers, with their own radio. In the next, a contingent of Australians was eager to hear some news. It was some time before I could get a programme in English, but there it was – an announcer with an Australian accent:

> It was announced from Batavia, Java, that the Dutch had capitulated on March 15th, 1942. Fighting had ceased throughout the Dutch East Indies. The British defenders of Rangoon were resisting Japanese forces. Sea battles were still raging in the South Pacific. Bombing raids by German aircraft are reported from several English cities...

Now we knew the score.

Back among the trees I asked Bill for his atlas. 'I didn't know the Dutch East Indies covered such a large area,' I said. 'If the distance to Darwin is 1,500 miles, the plane will have to fly over this string of islands, now occupied by the Japs, then 500 miles over open sea. Phew, a risky journey!'

Being ground crew, the five of us were not eligible for the draw, but we had volunteered to assist in manhandling the plane onto the runway. At 5.00 am we joined the thirty or so other men alongside the plane, only to discover the fuel tanks had been ruptured and the tyres slashed. There was now no chance of it taking off. The officer in charge spoke:

'I realise the disappointment and annoyance of those who may have got away. This must have been done by some who thought the Jap threats would be carried out. Should anyone hear anything regarding those responsible, let me know.

'Those who filled in the trenches across the runway, get the spades and dig them up again. The rest do as much damage as possible to the plane. Setting fire to it would be easier but would attract too much attention.'

By dawn there were enough holes in the runway to stop any Jap planes landing. Afterwards we went for breakfast. It was Bill who expressed his feelings: 'Maybe the outcome was for the best. It could have been a suicidal journey, and if the Japs had carried out their threat, 160 men were liable to be shot.'

The first sight of our captors came a few days later, when a troop of soldiers arrived, who, with a great deal of grunting and shouting, marshalled us into groups of sixty. Jap officers came in cars. Their Samurai swords threatened to trip them up as they walked to the line of tables. After they were seated, each of us was curtly told to write name, rank, number and trade on the sheets of paper. There was some table thumping when they realised our trades had not been written down, which our officer had told us not to divulge. A meeting with our officer resulted in a lot of shouting in Japanese, but it was finally accepted that no mention of trade was to be made.

A speech through loudspeakers from a senior Jap officer, in very poor English, told us that Imperial Japanese soldiers would not have surrendered as we had done, but would have been expected to commit hara-kiri, but if we worked hard to earn our food we would be put into camps and treated well, with little interference from the guards, providing all orders were carried out. We were called on parade at dawn. After some language difficulties, we understood they wanted us in the same groups of sixty as on the previous day. After numerous counts by the guards, who seemed unable to count, we were first formed in ranks of five, and then changed to four, until they were finally satisfied. Our first task was filling in the trenches again. As Bill remarked, 'They must know we're expert at this.'

Not being too keen to over-exert ourselves, the guards kept shouting 'Kura, kura', which we took to mean 'Faster, faster'. This caused Jock to retort: 'Oh, shut up you silly little man, we don't understand you,' or something similar. Even if the guard had knowledge of English, it's doubtful whether he would have understood Jock's broad accent. At midday we learnt a more pleasant Jap word – 'yasme', meaning rest. Work ceased as darkness fell, without the job being finished. The first time we filled in the trenches it took only a couple of hours and about the same time to dig them up again.

There was room for us to move into the permanent buildings, now the Dutch and Australians had been transferred, presumably to another camp, and this gave me a chance to listen to the radio again, but there was nothing to cheer about.

'The Japanese are still advancing into Burma ...'

'Oh, switch it off,' someone shouted. 'It gives us the willies, and don't put it on again until there is some good news.' A sentiment echoed by several others.

After a few days we were called on parade at dawn, with all our belongings. The farcical effort of counting took quite a time. Then a Jap officer, with a better mastery of English, addressed us: 'You will be going to a new camp where it will be possible to grow much of your own food. Working parties will be expected to carry out light work as ordered by the camp commander.'

Trucks were lined up ready to transport us to the new camp. Reg said, as we climbed aboard, 'I wonder where we are going. It doesn't sound too bad. Roll on Christmas, when it should be all over.'

After about two hours we arrived at another airfield. 'Blimey, are we going to dig the runway up to grow our food?' quipped Jock.

The usual farce of a count by the five guards in charge of the groups of sixty followed. They finally agreed we were all there, and handed us over to new guards. There was a striking difference between these and the small, one-star Jap soldiers who had now left. They were taller, and without any mark of rank on their uniforms. We later learned they were Koreans. So, this was Jogjakarta.[1]

Our accommodation was the former Dutch barracks, which were devoid of any bunks or bedding, to enable the maximum number to be packed in. I was thankful for my blanket to sleep on instead of the bare floor. Our skill at filling in trenches must have been noted because the first job for our group was just that. Other parties were unloading 500lb bombs and cans of petrol from railway trucks. As we made our way to the cookhouse for the midday meal a fire broke out in the railway sidings, spreading to some buildings.

'Well, that's some petrol they won't be able to use,' I remarked gleefully. 'But I hope they got the bombs well clear before the fire started.'

No sooner had we got our meal when a real panic set in among the guards, with *'Kura-kura'*, and a new word, *'Speedo-speedo'*, as they pushed and shoved us towards the parade ground. When we had been lined up a Jap officer stood on a box in front of us, flanked by a squad of soldiers with fixed bayonets. He spoke in what could just be made out to be English: 'Any form of sabotage is a crime against the Emperor, and the person or persons responsible will be severely punished.'

An RAF officer, escorted by two soldiers with rifles, was brought before him. 'That's Flying Officer Taylor,' whispered Bill.

Taylor's cap was removed and the Jap officer spoke to him. 'You arranged for the petrol to be spilled, which caused the fire. It could mean your death,' snorted the Jap, placing his hand on the shaft of his sword.

'Oh God, not that,' ran through the ranks. The soldiers raised their rifles to deter any movement forward.

The officer went on: 'Let this be a warning. There will be no reprieve next time, but you must be punished.' He proceeded to strike Taylor in the face with his fist. There was muttering from the assembled men.

We all felt revulsion having to watch one of our officers being beaten, but also some relief that the original threat had not been carried out. We knew corporal punishment was allowed in the Japanese Army; a high rank could hit a lower one. Up until now it had not been used against us, but would this incident change things? We were ordered to clear up after the fire, removing burnt-out trucks, replacing twisted rails and sleepers, and our fears that the beating of our officer would be a signal to the guards to do the same to us became a reality. At the least excuse it was bash, bash, and it was obvious they got immense satisfaction doing it.

Bill and I were detailed to collect supplies from town, accompanied by two Japanese soldiers. It was a welcome break and a chance to see something of Jogjakarta, a busy town. The European influence could be seen alongside the Asian buildings. Dutch ladies mingled with the natives in and about the variety of shops and stalls. Soon the truck was loaded, but before setting off on the return journey, the Japs allowed us to buy things for ourselves. Not having had chance to spend much before, we still had some Dutch guilders, which the traders gladly accepted. We bought 2 kilos of tobacco, as well as bananas and papayas.

Back at camp, after unloading the goods for the Japs, we took two sacks of rice to our cookhouse. So far, our food supply was okay. There were large stocks of tinned meat and vegetables, potatoes were substituted with sweet potatoes and yams, but flour and sugar were in short supply. Our cooks' first effort at cooking rice was disastrous, resulting in a gooey mess. Of our own goods, the tobacco was the most sought-after item and was difficult to share out. We took enough money from that to pay for all the goods, so shared the fruit out as fairly as possible.

'Let's hope we get chance to buy some more,' said Bill wistfully. 'It was a nice change to get out of camp.'

It was at the cookhouse that I made a bad mistake. Thinking we still had some rights, I reported to our officer that a Korean guard had taken some of our sugar. He reported the guard to the Jap officer, who promptly beat him in front of the assembled prisoners. It was a few days later that I realised my error in reporting the Korean guard. He was put in charge of a working party, and went through the ranks until he found me, having deduced it was I who had brought about his disgrace. In the days that followed the routine was the same, picking me for his working party, and he needed little excuse to hit me when he felt like it, which was often. There was no chance now of going on the supply truck; my personal persecutor saw to that.

The days passed with tedious monotony: parade at dawn, a meal break at midday, finish work at dusk, queue for a meal, then to bed, seven days a week. It became difficult to know what day it was. Growing our own food was never mentioned. On parade, the other chaps tried their best to keep me away from my tormentor, but rarely succeeded, and sometimes they were hit for their efforts. The guards, having realised there would be no recriminations against them for using corporal punishment, needed little or no excuse to lash out at us, even with their rifle butts. Should anyone retaliate, other guards joined in.

Relief from my satanic guard came in the form of my first bout of malaria. Sometimes cold and shivering, unable to get warm even in the tropical heat, other times I'd be streaming with sweat. I had no appetite for food, but drink was essential – a severe problem during the day while on my own. Bill and the others did all they could in the evenings to tempt me to eat.

'Come on, Taz, you must eat something, or you'll just fade away,' chided Bill.

Thankfully, quinine, in small doses, was still available, and after a few days the fever subsided, leaving me weak but able to do light duties around the camp. With the return of my appetite I was soon fit enough to go back to the main working parties. Had my tormentor forgotten me? I hoped and prayed that he had. No such luck … he found me again, and I knew what I could expect by the obvious look of satisfaction on his face. Were his blows harder? Or was it I that was weaker? It was with a certain amount of relief that we were told by the newly appointed Dutch interpreter that we would be moving to a new camp. 'The only work you will be expected to do will be to create gardens to grow your own food,' he told us.

'Let's hope that's true this time; I like gardening,' said Ginger.

'My only hope is that I finally lose my pet guard,' I said.

It was at dawn the following morning that we paraded with our belongings. Mine were my blanket, eating utensils and radio in my side pack. After the usual incessant counting we set off for the railway station, where we boarded open trucks, tightly packed, with standing room only. We arrived several hours later at a small station, from where we were marched to our new camp, a former girl's school, The Lyceum.

For hours we stood on parade, weary and hungry, not having eaten since leaving Jogjakarta, and with no protection from the tropical sun. For the first time, our belongings were searched, the guards taking away any knives or weapons. One man had a large parang strapped to his back, under his shirt. Our wristwatches and anything the guards fancied were taken. Fearing I would lose my radio, I quickly took all but the radio from my side pack, and slid it to Bill, who had been searched, while two Koreans gloated over their booty. The guard took my watch and, looking at my cigarette case, said, 'Fujiama', and to my surprise handed it back to me. It was then that I realised the mountain portrayed on the case was the Japanese sacred mountain. I said to Bill: 'It's strange he didn't take that. I would have thought he would have been pleased to own it.'

'Maybe you should have had Fujiama tattooed on your arm in Cairo. They might have let you go free,' replied Bill.

We soon realised that the comparative honeymoon was over. We were packed into native-style huts – bamboo frames covered with atap, a type of thatch made from banana leaves. Along each side, the full length of the hut, a raised platform of split bamboo was our resting place, with no more than 18 inches between each man. Several thousand men occupied the camp – some Australians and Dutch, but mostly British. Nowhere within the confines of the camp was there room to create gardens, not even between the huts. Jap officers and soldiers were billeted in the permanent buildings, while the Koreans were separate in the classrooms.

A new order was issued: we must now bow to the guards, no matter how far away they were. Failure meant immediate Bash! Bash! On one occasion a tall Australian, having failed to bow to a guard, received a thump from him, which he returned with interest, knocking him down with a well-aimed blow. Two other guards rushed over and forced him with their rifle butts before a Jap officer. All the men were called onto parade, and we had to witness the luckless Australian being beaten unconscious.

No food stores had been brought from Jogjakarta. We now had to manage on the meagre rations allocated by the Japs – watery rice for breakfast, boiled rice with thin vegetable stew for midday and night – leaving us hungry within a very short time. Our conversation inevitably turned to food 'like mother used to make' … home-made bread with lashings of butter, meat and potato pie, followed by suet duff and custard.

'Taz, did you ever go for a tripe and onion supper at the shop opposite the Gaumont cinema?' asked Reg.

'Yes, with mushy peas and brown sauce.'

'I never tried haggis,' said Jock, 'but I could manage some now.' And so the talk went on. Small parcels of food were thrown over the perimeter wall by Dutch ladies, but the chance of being at the right place at the right time was remote.

'Look, isn't that lad in the cage from 211 Squadron?' asked Jock.

'Yes, its Spud. I wonder what the poor devil has done to deserve that treatment,' I replied.

His wrists were tied to his ankles, and a boulder placed on his knees. Razor-sharp strips of bamboo had been put behind his knees, and blood was running down his legs. The guards seemed to vie with each other to devise more sinister forms of torture. Another contraption was the hot box – a solid wooden box, only high enough to allow a man to crouch. The door was shut, cutting off a supply of air. The heat must have been terrible, and the stench made us gasp as we walked past, hurried on by the guard. There was no way we could tell who was being punished. Whatever the crime, there was no excuse for such barbarity against prisoners of war. Realising there was no way I could assist the poor devil, I prayed for his early release.

The only supply of electricity was in the school buildings, so I had been unable to use the radio. This was to change when some chaps were told to fit power plugs for the Japs. They took the opportunity to run a cable to the nearest hut, explaining to a curious guard that it was a necessary earth wire. Extreme care had to be taken when listening in; we were very close to the main buildings. The news was far from good, and our hopes of being freed by Christmas took a distinct knock when we realised that it was now December. We had lost all track of time, with each day being a repeat of the previous one. My twenty-first birthday in June had passed unnoticed.

The huts had become infested with bugs, lice and fleas, causing discomfort to all except me. My blanket lived up to the claim on the label. I would wrap it around me and sleep undisturbed through the night, while the others suffered purgatory. Often the guards would have a snap search of the huts, turning us out on parade in the middle of the night, keeping us there for hours. The radio was always well hidden, underneath the bamboo platform, or on the lintel above the door. The guards never thought to look up.

Again, we were moving to a new camp. Only those with broken limbs failed the so-called medical. The painstaking count as dawn broke and the search of our few belongings passed without incident. Bill assisted me with my radio. Again we were told the only work would be growing our own food. We'd heard that before!

Chapter 5

Garden of Eden

Our spirits were somewhat lowered as torrential rain began to fall. We marched throughout the day, stopping at kampongs where the guards ordered the inhabitants to supply us with food. At one point, the sole of my right shoe parted from the upper, making it difficult to walk. I stopped to remove it, but had a job untying the lace. A guard came running back to collect me, shouting the usual *'Kura-kura, speedo-speedo!'* With a blow from his rifle butt he sent me sprawling. I rose slowly, seeing a flash of gold fillings in his teeth as he snarled, threatening to hit me again. It was as well that he didn't understand what I called him as I bowed and carried on walking. I managed to discard the other shoe without stopping. Soon my tattered socks fell apart. It was hard going with my bare feet sore and blistered.

Darkness had fallen by the time we reached our destination, a floodlit camp. For hours into the night we were kept on parade while the guards counted, counted and counted again. All round, men were collapsing from fatigue and hunger, only to be kicked until they rose or remained on the ground unconscious. Our belongings were searched, but with Bill's help, standing next to me, I was again able to slide my side pack containing the radio to him. Finally, we were told to find ourselves space in what appeared to be overcrowded atap huts. The guards, with a lot of shouting and lashing out with sticks, forced the men closer together, until we each had a few inches to lie on.

Reveille was sounded before dawn. Only the extremely sick were excused from parade. The Dutch interpreter told us:

'This is Jaar Mart camp, Sourabaya, a former Dutch barracks for a thousand men, now there are ten times that number, and the discipline is extreme. You must bow to the guards at all times. In future you will number off in Japanese numerals. You will learn the Japanese prayer praising the Emperor, the Son of Heaven, to be spoken each morning as you bow to the east.'

While in the queue for breakfast, slips of paper were given to every fifth man, bearing the Jap numerals *ichi, ni, san, shi, go*, as well as the Japanese prayer. The rest of the day we spent learning the numbers, as we had no illusions as to what would happen should we say the wrong number on parade. We also thought it necessary to learn the prayer, in case a guard should ask anyone to repeat it. At the morning parade the numbering went fairly well, and our version of the prayer, which would have been unsuitable for ladies' ears, went unnoticed. Our dream of a garden camp was shattered on being told that working parties would be employed on the docks.

After the usual watery rice for breakfast, we boarded the waiting lorries. There were thirty in each lorry, with two guards in charge. A Korean, whose name was Kasiyama, spoke perfect English, having been brought up in an orphanage in Hong Kong. He disliked the brutality being meted out by other guards, and if we did our work well, everything would be fine. On the 3-mile journey to the docks, along the roads lined with hibiscus trees in full bloom, Dutch ladies threw packs of food to us as we passed. Kasiyama also allowed the lorry to stop alongside native traders, where those who still had money could buy food. We stopped by two Salvation Army ladies, who told us they were from Pudsey and had arrived in Java from Singapore.

The work on the docks was hard, loading drums of petrol, boxes of ammunition, bombs and torpedoes onto merchant ships, stopping at midday for a meal of rice and vegetable stew. The afternoon was the most difficult time for those of us who had no footwear; our feet were still sore and tender, and walking on the concrete dockside and steel gangways, heated by the tropical sun, was extremely painful. The lorries returned at dusk to take us back to Jaar Mart, where the parade was over much faster, being able to number off ourselves.

Kasiyama was the favourite guard to work with. He allowed those with money to buy food from the natives, but it was not possible to be on his party each day and my chances were reduced by the appearance of my loathsome Korean, 'Basher', who searched for me each morning, often without success, having less time to go through the ranks. The days passed with monotonous repetition, and we were completely unaware what day it was or even the month of the year. The Salvation Army ladies waited each morning with their welcome packs of food, but I was unable to speak to them again.

It came as a painful shock when we realised the guards had been taught English swear words. It had always been our habit to blaspheme when speaking to them, but now words like 'cooking' and 'basket' could so easily be misunderstood. Guards prowled amongst us as we recited the morning prayer and if a wrong word was detected, the culprit would be taken before the big powerful Jap, Gunso Mori, who took pleasure in beating prisoners with his fist or with the bamboo stick he always carried. We soon learnt to go down from the first blow to escape further punishment.

I'm sure it was no coincidence that the swearing purge came at the same time Kasiyama was made official interpreter. What a turnaround! He no longer allowed the lorries to stop to buy food, but worse still, he invented misdeeds by men in his working party. While he didn't carry out any punishment himself, he reported the alleged 'offender' to Gunso Mori for the usual beating, while the luckless person hadn't any idea what he had done wrong. What seemed to be a cynical co-operation between Kasiyama and Mori caused them to be dubbed 'Blood' and 'Slime'. This change came as a nasty shock to us. No one was now eager to be on Slime's working party, as was the case before. Now there was the dread of being picked and no chance to buy extra food from the natives, only the likelihood of one or more providing pleasure for Mori.

It was not easy to keep in contact with my four mates, as we had been unable to get into the same hut. I would see one or the other sometimes on parade or on working parties. Bill had gone down with his first attack of malaria. He was in hut six. After returning from the docks, I went to see him, taking some of the food supplied by the Dutch ladies, but he was unable to eat it. He was shaking all over and couldn't get warm, so I fetched my blanket for him. The next few nights I realised how lucky I was to have that vermin-proof blanket. Now the bugs seemed eager to sample a fresh supply of blood.

Bill was soon back on his feet and returned my blanket, saying, 'Thanks, Taz, it really does keep the beasties away.'

'Yes, it does. I know now what it's like for you others. I've hardly had any sleep without it,' I told him.

I went down again with malaria. Fortunately, I was treated by a Dutch medical officer who had been stationed at Jaar Mart prior to the capitulation and had been able to retain some medical supplies, including quinine. The Dutch had occupied the main hall and been able to bring some home comforts with them, including bedding, clothing and footwear. A degree of overcrowding was caused when civilians were brought in later.

My reason for visiting the main hall was to find somewhere to listen to my radio. The single light bulb in the huts stayed on day and night, so there was no way of connecting up to the supply. Most of the men were working on the docks, except for a few who were ill. One man, who had worked for an oil company, spoke good English. To my question he replied, 'Yes, there are power points here, but care would have to be taken as the Jap guard room is next door.'

'I'll go and fetch it while most of the guards are on the docks,' I said.

In my haste when returning, I failed to bow to a guard and received a hefty clout for my error. I heaved a sigh of relief when he did not look into my side pack. The very thought made me sweat. There was no news on the radio, only music. There was no point in taking further risks so I decided to return later, and went back to my hut, this time with more caution than I had shown before. I returned the radio to its hiding place, on a lintel above the entrance, behind a strip of atap. So far there hadn't been any snap night-time searches.

Despite the heavy toil it was better to work on the docks to obtain the increased food rations and the fifty cents (6p)[1] per week now being paid. There was little opportunity to buy from the locals. On rare occasions, out of sight of the guards, a banana could be bought for ten Dutch cents, but cost twenty cents with Japanese notes. Many times, I thought of the Dutch notes blowing about the road in Tjilatjap.

The soles of my feet were becoming hardened, and the discomfort from the heat was less noticeable. I had to use my tunic to patch my shorts to retain a degree of decency, which resulted in severe sunburn on my shoulders. Packs of food were still being thrown over the wall of the camp by Dutch ladies, as they were at The Lyceum, and one night I was walking near the wall when a large pack hit me. My lucky day! I rushed over to hut six to share it with the others. It came as a surprise to find a message inside, written in Dutch. Bill, speaking with his mouth full, quipped: 'It's double Dutch to me.'

'Yes, me too,' I replied. 'I'll go over to the main hall and ask the chap I spoke to before for a translation.'

He told me: 'We have seen similar messages in the last few days. It seems unbelievable.'

'Well, what does it say?' I asked.

'On a day to be fixed, the ladies will be allowed to visit us in the camp. This has been ordered by the Emperor of Japan in celebration of his birthday. They want lists of things we are most in need of, apart from food and clothing.'

'I think our priorities would be soap, toothpaste, razor blades, tobacco and paper,' was my reply.

'These things are already on our list, plus bandages, disinfectant and any medicines that may be available,' he said.

Back with my mates, they greeted my report with scepticism.

'This lot of Japs would never allow it,' was Reg's pronouncement, adding a more colourful description of our captors.

This talk led to suggestions of other things we would like to include on the list, things we had taken for granted before being taken prisoner but were not now available: milk, sugar, bread, butter, potatoes, cake, biscuits, cheese, jam, fish, bacon, eggs, and numerous lesser items such as sweets and chocolate. Tea was plentiful because Java tea, which used to be exported to England, was not to the taste of the Japs.

Some time passed without any change in the routine. Nothing more was heard about the open day, and we began to think it was pie in the sky. On parade one morning, we were addressed by Kasiyama: 'Today is the birthday of His Imperial Highness, the Son of Heaven, Emperor of Japan. He has generously decreed that there will not be any working parties today. At ten o'clock the camp gates will be opened to allow the ladies to visit their men folk.'

Hundreds of ladies swarmed in when the gates opened, struggling under the weight of the parcels and cases they carried. It seemed strange that there was no check on the goods they brought in. We had no option but to stand aside while the ladies sought the person they had come to visit. To the thousands of British and Australian prisoners, this open day didn't appear to offer any relief.

I spotted the bonnets of the Salvation Army ladies among the crowd, just two English ladies to visit so many men, staggering through the crowd with their heavy cases. By the time the four of us reached them their goods had been distributed, so we stayed to talk with them. Guessing their ages wasn't easy – probably about 30. Anne was the taller of the two, while Susan had the darker hair. Both were single, and had volunteered for overseas service in May 1940. We knew they came from Pudsey, having spoken to them on the way to the docks. Their journey took them to Cape Town, Cairo, then to Bombay, followed by a long journey by train and bus to Madras. They sailed to Singapore and went up into Malaya.

'Wasn't it dangerous for two young ladies travelling through those foreign places?' asked Bill.

'We were not alone; there were four officers with us until the first air raid on Singapore, when we were evacuated with the women and children. We have no idea what happened to our companions,' explained Susan.

'How did you arrive here?' I asked.

'We landed at Batavia, and came here by train in the hope we could get a boat to Australia,' said Anne.

All too soon the order came to clear the camp. As we said goodbye to Susan and Anne, wishing them Godspeed and the hope that everything would turn out right, a Dutch lady, who had been unable to find the person she had hoped to visit, gave us the contents of her bags. There were bananas, papayas, lychees, hard-boiled eggs, home-made cakes, tins of condensed milk and corned beef, blocks of brown palm sugar, cigarettes and bars of soap. The lady didn't speak English, so we expressed our gratitude to the best of our ability. She was crying as she left. We shared the fruit among those gathered around, and put the tinned goods into the cookhouse. The soap became a communal asset in the following days.

After the last ladies had left, we were called out on parade. The counting took hours, and all hell was let loose when it was decided two men were missing. Finally, the Dutch medical officer solved the problem. Two men had been sent to hospital the previous day, after an accident on the docks.

It would not have been difficult to walk out with the ladies, but the prospect was daunting as all Dutch males had now been put into camps. The sight of a white man walking the streets, without shoes or proper clothing, would inevitably have attracted attention. There was no certainty of assistance from the natives, who were themselves threatened if they helped us.

The reason for the open day seemed somewhat obscure; we could have understood it better if the Japanese had suffered a major defeat, but the news on the radio did not indicate this. Ships had been sunk off Ceylon and the advance by the Japs towards India continued. Their only setback so far was that they had been unable to take the Solomon Islands.

Chapter 6

Danger

It was after dark when I went across to the Dutch quarters, and having no news from my radio, I sat talking to a man called Henry (I couldn't pronounce his surname). What he told me came as a surprise: 'The ladies smuggled in some arms and ammunition, which are now hidden behind the panelling in the main hall. There is also a quantity of rifles and other weapons that were hidden when we capitulated. It is hoped that a mass breakout can be achieved, and the takeover of ships in the docks.' This was a wild plan that might just work, should the warship in the harbour withdraw.

Normal routine returned the following morning: parade, count chant, then working parties. The guards seemed more on edge than usual. The reason became clear as we drove through the gates. A group of Japs, with the aid of sticks and rifle butts, were forcing the waiting ladies back to prevent them from throwing packets into the lorries. Anne and Susan were among them. Further down the road our lorry stopped while the guards dispersed another group, with an unnecessary degree of violence.

Back at the docks, the ship we were working on – a former British cargo ship built at Barrow-in-Furness, possibly before the first war, and now named the *Amagi Maru* – had wooden steps leading into the upper holds and platforms over the sides. We failed to comprehend the significance at the time. Those upper holds were left empty, and we moved to another ship.

As the days passed, more and more we missed the extras the ladies had thrown to us. The number waiting had declined day by day, until only Anne and Susan attempted to get supplies to us. We pleaded with them to cease, fearing for their safety after seeing the brutality used against the other ladies, but they took no notice. Returning from the docks, we were horrified when we saw them standing alongside the gate, guarded by two Japs, without their bonnets. Their heads were shaved. They must have been standing there all day in the tropical sun. The sight of those Salvation Army ladies was indelibly printed on my mind. While Gunso Mori had made it clear he had no respect for us because we had allowed ourselves to be taken prisoner rather than commit suicide, their only 'crime' was helping, to the best of their ability, the relief of suffering, as was their calling. During the following days, there was no sight of Anne and Susan, or, for that matter, any Dutch ladies. We learnt later that all white women and children had been confined to internment camps.

One night around midnight, the guards came stamping through the huts, turning us out on parade with the help of sticks and rifle butts. We could see that, in addition to the Korean guards, there were a large number of Jap soldiers with fixed bayonets. This was something special. After a long count, Kasiyama climbed onto a box and said: 'I overheard two Englishmen talking about something that could only have come from a radio. We want that radio. Now! There will be no reprisals against anyone if it is brought to me here. Should it be found by the guards searching the huts, serious consequences will result.'

Although a good many knew of the radio's whereabouts, no one spoke. Jap soldiers came along the lines, threatening injury by jabbing their bayonets at us, but failed to get any information. It crossed my mind to take full responsibility, as the whole hut would suffer if it was found. Bill, standing next to me, must have realised what I was thinking and whispered, 'Don't say anything, Taz; they won't find it.'

As the Japs had no inkling of the existence of the radio before the open day, would they assume that it was brought in by the ladies and so concentrate their search on the Dutch quarters? If so, there was a grave risk of the arms cache being found. I had not repeated to anyone what Henry had told me regarding the arms behind the panels. Judging by the commotion coming from that direction, something had been found, so nothing would be gained if I handed in the radio now.

The first glimpse of dawn was showing when we were allowed back into our huts. Guards stood at each end of the hut. I warned my mates not to look towards the radio, or the game would be up. Checking after the guards had gone revealed the radio was still there, but it dawned on me that in future it would be too risky to use it; the Japs must have realised that the only power points were in the main hall, and would keep a special watch. In what we thought was sheer spite, they took all our plates, mugs, forks and the knives and watches that had been missed during searches at The Lyceum. But still they left my cigarette case. 'Why?' I wondered. There was no time to rest. We were due on parade again for the working parties.

At breakfast we had quite a problem: how to collect it without utensils? Some chaps had half coconut shells, although even by sharing them there was not enough time for everyone to get some wet rice and tea. Many had to go to work without food.

The Dutch were still on parade as we set off for the docks, and an armed guard was posted at the entrance to the main hall. The guards were in a vile mood, and vented their spleen on us at the least excuse. Our weakness and hunger gave them plenty of opportunity as we struggled with the boxes of ammunition at the docks. The lorries arrived to return us to camp as darkness fell. Was it another display of malice that kept us on parade longer than usual? At last we were dismissed to get our evening meal.

Although more coconut shells had been picked up on the docks, there still weren't enough to go round, but unlike the morning and midday, there was no time limit, so everyone was able to get a share. The main hall was in darkness, still with armed guards outside, but there was no knowing what had gone on, or what had happened to all the Dutch men. Now for some much-needed sleep. The bugs disturbed no one that night.

A couple of days of comparative calm followed, although the guards were still on edge, now with fixed bayonets, hitting out if they thought we weren't working hard enough. At the following morning's parade, Kasiyama spoke: 'You are being moved to a new camp, to be self-supporting, with food you will grow in the gardens ...'

I heard Jock's voice, just along from me. 'He must have brought the script from The Lyceum.' Unfortunately, a guard heard him. Bang – Jock received a hefty clout.

Kasiyama carried on speaking: 'with no interference from the guards. Only the fittest will go, following a medical check by Japanese doctors.'

The medical was as before, a walk past the seated officers. This time our step was not as brisk; we were not too keen to go, as each of our previous moves had resulted in worse conditions. Those selected, including me, were told to wait in their huts, and each man's belongings would be searched as we left. Not much to search now. This time I dared not take the radio.

We were assembled in groups of 500, and as there were no lorries present, we assumed we would be walking to wherever we were going. The first of the four groups set off, followed by the next one some thirty minutes later. We had travelled along this road many times; we knew we must be going to the docks. Would we now find the illusive garden camp?

Our spirits were at a low ebb and there was no singing now. Reaching the docks, there was no sign of the previous groups as we stopped alongside the *Amagi Maru*. Now it was clear why those steps had been put into the holds: we would be leaving Java, by sea, but not in the manner we had hoped and prayed for.

Chapter 7

Sea Cruise to Paradise

We boarded the *Amagi Maru* and filed down the wooden steps into the battened-down hold, which was illuminated by a single electric bulb. It was difficult adjusting our eyes to the gloom after coming out of the bright sunlight. It soon became obvious that if 500 men were to be packed into this hold, precious little room would be available to each one. With a lot of *'Kura-kura'* and thumping with rifle butts by the guards, the last man was finally pushed in, leaving us only sufficient room to sit with our knees under our chins. The only toilet facility was a cut-down oil drum in one corner. We had to clamber over each other to reach it. The wooden platforms over the ship's sides were also latrines, but only two men at a time were allowed on deck. The engines started and the ship moved away from the dockside. But we were not on our way yet, as very quickly the engines stopped and the anchor was lowered.

It was with extreme difficulty that the food was distributed when the first meal was brought to the bottom of the steps – a mixture of watery rice and some type of vegetable. Many spilt their meagre ration as they struggled to return to their space. The heat and stench were overpowering, made worse by the lack of ventilation and intense heat. The supply of water was far from adequate, being just a few drops in our coconut shells twice a day.

I knew that there were several other ships at anchor in the harbour, but I had no idea if any prisoners were aboard them. Six men at a time could now use the deck latrines, giving us a chance of a short spell of fresh air. As I reached the top step to go on deck, there was a violent explosion, throwing me backwards onto the men following. Fortunately, no one was injured. Reaching the deck again, I could see the ship nearest to us was on fire and had a large hole in its side. It sank in minutes. Our bow was now pointing to the shore, having been turned around by the blast. Debris was falling all around us and the guards hurriedly pushed us back into the hold. If there had been prisoners on that ship, their chances of survival would have been nil, as ours would be in a similar catastrophe aboard this ship, knowing the contents of the lower holds.

During the few days we lay at anchor a number of men developed diarrhoea, which made matters much worse, as excreta fell on us as they made their way to the latrines. A few of the more severe cases were allowed to stay on deck. From the time the ship got under way, until we dropped anchor again, I have no recollection of the journey. I went into a stupor, unable to process what was happening around me. Eventually, when the ship docked it was like waking from a deep sleep. I could see again the squalid conditions and inhumane way that we were being treated. I could smell and taste the excrement that was surrounding us in the hold ... the incessant swarms of flies feasting on the accumulative mess and festering wounds on bodies.

Up on deck I could see we were anchored in a picturesque natural harbour, but we had arrived during an air raid. Bombs were falling from high-flying American planes, some too close for comfort. Whilst we didn't relish being on the receiving end of Allied bombers, it raised our spirits somewhat knowing we were within range of our own aircraft. An overzealous Jap gunner opened fire on a plane taking off from what must have been a nearby airfield, one of their own, but he missed. I chuckled at this fool.

As darkness fell, the ship was on the move again; obviously we had not reached our destination. Torrential rain began to fall, which was not unwelcome. The covers had been removed from the hold and it was a treat to try to remove some of the accumulated filth of the journey. After a short time, still in darkness, the ship moored alongside a jetty. With the usual shouting and thumping from the guards, we were herded ashore. We made our way along the wooden jetty by the light of storm lanterns, wishing by now that the rain would stop. It was not until we lined up to be counted that I realised others besides our 500 had arrived on the *Amagi Maru*. We later discovered that the number was 2,050.

In the darkness we couldn't see any buildings. Maybe they were further inland, on higher ground, away from this open clearing, which was ankle-deep in mud. Many men were too weak to walk from the ship and had to be carried ashore, but without any form of shelter there was no option but to leave them lying in the mud. The knowledge that Korean guards Blood and Slime had come with us did nothing to improve our

44

morale. Now Kasiyama was addressing us: 'Gunso Mori sends you this message. You are here to die. But not too quickly as you will build an airstrip for the Imperial Japanese Air Force on this island. As you have not worked for fifteen days you must begin at once to unload the ship.'

Back at the ship, the drums of oil and petrol were pushed over the side into the sea and then floated to the shore. The crates of ammunition and other supplies were manhandled along the jetty. Daylight came, with still no respite from the torrential rain. A number of men had been injured as they struggled with heavy crates without mechanical aid, and some had collapsed from exhaustion. It was with relief that we heard that the bombs and torpedoes did not have to be unloaded. The usual disgusting pap was supplied from the ship's galley. It was cold by the time we had found our makeshift eating utensils. During the midday break, our medical officers told us they had persuaded the Japs to allow some men to work in the camp, erecting the remaining huts to provide shelter for the sick first, then cover for those still fit enough to work.

This Island was Haruku, and the harbour we had anchored in was Ambon, some 600 miles north of Darwin, we were told. So, this stretch of mud was the camp site. There was nothing here but two unfinished huts – just a bamboo framework, without walls or roof. This type of building was constructed without nails, the bamboo poles being tied into position with rattan, thin strips of cane, and clad with atap panels made from palm leaves. While there was an ample supply of material, our skill at using them was limited by our weakened state. We had to clamber up makeshift ladders. By nightfall, one hut could offer some degree of shelter, but the sick still had to lie on the wet ground. Water was diverted by digging a trench the length of the hut and banking soil against the wall. Two men had already died. The rain, which had been so welcome at first, was now a positive menace. There was no way latrines could be dug with the water rushing through the camp site. Our suggestion to erect platform latrines just off the shore was turned down by the Japs.

It was impossible to start fires for cooking; there was no dry wood, and a request for oil was refused. This was the situation on the second morning on Haruku, after a wet, uncomfortable night trying to snatch some sleep in the lee of the one hut. More men were rendered incapable of work through exhaustion and hunger. Now more than half the men had contracted acute diarrhoea, and due to the lack of latrines, excreta was spreading throughout the camp site. A hundred men were detailed to finish unloading the stores from the ship. Another group set about finishing the first hut by putting bamboo platforms along each side to provide dry resting for the sick. There was no means of drying the saturated clothing and blankets.

The second hut was soon completed, and the cookhouse finally erected. It still wasn't possible to start the fires. A ration of watery rice was brought from the ship, made even more watery by the rain as we queued for our meagre share. The work on the remaining huts was actually progressing well, despite the awful conditions. The cleared area of the camp was surrounded by tall coconut palms, interspersed with smaller trees and shrubs, with more on the higher ground away from the shore. The thought occurred to me that maybe there were edible fruits waiting to be picked. But how would I know which were edible? I approached Bill and the others who were still fit enough to work, and they agreed we should take a look. There were no problems with the guards; they had kept well away from the camp site, only supervising the unloading of the ship.

There were small red berries on some shrubs, rather hard, but they tasted all right. Some larger yellow fruit were sweet and appetising, but there were only green bananas. We looked longingly at the coconuts but were unable to reach them. On a large tree there were some green fruit with prickly skins, as large as rugby balls, like the ones we had seen on stalls in Sourabaya, but they too were out of reach. Olive-green, plum-like fruit we knocked down with a bamboo pole. The flesh was bitter but after eating the kernel we were violently sick, fortunately without lasting ill effects. We learnt later they were the fruit of rubber trees. The area was soon devoid of any fruit.

During the next few days, despite the decreasing number of men fit to work, the remaining huts were completed. For the first time since our arrival, everyone could sleep under cover. The following day the cookhouse fires were started and we looked forward with pleasurable anticipation to a more substantial meal than we had received so far. As we queued at midday, the rain finally stopped. Now the most urgent task was to dig latrine trenches. The ground soon dried out in the tropical heat, and the camp site had to be cleared up as fast as possible. Clothes and blankets were laid out to dry, with the hope that the parasites we had brought with us had been killed off. That night, I realised that my blanket had retained its resistance to pests, but the others soon surmised that it would take more than a prolonged soaking to get rid of them.

The condition of the sick was fast deteriorating, with some showing signs of dysentery. These were isolated in one hut in an effort to stop it spreading. Without medical supplies, the one Dutch and two British medical officers were powerless to check it. Even a request for disinfectant was turned down by the Japs. While the filth had been spread around the camp, the guards had been reluctant to come close, only giving orders from beyond the stream. Now, with the camp much cleaner, we were called on parade. It was the first time we had seen the Jap officer we had named 'Yellow Boots' while at Jaar Mart. Here he was camp commandant. His rage was conveyed to us by Kasiyama when less than 600 turned out on parade: 'There will be no laziness in this camp. No work! No food! We want 1,500 men to start work building the airstrip tomorrow. The guards will go and turn out those who are idling in the huts.'

Many of those on parade were unfit for work, being weary and weak from hard work, exposure and lack of food. Guards were sent into the huts to drag out the sick, despite the pleas from the medical officers. The men were pulled off the bamboo platforms and beaten and kicked to get them on parade, but most just collapsed, too weak to climb back again, and had to wait until we could assist them. Four more men died that night. Both Jock and Ginger had gone down with acute diarrhoea. It was distressing to see these young men reduced to quivering wrecks through deliberate neglect, knowing we, who were still on our feet, were unable to ease their suffering. More cases of dysentery were diagnosed, and a second hut was taken over as an isolation hospital. Only 450 men were able to turn out for the working party. Some of the men who had been injured while unloading the ship had been kept back, on the medical officer's order, to look after the sick. This arrangement did not please Gunso Mori, who insisted they be brought before him. Even he had to agree they would be useless on the working party – some hobbling with makeshift crutches, others with arms in slings, and some with feet or legs bandaged with torn-up shirts.

We walked slowly and wearily up the rising ground, away from the camp, and we realised this was not an uninhabited island as we had first thought. As we passed a native kampong, the women and children watched us with curiosity. Soon a shallow valley came into view, with tall cone-shaped peaks at each end, which we later learnt was coral. So this was where the airstrip was to be built. The idea was to cut down these peaks to infill the valley. After forming into groups of twenty, we were given 2lb lump hammers, a cold chisel and a small, flat coolie type of basket. As the basket was filled with chipped-off coral we carried it down into the valley. This primitive method would have been laughable anywhere but here. The coral was hard and flew in all directions, painfully cutting into the flesh. Walking on the jagged rock with bare feet was an additional discomfort, plus the occasional blows from the guards who thought you were not working hard enough. The working parties dwindled daily. The first men to die had been buried in bamboo coffins, but when the daily death toll reached ten or twelve, they could only be buried in rice sacks. They were buried by the working party when they returned to camp in the darkness.

Now eight huts were occupied by the sick. As the dysentery outbreak reached epidemic proportions, the many sick were moved to other huts as their condition deteriorated. It seemed that the only way out of hut eight was via the burial party. It was difficult to keep track of my mates. Jock and Ginger had been moved to an isolation hut and I was unable to find them in the badly lit huts. Reg was the next to succumb to dysentery, whilst Bill had another bout of malaria.

A new menace appeared in the form of a plague of flies breeding in the open trench latrines. This could have been easily overcome by the use of petrol or oil, but our request for these was turned down by Gunso Mori. The solution, as translated by Kasiyama, was that 'each sick man must catch a hundred flies each day before they could receive any food'. Whilst most were too sick even for this task, catching the flies was left to the walking sick, mostly men suffering from what had been small cuts on their legs and feet caused by the flying coral, which had remained untreated and were now large, expanding, festering sores. The bluebottles were easy to catch over the latrines with nets made from remnants of mosquito nets and were killed by immersion in hot water. This had the effect of sterilising them and keeping them whole, ready to be counted into lots of 100, which were then wrapped in leaves. These packs were distributed to the sick men in the first six huts, knowing guards wouldn't go into huts seven and eight. After the guards had looked at some packs, they were surreptitiously passed to others. It didn't occur to the guards to take them away and they were reused the next day.

When the turnout for the working party could only muster 100 men, work on the airstrip was suspended. These men were now able to make some improvements around the camp. First a channel was dug from the stream to divert water through the latrines and then down to the seashore. Some prisoners made useful articles to use from tins and bottles that the Japs had thrown away.

I did what I could to assist the sick by washing them down, but because it was impossible for them to reach the latrines, they were just as bad a short time later. I found Jock in hut seven. It was heartbreaking to see these young men lying in the filth of dysentery. Ginger was in an even worse condition than Jock, with maggots extruding from every aperture of his body. It was obvious there was no chance of him surviving. He died that night. I sat and cried.

The medical officers worked long and hard, in atrocious conditions, without proper medications. They prepared concoctions from leaves and roots for the patients, not so much as a cure, but with the hope it might increase their will to live. They washed and cooked maggots, then pounded them into a paste, which they fed to the worst cases. Pure protein! Another idea proved a real breakthrough for treating the horrific sores that spread so quickly from small cuts. Maggots were placed on the open wounds and held in place with leaves. The maggots ate the pus, allowing new flesh to grow.

The Japs then decided to return several hundred non-dysentery cases back to Java. These included those suffering from beriberi, a complaint caused by lack of vitamins, in which their bodies filled with water to grotesque proportions. Also, some with broken limbs were sent back.

The men were dying too fast even for Gunso Mori and had reached twelve a day, when the rations for the sick were increased. Ketchinegue beans, a light green vegetable rich in protein, and tempi, a pink paste made from fish, were added to the rations. It was soon possible to notice an all-round improvement among the sick. Fewer were being taken to the last hut. Although deaths still occurred daily, it seemed the peak had at last been passed. Bill was back on his feet, but was still very weak, but he, like me, had not contracted dysentery. It was Jock who now caused us the greatest anxiety. He had not been too ill and we fully expected him to pull round, but now he was unable to keep any food down. We took it in turns to sit and talk to him, telling him how his parents and sister would be praying for him, in the hope that he would improve and regain the will to live, but he just lay there, in a state of lethargy. He died a few days later. Bill wiped a tear from his eye and said, 'It seems Gunso Mori could be right; we are here to die.'

'Don't even think like that,' I replied.

With the resumption of work on the airstrip, differential rationing was reintroduced to encourage more men to return to work. The Japs must have realised that to remove these peaks with 2lb hammers could take ten years or more. We had made little impression so far. Now explosives were brought in. We drilled the holes and Jap sappers set the charges, which they detonated without warning, often causing injury. This meant much harder work moving the larger quantities of coral, and the distance to carry it increased daily. I then went down with another attack of malaria, which proved much more difficult to shake off, leaving me weak and unsteady.

It took me longer than usual to be able to return to work and back on full rations. The expanding stretch of white coral also caused me to go blind. One moment I was walking along the airstrip quite normally, and then, complete blindness. I was taken before Jap doctors to be examined. They ordered that I be put into a punishment hut with a guard outside. There were three other chaps in the hut, also blind. The hut was small, maybe 4 yards square, completely bare, without any toilet arrangement, and no means of going to the outside latrines. Lofty Topp had been there about a week. Ted Wilson and Jack Cowan had come in the previous day. A single meal was brought, probably around midday. We could hear the working party getting their meals but had no way of telling whether it was morning or evening. Each day we were taken before the Jap doctors, stepping into a tray containing disinfectant before entering the hut. They didn't seem to examine our eyes, but just placed obstacles in front of us, which we fell over, and then returned us to the hut. After a few days my sight returned as suddenly as it had gone.

Having already been before the Jap doctors, I waited until I heard the working party getting their meal, and in the darkness loosened a piece of atap and slipped out to join the queue at the cookhouse, returning with the food in a banana leaf to share with the others. I was fully aware of the consequences should I be caught. The following day I needed to know what tricks the Japs played when we went before them, so I arranged to go through last. I fell over the two boxes, turning the wrong way as

I got to my feet. Next, two fingers were thrust towards my eyes. But I was ready, and I did not blink or flinch when a blow was aimed at me. For good measure I fell over a box on my way out. I again fetched food from the cookhouse in the evening. In the morning I climbed through the atap and ran straight into the guard's rifle-butt. He had gone to the back of the hut for a smoke. Taking such a chance, just to get some of the awful ongle-ongle now being served for breakfast, was, in hindsight, pretty stupid. This purple gelatinous food was made from the pith of the sago palm, tasteless and with little or no nutritional value. I was taken to Gunso Mori and Kasiyama in front of the working party parade. Kasiyama got onto his box and said: 'This man must be punished, not only for failing to work, for which he gets fed, but worse still, attempting to portray our doctors as incompetent. In fact, they knew from the first day that he was not blind, and the guards were told to watch for him coming out of the hut. This morning he did.'

Mori came in front of me, a sadistic sneer on his face. He must have seen the hate and loathing showing in my eyes. From past experience I decided to take just one hit and stay down. He hit me. I felt myself falling, falling …

When I came round I was on my bed space with a medical officer examining my face. Nothing was broken. Bill and Reg came to see me after work. When they had fetched some food, we sat talking. I told them what had happened: 'I was blind for six days, but my sight returned soon after a visit to the Jap doctors, so I fetched food from the cookhouse for the four of us. Yesterday I fooled the doctors and again got some food. Then this morning I was daft enough to try to join the breakfast queue. You know the rest.'

'The others were beaten up for not reporting you too,' Bill told me.

I felt really guilty for causing them this extra suffering.

Having lost all track of time, not knowing the day of the week or the month of the year, there was one question that no one could answer: had the second Christmas passed, and was it now 1944? The monotonous sequence of work and sleep, day after day, plus the routine burial of several unnamed men after dark, was broken only by my frequent bouts of malaria. I was finding it much harder to recover from these attacks, and the accompanying depression made me realise how easy it would be to give up the fight and slip into oblivion. These thoughts had to be dismissed quickly.

'What's going on?' I asked Bill as Kasiyama mounted his box in front of the waiting working party.

'I don't know,' he replied. 'Who are those two chaps standing between the guards?'

Kasiyama was about to answer our questions. 'You all know the sentence for attempting to escape is death. These two Australians stole a native boat but didn't get far. They will face a firing squad later.' A murmur of dissent ran through the ranks. It was obvious that any reaction from us would have resulted in the Australians' immediate death.

This being my first day back working for some time, I had never before seen a new building, surrounded by a high fence. It was some distance from the native village. Bill suggested that they were bringing in the Geisha girls, as no prisoners had been used to build it.

At first glance it would seem that the airstrip was finished. The blasting had ceased, and the two coral peaks had been flattened. Now surveyors and engineers had been brought in for the levelling and grading of the strip. These Japanese were a different class from any we had so far encountered. Whilst they could not be called friendly, they did object to the Korean guards striking us.

Our work now was much lighter. The pressure and panic had gone. We filled our baskets from the remnants of the peaks and placed the coral where the surveyors indicated. The two steamrollers now in use completed the process. We had more breaks from work as the number of air raids on Ambon increased, the American planes flying high over the length of the airstrip. Each time the sirens sounded, we raced for the cover of the trees. It was something of a puzzle why no bombs had been dropped on us. The Yank pilots must have reported this white gash across an otherwise green island.

A number of native workers could now be seen at the far end of the strip, possibly constructing parking bays amid the trees. We were not allowed to contact them. One morning everything seemed to be normal. The natives were working at the far end and we were much closer to them now as the levelling advanced along the airstrip. Suddenly, there was a lot of shouting by the guards as the natives disappeared among the trees, refusing to return to work. Soon the sirens sounded, and we all rushed to the shelter of the trees. As the wail of the sirens died away, the throb of aircraft engines could be heard … then the thump of an exploding bomb some distance away, followed by another, much nearer. We moved further back into the trees as a string of bombs rained down onto the airstrip. The Yanks did know what was being constructed. When the all-clear sounded, we trooped back onto the strip to examine the damage, which was surprisingly little, only shallow depressions on the hard surface. Some palm trees had been damaged by bomb fragments.

The natives were back working, which raised the question, had they had a premonition that this raid was to be directed against Haruku before they fled prior to the sounding of the siren? At first, I thought there had not been any casualties among the prisoners or natives but learnt later that one man had been killed and several injured, and some damage was done to the native village. The new building had received a direct hit. We were not told the fate of the occupants. In the following days, when the natives ran into the trees, we all followed, the guards making no effort to stop us.

Returning to camp one evening, we were told a volley of rifle shots had been heard in the afternoon. The sad death of the two Australians was confirmed by Kasiyama the next morning.

After such a long time it came as a severe shock to find myself face to face with my bestial Korean guard, Basher. By the look on his face he had not forgotten me and picked me for his working party. My best bet was to stay near to the surveyors, using a rake to level the baskets of coral as they were brought. Basher was eager to get me away from there in order to vent his spite on me. He took my rake and gave me a basket, indicating that I was to fetch coral. Now was his chance. Meeting me on the way back, now with a stick in his hand, he stopped me, complaining that my basket was not full enough. The first blow hit my shoulder. Dropping the basket, I raised my left arm to protect my head. Again, his stick lashed out, giving me a stunning blow to my wrist. It began to swell immediately. Back at camp, the medical officer told me a bone had been broken and I must keep it in a sling in the hope that it would mend itself in time.

I was given the job – along with Brummy Jones, who had a similar injury – of taking the midday meal to the men on the airstrip. Carrying a container on a bamboo pole was an easy number, entitling us to full rations. On one trip we were met by an Australian who told us not to go near one of the steam rollers, as he had fastened the safety valve down. A minute later, with a terrific roar, the roller exploded, the flywheel being blown high into the air. That roller would not work again, we laughed. It was also laughable to see the guards rushing round picking up the debris as if to stick it together again.

After a while I realised that the bone in my wrist had healed, but not wishing to lose my cushy job, I told no one and kept my arm in a sling. Everything was fine until I made a stupid mistake. With a guard standing beside me, I lifted the pole from my shoulder with my left hand. He went berserk. He grabbed my left arm and for a while I thought he was going to break it again, and then he began slapping me around. Then it was another painful meeting with Gunso Mori. Maybe he wasn't getting any satisfaction delivering a single blow. By his standards, I received just a gentle punch, but went down to avoid any further punishment. Some days later, Kasiyama was on his box again in front of the working party.

'What the heck do you think he's going to rant about now?' asked Bill.

'We'll soon find out,' I replied.

'With the airstrip almost finished, half of you will be leaving on the ship now alongside the jetty.' He went on, 'The sick will go aboard first. Those to the right of the guard will collect your belongings; the rest will carry on working.'

I was on the right. After several hours we lined up along the jetty and boarding began. A single guard kept count as they boarded in front of us. Bill, Reg and I had managed to stay close to each other, but after Reg started to mount the gangway, followed by a ginger-haired lad, the guard indicated that was all for this ship. Bill and I were left on the jetty, disappointed that we had been parted from Reg. 'See you soon, Reg. Good Luck!' we shouted. We went back to the camp.

Several days later, Kasiyama made an announcement: 'Today the airstrip will be opened officially by the Emperor of Japan, the Son of Heaven. When the plane lands, you must all lie on the ground. Anyone looking up will be severely punished.' The plane arrived and we all knelt on the ground with our heads on our hands, including the guards. I, being well to the rear, took a quick look and saw a small, dapper Jap, dressed in a morning suit complete with top hat, accompanied by several high-ranking officers. After a short ceremony they all departed. The whole visit lasted less than thirty minutes. I could imagine the panic had there been an air raid. Bill expressed his opinion of the visit: 'I can't believe the Emperor would come from Tokyo to this small island, within bombing range of Australia.'

'Neither can I,' I replied. 'All the guards seem convinced that it was the Emperor. Even if they had seen him, I doubt if they would have known if it was him or not.' Kasiyama told a group of us we should be proud that he honoured us with a visit.

'Some blooming honour,' I thought.

There was now another ship alongside the jetty. 'Bill, do you think this is the one that will take us off Haruku?' I asked.

'Most likely,' he replied. 'Some men are already loading equipment now the airstrip is complete. While it will be a relief to get away from here, I've an awful feeling of fear and dread at the thought of another sea journey.' He echoed my inner feelings. There was no one in as good a physical condition as when we left Java, maybe more than twelve months ago. We had just existed on inadequate food rations, been used as slaves, suffered with many diseases and treated with sheer brutality. This, in turn, caused debilitating illnesses and had reduced us all to a pitiful state. Yes, it was time for us to leave. With a thought for all those who would be left on the island, Bill and I lined up with the others along the jetty, to be counted as we embarked.

Chapter 8

Hell Ship Journey to the Show Camp

The conditions were the same as on the *Amagi Maru*. Packed in the one hold, the 600 prisoners had only room to sit, and the heat and stench quickly became unbearable. Soon the first men died. Their bodies were taken to the foot of the stairs – an extremely difficult task through the crowded hold – then taken onto the deck and put over the side without ceremony. I must have had a guardian angel watching over me, because apart from the first few days, I cannot recall the rest of the journey as, again, I went into a stupor. Was this a form of protection against the horrors around me?

The strident shouts of the guards, who came into the hold wearing face masks, brought me back to reality. The engines had stopped. This was where we were to disembark. The guards punched, kicked and clubbed us, to force us, half walking and half crawling, out of that stinking hold. We were alongside the dock at Surabaya, Java. The count on the dockside revealed that only 318 men had survived the journey. There was no sign of Blood and Slime.

A Jap officer addressed us: 'You have been fed for the past sixty days without working. This loss of time will have to be made up in the near future.' We stood there, our clothing for the most part being shorts made from rice sacks, gaunt figures, apart from those bloated by beriberi. We presented a pathetic sight.

There was a discernible change of attitude towards us by the new guards who had taken over. There was no shouting or bullying. We were told to sit down. Then, surprise, surprise, each of us was given a small pack of native-style food, consisting of rice, sweet potato, some meat, small sardine-like fish, and a hard-boiled duck egg topped with chilli sauce. This was followed by hot tea and a banana, brought to us where we sat. Our spirits rose somewhat after that first solid meal for ages. There is no doubt we could all have eaten the same again, but we were thankful for small mercies.

A different Jap officer spoke to us, in quite good English: 'You may stay seated. It is only a short walk to the railway station where you will board a train to go to a rest camp to recuperate, with good food and no work.' This was hard to believe. We had heard similar statements before, and, as yet, not reached this utopian camp. Anyhow, the beginning showed promise. Maybe the worst was over. We boarded some open trucks and were allowed room to sit, unlike the last train journey, which had standing room only. Here was a different attitude. The train stopped after a few hours and another meal was distributed by the guards. We arrived at Bandoeng station and transferred to waiting lorries as darkness fell.

On arrival at the camp we were surprised to see it so well lit. After a leisurely count, we went into three empty huts – just 106 men in each hut. Sheer luxury! Huts of this size usually housed 200 men. The quantity and quality of the food from the cookhouse was an even bigger surprise: fried rice, with thick meat and vegetable stew, and a small loaf of bread between two men, washed down with sweet tea. We had at last arrived at what seemed to be the ideal camp.

Rising at dawn after a sound, undisturbed sleep with no pangs of hunger, we were able to stretch full length and move without making contact with the men on either side. We waited for the call to go on parade, which did not come … only the sound of a bell, which a guard indicated was a call for breakfast. This was soft boiled rice with grated coconut, sweetened with gula jawa, a brown palm sugar. No one seemed to mind us having second helpings. The men already in the camp, who had been unable to contact us when we arrived during the night, were full of curiosity as to our condition, which was understandable as they looked extremely fit and were still well dressed. Many questions were fired at us: 'Where have you all been?' 'How did you all get into such a state?'

A guard walked by. We bowed. 'What was that for? We don't do that here.'

We had to explain what had happened at other camps. I was more interested in the whereabouts of Reg and asked, 'Have any others come here from Haruku?'

'Yes,' one of the men replied. 'A small ginger-haired fellow arrived a couple of weeks ago. He thought he was the only survivor when the ship he had left Haruku on was sunk.'

'Where is he now?' Bill asked.

'In his hut with an attack of malaria. I'll take you to him.'

Walking through the camp, Pete, our guide, pointed out the various activities that went on. There was a tailor's shop where clothing could be repaired, and a cobbler's shop that repaired shoes and made sandals and wooden clompers. Soap was made from coconut oil and wood ash. Nearby was a plant for manufacturing coconut oil. There was also a print shop issuing camp news and advertising goods for sale and exchange.

Most men worked in the gardens growing vegetables. Whatever work they did they received regular pay for, which could be spent at the camp shop. Here could be bought home-produced goods, along with native produce, such as fruit and tobacco. The Japs allowed a weekly trip outside the camp for this purpose. Reaching the sickbay, we immediately saw the ginger-haired fellow. He told us his name was Don Sharp, of 211 Squadron.

'Don, did you know Reg Webster? He was 84 Squadron.' I asked. 'You were the last to board the ship in Haruku, and Reg was in front of you.'

'Yes, I knew him, but don't know what became of him. Several men died on board before the ship was sunk,' he replied. 'After the explosion I found myself clinging to a piece of wood, not far from land. Another chap joined me, but he slipped away and I was unable to save him. It was not long before a native boat picked me up, and I was looked after at a native village for several days, until some Jap soldiers brought me here.'

'Maybe others survived and have been taken to other camps?' suggested Bill.

We left Don knowing there was little chance of finding out what had become of Reg. Strolling back to our hut, we stopped by the camp shop and looked longingly at the array of fruit being offered for sale. There were bananas, lychees, papaya, pineapples and others we did not know the name of. I felt as if I was living in a dream. No interference from the guards. No bowing. No beatings. And above all, much better food, but even here there were no medicines available.

The following day, the camp newsletter was distributed. This carried a brief outline of our life as prisoners and an appeal for clothing and footwear for us. A distribution point was set up and soon an assortment of shirts, shorts and clompers was ready for us to collect. The clompers I tried on were difficult to walk in. Being barefoot was not now a great hardship. The shorts, which had been made by the tailors from white flour sacks, were very welcome.

After three days, a wire fence was erected around our huts and we were not allowed to mix with the others. It had been found that we had introduced vermin to the camp, something previously unknown. The standard of food remained high and was brought to our huts, instead of us having to go to the cookhouse. We were not prevented from speaking to the others through the fence and they were very generous with their gifts of fruit and tobacco. The better food and rest were having the desired remedial effect, and the improvement in our health and spirits was noticeable, even after one short week. I went down with another bout of malaria but thankfully it wasn't as severe as the previous attacks. This was possibly due to my improved physical state and the fact that there was no reduction in rations for those who were sick.

It came as a surprise when a newsletter, printed in English and dated July 1944, was issued by the Japs. The headline read: 'The fall of Imphal is imminent. The Imperial Japanese Army is within 10 miles of Imphal, on the Burma Indian border, and it is expected to fall within the next few days.'

'Blimey, I didn't think they had got as far as that,' I remarked to Bill.

Then followed an invitation to join the Japanese Army as non-combatants, to gain our freedom, and speed the end of the war.

'They must be joking,' was Bill's reaction. 'Do they really think they could persuade us to join their lot?'

A news item was headed: 'This is what the Yanks are doing to your womenfolk back home. The wife of one of our prisoners who lives in Long Eaton, Nottingham, has given birth to twins, fathered by an American sergeant.'

'This report stinks. Are they trying to convince us that they have got tabs on all our next of kin?' I said.

The next issue, a week later, proclaimed: 'The British garrison is preparing to surrender as Japanese forces advance within 16 miles of Imphal.'

'Bill, didn't last week's sheet report the Japs were within 10 miles of Imphal?' I asked.

'Yes,' replied Bill. 'Either Imphal has been moved 6 miles further back, or the Japs are advancing backwards.'

The first parade in the three weeks we had been at Bandoeng was called after breakfast. It was said that only the fittest need turn out; those suffering from beriberi, malaria or injury could stay in their huts. Two hundred and fifty men were required to move to another camp, which was run on similar lines to Bandoeng, and were leaving the following morning. The names of those on parade were taken. I prayed for another attack of malaria. I liked what I had got here, rather than some unknown camp. Why had I so quickly shaken off my recent bout?

In the morning I was shaking all over, so I stayed in the hut, but as my name was on the list from the previous day, a guard was sent to fetch me. I was able to convince him that I was ill and thought I had got away with it, but I was unable to fool the Jap doctor with his thermometer. Collecting my few possessions, I joined the parade, fully expecting to land in trouble, but there were no reprisals.

We boarded the waiting lorries to drive us to the station. The train journey was similar to the previous one from Sourabaya – no overcrowding and with frequent stops for meals and to stretch our legs. Under different circumstances this could have been a pleasant journey, passing through the wonderful scenery of central Java. We arrived at Batavia late in the afternoon, and then it was a short walk to what I recognised as the former Dutch barracks where we had received our first pay in guilders, so long ago: Cycle Camp. This had been the depot of the Dutch army, the Bicycle Regiment.

It soon became clear that our holiday was over. Our Bandoeng guards counted us and handed us over to the new guards. They counted us again and again, finally satisfied that there were 250. Meanwhile we could see the other inmates, who certainly didn't look anywhere near as fit as those in Bandoeng. And they bowed to the guards. A further contrast came when we were packed into what seemed to be already overcrowded huts. The guards lashed out to force the men closer together. The evening meal was no better than those on Haruku. During the allocation of bed spaces, Bill and I became separated. I was alongside a fair-haired chap, whom I had seen somewhere before.

'I'm Geoff Lee, otherwise known as Taz. Were you in Jaar Mart?' I asked.

'Yes, then I went to Haruku,' he said. 'I was returned to Java with a small group of sick men, and have been here ever since. My name is Claude Thompson, from Auckland, New Zealand.'

After I had outlined my movements, I asked, 'Are there any others here from Haruku?' hoping he might know the whereabouts of Reg.

'Only those who arrived back with me. Some died on the journey.' So it didn't seem likely that Reg was here.

Claude told me they were working on the docks, loading ships. Now that our group was integrated with the others, it was reasonable to suppose that we would also do the same work. The morning parade was followed by the routine chant and bow to the east. I had forgotten the words of the chant and was thankful that no guard came close enough to notice. We set off to walk to the docks, along the road bordered by flowering trees that I had seen on my arrival in Batavia from Sumatra. I would like to say we marched, but that would be a travesty of the truth. Some men struggled along wearing clompers; a few still had remnants of shoes, while most were barefoot.

The work was heavy and reminiscent of Surabaya, loading ammunition onto ships, while the guards ranted and raved, lashing out with sticks to make us work faster. Something that I had seen before gave the impression that another sea journey was in the offing: wooden steps into the holds.

During morning parade on the third day, a Jap officer addressed us: 'A certain number will be leaving this camp. Only the fittest will be going, after a medical examination. Collect your belongings and return as quickly as possible.'

Bill caught up with Claude and me. 'He forgot to tell us we would be going to a garden camp,' was his sarcastic remark.

The examination was as we expected it to be, just a walk past two seated officers, only being failed if one's injuries were obvious. We walked down to the docks for the last time. Was it my fear and dread of another Jap-style sea cruise that caused my mind to go blank? I have no recollection of boarding the ship, or of the journey. The next thing I remember is when the guards came into the hold to move us out, in their usual manner.

Bill was alongside me and I said, 'We must have arrived, but goodness knows where we are.'

'Blimey, Taz, those are the first words you have spoken since we set sail a few days ago. You acted the same way on the two previous journeys – capable of normal functions, but aloof regarding your surroundings,' remarked Bill.

'Were there any deaths on board?' I asked.

'Not to my knowledge,' he replied. 'Someone who had been to the deck latrines earlier said he recognised the skyline of Singapore.'

Although the guards kept thumping and kicking us to get us out of the hold, for some reason only a few at a time were allowed onto the deck.

The reason for the hold-up became clear as I reached the head of the steps. Six men at a time were lined up with their backs to the dockside and told to drop their shorts and bend over. A Jap inserted a glass rod into the anus of each in turn to check for dysentery.

There was nothing hygienic about the process, the rods being wiped on paper before being used again.

'It looks as if they are trying to spread disease,' I said to Bill. 'How will they know which sample came from which man?'

This provided hilarious entertainment for the populace ashore. It was hours before all the men had gone through this humiliating health check.

Then we set off walking to what we discovered was River Valley camp.

Chapter 9

Down But Not Out

River Valley was far from being a luxury camp. A stinking open drain ran along one side, over which were the latrines. The huts were of the usual type and were grossly overcrowded. The food was so bad that if one picked out all the foreign bodies from the meagre ration of rice there wouldn't have been much left. Again, unable to work through a recurrence of malaria, I was back on half rations. With the improvement brought about by the three weeks at Bandoeng fast wearing off, my spirits were at a low ebb. When would it all end? What was happening outside? Would Gunso Mori's prediction become a fact?

When I got back on my feet I got talking to a group of Australians. They had got away from Singapore in a small boat and reached the east coast of Sumatra. They had sailed up the Singingi River but could get no further than Rengat. They set off to walk, heading westwards, and arrived at Padang, a port on the west coast. The Japs had got there before them and the Australians were taken prisoner. Later they were taken to Medan, on the northernmost point of Sumatra, and were set to work building roads. After a month or two they were put aboard the Dutch coaster the *Van Waerwijck*, which was torpedoed in the Malacca Straits. The survivors landed in Singapore. I was told that two other ships carrying prisoners from Java to Singapore had been sunk.

Although it was sad that our own men were being killed by action from Allied submarines, it did show that the Japs did not now have complete control of the seas. We had, however, no means of knowing what else was happening in the outside world in this month of August 1944. Near River Valley camp was a nightclub called The Great World, I was told. Its blazing lights made it clear the Japs had no fear of air raids on Singapore. Each evening, music drifted through the still night air. One haunting Malayan song could be heard quite clearly. It was called *Terang Bulan*, which someone said they thought meant 'moon over the river'.

63

Back working on the docks, loading lorries from the godowns, we came across some Red Cross parcels date-stamped June 1943. As there seemed little chance that the Japs would distribute them after so long, we thought up a scheme to do the job ourselves. The drawback was that we could not conceal any goods under our tattered clothing. First the guard at the door had to be removed. This was achieved by two men dropping a case of tins which broke open. These large tins contained an edible seaweed, part of the Japs' staple food, which was now rolling along the dockside, with the guard chasing after them to ensure they were all recovered. He was not pleased and showed it. This gave us some time to remove some parcels by making an opening into the back of the stack, where parcels could be opened out of sight. When the midday meal arrived, each man would collect one tin of food and drop it into the stew pot as he received his ration. At the end of the meal the lid was put on the stew pot and put back onto the lorry to be returned to the cookhouse.

This method worked well, and the contents of several dozen cases were delivered to the cookhouse. Even with this additional food, the improved quality of the evening meals was hardly noticeable as it was being shared by so many. It was my error that put a stop to this supply. I dropped a tin of bacon, which rolled past the guard. The look on his face would have been laughable under other circumstances. When I had retrieved the tin, the guard called me to him to give me a hefty clout. He then indicated that he wanted to know from where the tin had come. We stood watching as he went to the back of the stacks and saw the empty cases, coming out a short time later obviously agitated. He spoke to the other guards, and then called us all on parade, leaving one guard in charge, the remainder going into the godown.

'Who do you think will get into trouble over this, them or us?' asked Bill.

'By the way they are acting, I think they are worried it will be them,' I replied.

We stood on parade for the rest of the afternoon, and then returned to River Valley, where no mention was made of the incident. 'As I thought, the guards dare not report the matter or they could be punished for neglect of duty,' I said to Bill.

The following morning, we walked down to the docks, passing the famous Raffles Hotel as usual. This appeared to be occupied by Jap officers and Italian naval officers, whose armed merchantman[1] was alongside the dock near to where we were working. The Italian sailors often passed us, pointing their fingers at us and laughing, probably making disparaging remarks about us. The guards must have worked hard the previous afternoon because there was no sign of the Red Cross supplies in the godown, but it was noticeable that they were more diligent than before, watching us closely to prevent such a thing happening again.

It was a surprise when one morning a German U-boat docked near us, with the German version of *Roll Out the Barrel* blaring out from its tannoy. Our guard, a small, bad-tempered Korean, lined us up and went along the line slapping each man's face. Before he got halfway along, two German sailors came ashore and, without a word, picked him up and dropped him into the harbour. He emerged minutes later minus his rifle, which would certainly cause him more trouble when he returned to the camp.

Another move was imminent. We were ordered to parade with our belongings and told again that only the fittest would be able to travel to the new camp. First, we had to pass a medical. At the new camp we would get to grow our own food, we were told. A long time and many sea miles had passed since that first 'medical' in Surabaya, but the routine was the same.

We set off for the docks, obviously about to face another sea journey. We stopped alongside a sort of river steamer.[2] There were no holds, so we were packed tightly on the deck, with hardly room to stand, let alone sit. Fortunately, my memory lapsed again. When my senses returned, I was in the water holding onto a bundle of latex. Nearby, our boat was sinking. I had no idea how long I had been on board the steamer, nor how many men it was carrying. There were other men clinging to debris. One man joined me, telling me his name was Tom Williams. There was land in several directions, and we were drifting towards a sandy beach just as darkness was falling. As we drifted through that long night, we kept talking to stop ourselves falling asleep and losing a grip on the latex.

'How long had we been at sea?' I asked.

'It must have been about nine o'clock when we left Singapore and around five o'clock when the boat went down,' he replied.

My side pack containing my blanket was awfully heavy and I thought of letting it go, but with a struggle I managed to get onto the latex. After I had told Tom about my movements, he told me what had happened to him: 'I was in Malaya with a light Ack-Ack unit when the Japs attacked Pearl Harbor, then as they advanced, we moved back to Singapore. I was injured in the fighting at Bukat Timor hill and was in Singapore General Hospital when Singapore packed in. A squad of Japs went through the hospital and bayoneted all those on the ground floor, killing 123. I was on the second floor. Later I was moved to Changi prisoner of war camp, where I stayed until a few months ago when I was moved to River Valley camp.'

'I'm worried about my mate Bill Woodhouse,' I told him. 'I don't know if he got on the boat as we separated on the dockside. Do you happen to know him?'

'No,' he said, 'but there were still some fellows left on the dockside when we set sail.'

The sky was getting lighter as dawn approached. Soon the sun rose above the horizon and, to our horror, there was no land in sight.

'Blimey, it looks as though we've had it,' said Tom.

'It doesn't seem too good,' I replied, 'but do you see those banks of cloud? Maybe they are hiding the land.'

'I hope so. We must be close to the Equator, and the sun is likely to burn the skin off our backs at midday,' he said gloomily. 'Let's try paddling towards the cloud over there; it seems the nearest.'

For what seemed like ages, we paddled, sheer desperation giving strength to our weary legs, until before us we could make out a coastline. With renewed effort we drew closer.

'Stop paddling, Tom, the tide's taking us in.'

Soon we reached shallow water and staggered ashore, completely exhausted.

With blistered skin and swollen lips from the effects of the sun and seawater, we crawled to the shade of palm trees and thick undergrowth. We looked longingly at the green coconuts, knowing the cool milk would ease our burning thirst, but we had no means of reaching them. The sun had not yet reached its zenith and I calculated that we must have been in the water for about sixteen hours.

Hunger and thirst drove us to make an effort to find some water and berries to eat in the undergrowth. There was a brackish stream further along the beach. Thirst made us take the chance of ill effects from drinking the water. There was an abundance of various fruits that were palatable. Three other survivors landed a short distance from us, two

English and one Dutchman. Arthur Lewis and Ron Rooksby were both RAF. We were unable to pronounce the Dutch name, so we called him Hank. He proved to be a godsend. He had lived in the Dutch East Indies for years and had a knowledge of which fruits and roots were edible.

I asked him: 'Where do you think we are?'

'That's difficult to say. There are a number of small islands off the coast of Sumatra, and we could have landed on any one of them. But again, in the time we were at sea we may have reached Borneo or the mainland of Sumatra,' was his reply.

Weary, but with our hunger somewhat satisfied, we lay on the beach as darkness fell. Sleep was elusive due to the strange, unfamiliar sounds coming from the jungle – the incessant two-tone call of some night birds, and the cries and screams of unidentified animals.

We all jumped up in a flash when we heard what must have been a large animal moving through the undergrowth, but we could see nothing. The sun rose from the sea, and we caught sight of some flotsam that had drifted ashore. A wooden crate had come to rest in the shallows. This proved difficult to open without tools, but eventually we succeeded with the aid of a rock. Inside were twelve tins with Japanese labels. We tried opening them with stones, but got nowhere.

Further along the coast a waterlogged boat had been washed up, a large hole in the bottom. Its only content was a Jap rifle, complete with bayonet, and a torn mosquito net. The rifle was unloaded and was thrown into the sea. We used the bayonet to open the tins, only to reveal brown Japanese seaweed. We made ourselves sick by eating too much, too quickly. We were now able to cut down long bamboo poles to dislodge coconuts and used the net to catch fish. Our puny efforts to start a fire by the reputed Boy Scout method were a dismal failure. The roots Hank found and the fish we caught would have to be eaten raw. This proved unnecessary as Hank did manage to start a fire. By striking the bayonet on a stone, the sparks ignited the tinder he'd collected from the heart of a small coconut palm. The fire was to be kept going all night, to deter any prowling animals. After eating our fill of roasted roots and toasted fish, we laid down to sleep.

At dawn we realised that our fire had attracted some unwelcome visitors. A troop of Jap soldiers were coming along the beach with fixed bayonets, ten in all, and one officer with drawn sword. They stopped some 10 yards in front of us, raising their rifles. As we stood with raised arms, the officer jabbered away in Japanese.

Hank said, 'I have learnt some Japanese. He is asking where we came from.'

As Hank stepped forward to speak, a shot rang out, which whistled over our heads. Was this the end for us? The officer turned to the lad who had fired, who didn't look old enough to be handling a loaded rifle, and by the tone of the officer's voice we guessed he was getting a rocketing. Again, Hank spoke to the officer, who replied with another tirade.

'He speaks too fast for me to understand all he says, but I gather he doesn't believe me,' said Hank. 'He says no Japanese ships have been sunk and we must have escaped from a prison camp.'

After looking at the damaged boat and picking up the bayonet, the officer indicated that he wanted me to open my side pack; none of the others had managed to retain any of their belongings. He looked at my cigarette case, and then returned it to me.

'We are to go with them back to their camp,' Hank told us.

There we were taken, one at a time, before a more senior officer, who spoke in broken English. The interrogation took several hours, interspersed with frequent blows when our replies were misunderstood. Eventually we were put into a small hut without food and with several guards outside. It was a long, sleepless night due to fear and hunger pains. Our talk was subdued, and it did nothing to improve the morale of my fellow prisoners when I told them about the shooting of the two Australians on Haruku for attempting to escape. We all knew it was a distinct possibility.

In the morning we boarded a lorry. Was this the last journey of the condemned? After several hours driving along a rough jungle track, we arrived at a camp with a dozen atap huts. There we were handed to the camp guards. We felt immense relief when they put us into huts occupied by English, Dutch and Australian prisoners. They told us this was Sumatra, and they were here to build a railway.

Chapter 10

The Railway

This was certainly no holiday camp. The food was as bad as any at Haruku. The first meal was very welcome as it was the only food we had eaten since the open fire on the beach. I spent the afternoon looking round the camp and soon realised that everyone was bowing to the guards. Most men were working on the railway. A number of sick in the huts had come from camps in Java, but none that I knew. No one knew Reg or Bill. Tom had found a mate from Cycle Camp, and Hank was with his Dutch countrymen.

My first sight of the railway was of a deep cutting. It was obvious that this had not been made recently. On the banks were stumps of large trees that had been cut down not long ago. Maybe Hank could explain if he knew whether the Dutch had started the railway before the war.

My first task was carrying rails, with six men to each rail. These were red hot after lying in the tropical sun, and they burnt our hands and shoulders. This was made worse by the guards' malicious insistence that the tallest men were at the ends of the rail. I was at one end and felt sorry for the shorter men in the middle. Even with sacking on their shoulders, the whip of the rail caused constant bruises and abrasions. To add to this, the heat was oppressive. A certain number of rail lengths had to be laid each day, but they were rarely completed before darkness fell. The distance then had to be finished by the light of torches and storm lanterns.

My first bout of malaria in Sumatra kept me off work for several days. Taking a steady walk around the camp, I caught up with Hank, who was limping badly.

'Hello Hank, what happened to you?' I asked.

'My toes were bruised when a rail slipped, but don't worry, they're better now. I keep limping because I don't want to go back working on the railway. I get full rations chopping wood for the cookhouse,' he told me.

We went to his hut, where I asked him about the cutting. 'Has there been a railway there before?'

'No,' he replied. 'In 1923, the Dutch oil company planned to build a railway from the oil fields at Palembang to the small island port of Pakenbaru. The idea was abandoned due to frequent flooding of the large rivers it had to cross, and the unstable swampy ground.

'The Japs must have found the plans, and from what I have been told they decided to build a line. This was not from Palembang but from Moearo, where a line from Padang, which is a port on the west coast of Sumatra, ends. This section was started in June. Work started at Pakenbaru in March, the rails and engines being shipped from Singapore. Do you see the advantage this line would be to the Japs? It would provide a quicker route to move troops from Singapore to the west coast of Sumatra rather than the long sea journey round the north or south of the island.'

'Yes,' I said 'I can see the advantages; that long coastline must be vulnerable to an attack from India.'

'It's more than a thousand miles long,' he told me.

To qualify for full rations, I had to return to work on the railway. What a Heath Robinson set-up! How did the Japs expect to succeed in building a serviceable railway where the Dutch had failed? The rails were laid onto sleepers, which were made from trees cut down in the jungle and roughly squared with an adze, which is a type of curved axe. Iron spikes fastened the rails to the sleepers, which were driven home by men with 14lb hammers. A Jap engineer indicated where the spikes were to be placed and his only aid was a wooden gauge.

I was put on the hammer gang, a job I did not relish. The hammer was almost too heavy to lift, never mind being able to swing it. A guard seemed to think a few clouts would give me strength to work harder. Even he gave up and took the hammer from me after I had fallen over several times. The engineer needed some men to carry out the job of lining up the track. Armed with crowbars, we had to move the track physically as he instructed, a bit this way, a bit that way, until he was satisfied the line looked straight. At the end of a long and tiring day I was also chosen for a burial party. This was becoming a regular occurrence.

After the usual breakfast of the awful ongle-ongle – that purple, gelatinous pap made from the pith of the sago palm – it was back to work. A railway truck carrying ballast was pushed onto the newly completed section and all hell broke out. The heads of the spikes were flying in all directions: the rails splayed, and the truck was derailed. The guards went berserk, shouting and lashing out at all and sundry. This was deliberate sabotage by the men knocking in the spikes. I had been told to strike the head of the spike again after it was gripping the rail, causing the head to crack. My puny effort with the hammer could not have done much damage.

Now for the task of clearing up the mess. First the truck had to be unloaded and manhandled back onto the undamaged track – a back-breaking job. New sleepers had to be laid and the rails refixed. Several men were injured in the panic. If the sabotage had resulted in a day's delay in the construction of the line, it would have been worthwhile, but that wasn't to be. We still had to complete the day's quota.

After leaving the oppressive heat of the cutting, we found a dramatic change in terrain and atmosphere. The damp, sultry heat caused profuse sweating. Working in the swampy ground was far more wearying. An added menace was the presence of leeches. They attached themselves to our feet and legs until they had had their fill of blood. The only way one could remove them was by brushing them upwards, otherwise a nasty wound could be caused.

Now I could see why the Dutch had abandoned the project in 1923. Truck after truck of rock was brought up in an effort to create a solid foundation, but to no avail. It just disappeared into the swamp. It would take a long time to cover a short distance at this rate. To overcome this setback, whole tree trunks were laid along the line of the track, and then more were placed across the line. This had the effect of holding the rocks in the right place and soon it was possible to see an embankment being formed. Only time would tell if it would carry a train.

This work carried on relentlessly, day in, day out, with no respite, and with the lack of proper rations we were all becoming weaker by the day. Many of the men were becoming more and more susceptible to diseases and malnutrition. Thankfully, after a while, I was given another task. I was now away from the swamp and was with two other RAF men felling trees in the jungle. Paddy McQuade, from Londonderry, and Dinger Bell, from Sussex, had been taken prisoner at Tasikmalaya.

No guards came with us into the jungle and one might think it would be a good opportunity to escape. But where to? We had no idea where we were in Sumatra and didn't know if any natives lived in the area, or if they would be willing to help us. We did know there were wild animals in the vicinity – tigers, black panthers and elephants, amongst others – hence the need to keep fires going all night round the camp. To avoid getting lost we had to keep within the sound of the rail construction. One advantage of working in the jungle was our knowledge of edible fruits, as this meant we could augment the meagre rations.

We worked hard during the morning, two on a cross-cut saw and the other with an axe, felling the required number of trees before the hottest part of the day. The falling trees disturbed a variety of wildlife. Snakes, scorpions and lizards came out of the undergrowth. The large, roosting flying foxes in the tops of the trees dived at us with shrill shrieks. Once we had to run when a hornets' nest came down with the tree, but fortunately none of us were stung.

The use of tree trunks as a foundation proved successful and the line advanced northwards daily. This meant a longer walk from the camp each morning before work could start, and still the same length of line had to be laid. On returning to camp in the darkness, an already weary group had to bury the men who had died in the last twenty-four hours. Many of these deaths were a result of the horrific injuries sustained while working. Without medication, crushed feet and severe wounds soon turned gangrenous. Rarely did we know the identities of those being buried.

We continued to have an inadequate food supply and it seemed short-sighted not to use fruits and vegetables that were growing in abundance in the jungle. The root vegetable we had eaten on the beach was plentiful, as was the yellow tomato-type fruit and the long, green banana-like plantain, which could be used as a vegetable, along with a variety of other fruits. I felt sure a small group, with some knowledge of what was edible, could vastly improve our food. After thinking it over for some time, I decided at the first opportunity to put the idea to Hank, who was now acting as interpreter. This chance did not come until I was again recovering from malaria. When I told him of my idea, he replied: 'Yes, that sounds like a possibility. I will put it to the Japs right away.' He soon returned.

'The answer is no,' he told me. 'The Jap officer said the men are lazy, going sick for no reason, causing derailments and other delaying tactics. His only concession was that he would allow any such food collected during midday break to be brought back to the camp.'

'I don't suppose I'd expect any more from the lousy devils. Are they too dim to see that with better food and some medication, illness would not be so prevalent?' I replied. 'As for laziness, it is they who extend the length of line to be laid if things run smoothly, and most accidents happen through sheer fatigue.'

It was back to laying sleepers on my return to work. The leeches were still a nuisance. I loathed their fat, slimy bodies. After queuing for the midday meal, there was no chance of picking any fruit from the jungle, so the Japs' concession meant nothing. A few days later, I saw Dinger and Paddy on the morning parade.

'Stay with us,' said Paddy. 'The chap who has been with us while you have been off badly cut his leg yesterday and we will need somebody else.'

Felling trees suited me – hard work, but out of the reach of the brutal guards, in the comparative cool of the jungle, sheltered from the blazing sun, with just a few rays penetrating the canopy of branches. One of us would cut a 'V' in the first tree with the axe, and then two of us used the saw. The one with the axe trimmed the branches from the fallen trees, ready for another group to drag them from the jungle. Eight trees a day was the quota, checked by a guard at the edge of the jungle. We managed to have enough time to collect some roots in the rice sack I had brought with me, depositing it at the cookhouse on returning to camp.

It was now time to move forward to a new camp, ahead of the line, making the journey to work shorter each day. In the distance, hundreds of natives could be seen clearing the route for the line laying. They must also have prepared our new camp. The swampy terrain was now past and working conditions much better on the solid ground. The introduction of a rail-laying truck, pushed by a diesel lorry fitted with flanged rear wheels and a four-wheel bogie in front, made rail handling much easier. Now, each day, a greater distance had to be laid, and more men were put onto tree felling.

The days passed painfully slowly, each a repetition of the previous one. Men were injured and many died. The frequent recurrence of malaria left me weak and in a depressed state. With no sign of this purgatory ending, it would be so easy to lose the will to live. But I didn't want Gunso Mori's prophesy to come true. I was going to survive.

The line advanced northwards, and when it reached the camp site a siding was laid. A steam engine was now brought into use, having successfully negotiated the swampy section. Soon it was time to move forward again to a ready prepared camp. This was already occupied in part by a group of Australians, who were building a spur line to a coal mine. Here, for the first time, independent fires were allowed in order to cook anything we could glean from the jungle. Numerous small fires were dotted about the camp in the darkness. Some of this extra food was given to supplement the rations of the sick. In return, some were able to make cooking utensils and knives from tin cans discarded by the Japs.

I was back working with my two mates. Paddy had been ill and was still not fit, but needed the benefit of full rations. We turned our attention to obtaining any sort of meat. Snakes were the most abundant, which we caught with forked sticks and baked in hot ashes. The problem of catching small mammals and lizards was overcome by using traps made from bamboo. A chap who had a broken leg made them for us. Sometimes a luckless dog, possibly from a nearby kampong, would wander into the camp, never to find its way home again, although we never had any contact with the natives. A further unexpected supply of food came from a large pond near to where we were working. Small fish with stubby legs walked out of the water onto the bank. Being slow movers, they were easy to pick up.

'If only we could catch one of those monkeys,' said Dinger, as he watched them leap about in the treetops. 'One would provide more meat than a dozen rats. But how do we trap them?'

'I recall reading in a boys' adventure book that they can be caught by placing something coloured in a jam jar tied to a tree,' I replied. 'It would grab the object and wouldn't let go, so was unable to withdraw its clenched fist.'

'There's only one snag,' chimed in Paddy. 'Where do we get jam jars? I've never seen any the Japs have thrown away.'

'If we take necks off bottles by the cold and hot water method, and leave a curve at the top, that should work.'

'What's this water method?' asked Paddy.

'I saw a chap making mugs that way. He put cold water into the bottle to the level required, then poured boiling water over the top, causing the bottle to crack at the cold water level.'

We fixed the monkey trap, containing a piece of coloured paper, to a tree. In the two days before we moved forward again, it did not tempt a curious monkey. There was no way we could retrieve the trap so we had to abandon it. A fresh trap was set up in the new location. At first it seemed to be a complete failure. Then, one morning, we arrived to find a monkey struggling to free itself. Success at last. When I skinned it that night I was completely nauseated; it looked so like a human baby. Hunger finally won and into the pot it went.

Often a guard shouted, with arms raised, 'Orang-utan' as we entered the jungle. We took this as some kind of warning.

Suddenly, Paddy shouted. 'Eh, look over there.' Standing upright in a small sunlit clearing were three animals with golden brown fur. One was about 6 feet tall, another a little shorter, while the third was about half size.

'A family of orang-utan,' I shouted. We dropped our tools and ran for cover in the undergrowth. Cautiously we returned to retrieve our tools. The ungainly animals had departed. We told of our fright when we returned to camp, only to be laughed at.

'Orang-utans are quite harmless,' we were informed.

Chapter 11

A New Danger

We were now told that the railway was to be finished by 26 June 1945. Not knowing which month it was, was this six months ahead or less? Had another Christmas passed unnoticed and still no hint of what was happening in the world outside? Oh for some sign to boost our flagging morale.

Thankfully there was no outbreak of dysentery, as in Haruku. But still men died daily. I was put with a group to go back down the line, where an engine had been derailed. This was a most hazardous job. Diesel lorries were fairly easy to return to the rails but it was the steam engines that caused the most agitation. Using only crowbars, tree branches and brute force, the heavy engine was put back on the rails while the guards lashed out with sticks and rifle butts. Several men suffered crushed feet and one man broke his leg. The track then had to be relaid. We were too weary to eat when we returned to camp late at night.

The next camp was situated near a wide river. An embankment was being constructed to reach a maximum height of 8 feet. The materials, mud and gravel, were brought up from the river. As a result, the rail laying was brought to a standstill. After a few days of this work, the heavens opened – torrential rain, thunder and lightning of such intensity I had not witnessed before. This caused the river to become a brown, muddy torrent, making it dangerous to get the material from the crumbling bank. It was not possible to get gravel from the river, so only mud went to build the embankment, which was then washed away by the heavy rain. The guards were reluctant even to go near the riverbank and for our own preservation we also kept clear of the water. If anyone had fallen in, there was no way he could be saved.

Even under these conditions it was expected that the work would carry on as fast as in the dry weather. With lots of *'Kura-kura'*, the guards lashed out unmercifully. It was also not possible to collect anything from the jungle as everyone was occupied building the embankment, and while the rain continued, there was no way individual fires could be lit back in camp. It was dismal. Even the protective fires round the camp could not be kept going in the rain, so it came as no surprise when a small herd of elephants charged through. There were no casualties, but they flattened the Jap cookhouse. Our delight that it was the Japs' camp that had been damaged soon faded when they took over our cookhouse.

For the two days it took to rebuild their cookhouse it was not possible to cook any quantity of food for the whole camp, and with the whole place awash with the continuous rain, no fires could be lit in the open. Because of the dire situation we were in we erected a small shelter of bamboo and atap, and dug a trench to divert the water. Soon a fire was going. The cooks were then able to supply a small quantity of food late in the day.

As the storms continued, little progress was made with the building of the embankment. Rocks were brought in a railway wagon from further up the line. The track was so unstable that engines could not be used, so the wagon had to be pushed to collect the rocks. At the end of one day's working, we lined up alongside the track for the usual count. A bolt of lightning struck the rails. A ball of fire rushed towards us, the force knocking us backwards in a tangle. The wagon had been lifted off the rails by the force of the strike and was hanging precariously above us. Thankfully it did not fall. We picked ourselves up, luckily without any serious injury, although my right foot was painful.

Back up the banking we found that a Korean guard, who had been standing on the rail, had died instantly. This gave the guards another excuse to vent their spite on us as we strained to return the wagon to the rails. They seemed to have the idea that we had caused the lightning to kill one of them. Or maybe they were disappointed that none of us had received serious injury? My ankle was now badly swollen and I was unable to work on the railway.

Behind the camp, the ground rose slightly and beneath a large rock outcrop a natural spring gushed out. It was the best water we had come across while in Sumatra. My job was to keep the cookhouse, which was now back in full swing, supplied with water. For the first time in days, the rain had stopped. The hot sun caused steam to rise from the ground. I set off to the spring with two containers, a steady stroll alone. I rounded the rock and froze: there was a growl and a flash of gold and black disappearing into the undergrowth. There were clear imprints of a tiger in the mud. I fled back towards the camp. When I returned later, I made as much noise as possible as I had to retrieve the containers to get water back to the cookhouse.

I did not see the tiger again, but decided that if this was its regular watering place, another time it might not run away. So some other means to get water to the camp would have to be found. In Java I had seen bamboo used as pipes, although I did not know how to remove the centre part of the canes ... but I guessed Hank would. Hank was still cutting logs for the cookhouse, so I put my idea to him.

'You cut twenty-five 10-foot lengths of bamboo,' he said, 'and I will make the pipes by passing a hot stone through the bamboo.'

The guards drew their water from the stream created by the spring. If they realised what our plan was, they would insist that the pipe be run into their camp to create a shower. The first two lengths were soon ready. Hank joined them together with short pieces of bamboo wedged tightly inside the main pipes. Placing the pipe in a trench for concealment, with one end in the pool, water could now be collected 20 feet away from the spring. During the next two days, the complete pipe was put in place, covered on the lower part by undergrowth. It proved to have more than one advantage: continuous supply of water for the cookhouse, a shower for washing, and the surplus water flowing through a trench to flush the latrines, thus helping to remove the flies' breeding ground.

With my ankle nearly back to normal and having eliminated my water-carrying job, I was back working on the railway. The river level had dropped, exposing quantities of gravel for the embankment construction. We had to use silly baskets which spilt out the gravel. It was particularly arduous carrying the heavy baskets and scrambling up the riverbank onto the embankment. We would then receive a blow from the guard if the basket was not full enough. Native ladies would have carried them on their heads, but when we tried that we were not successful.

With the rail laying moving forward again alongside the river, I was back on tree felling and thankful of the opportunity to gather extra food. It was evident from the weighty rice sacks being carried back to camp that the monkey traps were successful. Ahead there was a bend in the river and the line followed the river course until we saw sight of a bridge. Above the convergence of the two rivers a large bridge was under construction. Native labour was being used. On seeing the primitive methods in use to build it, it was a relief to know that we weren't going to work on that bridge. The pile driver was an iron weight attached to a long rope which ran over a pulley supported on a wooden tripod. Twenty men raised the weight and let go on a given signal. The backlash often knocked men into the river as there was no protective rail. The thought crossed my mind: had they been forced to work during the tropical storms? If so, how many had drowned in the flooded river? There was no way of finding out.

Line laying stopped as it neared the bridge. Now everyone was put to the task of loading a wagon with gravel from the river. We got into lines to pass the baskets along from one to another. This met with disapproval from the guards. *'Ichi mens, ichi basket.'* (One man, one basket.) This meant hundreds of men climbing up the bank, getting in each other's way. The first wagon was loaded by late afternoon. A diesel engine was coupled to it, setting off with a dozen of us sitting on the gravel. We talked as we travelled along, at not much more than walking pace. There were two matelots in the group – Dave Colhoune, of HMS *Sultan*, an Irishman who was much older than any of us, and Joe Tivey, from HMS *Prince of Wales*. It was now getting dark.

'Blimey, how much further?' Joe asked. 'It'll be blooming late when we get back to camp after unloading this wagon and I'm hungry now.'

'Let's chuck some off now.' I suggested. 'The guard in the cab won't notice.'

At last the train came to a halt. The guard was carrying a torch and indicated that we were to put the gravel between the sleepers. Luckily he returned to the cab without looking in the wagon, where he would have seen that half of the gravel was missing. As the train moved slowly forwards it was to our advantage to get rid of the gravel as fast as possible. Most of it was thrown over the sides and only a little went between the sleepers.

Three journeys were made each day. On one occasion, the last group had the misfortune to have their wagon derailed and had to re-lay the track in the darkness. The native workers had now finished the bridge and moved away. Now line laying could restart. One of the most difficult jobs was the handling of the rails. The men had to step over open spaces to lay them in the correct position. But it was even more difficult and hazardous for those driving in the spikes, standing on the narrow walkway, swinging 14lb hammers. Many fell into the river, including some guards who got in the way. They were picked up by a boat downstream from the bridge.

We moved to a new camp nearer the bridge, which the natives had just completed. There were the usual nine huts, each housing seventy-five men on the split bamboo platforms running the length of the hut. The cookhouse was some way away, while the guards' quarters were on the opposite side. We missed the spring water. Now all the water had to come from the river and had to be boiled before drinking.

While the line was being built, before reaching the bridge, the surrounding jungle had offered some protection from the direct rays of the sun. Working on the bridge we were out in the open and the sun was beating down on us from a clear blue sky. It caused a great deal of discomfort to all of us. The rails were too hot to handle and caused burns, even through the rice sacking we wrapped around our hands. It suited me again to be put on tree felling on the far side of the river, with the advantage of more food and being well away from the brutal guards.

The line had almost crossed the bridge when I again went down with an attack of malaria. Someone brought me tea and ongle-ongle before leaving with the working party. The tea was welcome but I couldn't eat. Now alone, a mood of dejection came over me and my mind wandered. Had Imphal fallen as the Jap newspaper had forecast at Bandoeng? If so, had the Japs overrun India? Who had won the battle of the Solomon Isles as reported on my radio in Jaar Mart camp so long ago? When would this ordeal end? Or would Gunso Mori's prediction come about for all of us, as it had for so many thus far? Thoughts like these had to be dismissed to retain my sanity, and I recalled what I said to my Korean tormentor Basher, on Haruku, many months ago: 'You will not kill me.'

I must have fallen into an extremely deep sleep as I did not hear the working party return. Now they were preparing to start another day. They left as it got lighter. After what seemed to be only minutes, I awoke to find it was getting dark, and guessed the others should be back soon. I waited in anticipation of some tea when they returned, but there was no sign of them. I dozed off again. Suddenly I was awakened by a screaming guard with a storm lantern. He pulled me from the platform, and I realised I was still the only person in the hut. With repeated kicks, and blows from his rifle butt, he forced me, mostly on all fours, from the hut and along the railway line towards the bridge.

The sight that greeted me was the most terrifying I had ever witnessed. The river was in full flood. The bridge was in imminent danger of collapse, due to the pressure of debris piled almost to the top of it. All the men from the camp were carrying flaming torches and were stretched across the river on top of the debris. The object was to steer tree trunks and branches between the bridge piers. Even my guard seemed somewhat taken aback by what he saw. He stopped thumping me and stood taking in the scene. I was wondering where all the water had come from. There had been no rain in this area for some time. Dawn was breaking as he forced me forward to the end of the bridge and indicated that I climb onto the rubble on a hanging rope. It must have been sheer terror that gave me the strength to hold on. My reluctance to let go of the rope brought a further blow from his rifle butt. Finding a firm footing, I moved under the bridge out of his reach, and there I froze, clinging to the timbers. The vibrations increased and, with a mighty roar, the bridge collapsed. My guard fell past me and I was swept downstream. Something hit the back of my head. I remember someone leaning over me on the bank, saying, 'There are only eighteen of us here.'

How I was saved from the water I did not know, nor by whom.

Chapter 12

Judy

'Hello, it's good to see you have woken up,' said a voice with an Australian accent.

'Where am I?' I asked.

'You were the only one here when we arrived a couple of days ago. There were some sick chaps in other huts, otherwise the camp was empty.'

'Were you on the bridge when it collapsed?' I asked.

'What bridge? We moved up here after finishing the line to the coal mine. We met a group coming from this direction.'

'Someone must have known me and brought me to my bed space. This is my blanket and side pack.'

'My name is Andy. Could you eat anything?'

'I'm Taz, and I'm dying of thirst.'

'I'll be back,' he said as he left. As I lay there alone I wondered how many had survived the bridge collapse. Andy returned with some hot sweet tea.

'Where did you get the sugar?' I asked.

'It's palm sugar from the natives working in the coal mine,' he replied.

A meal was brought to me later – not the usual cookhouse food, but clean rice with meat and vegetable stew, with a few fried fish. This kind of food was given to me in the days that followed and my strength began to return. Taking a stroll around the camp for the first time since the bridge incident, I was surprised to see a chap walking with a fairly large but thin brown and white dog. Naturally I was curious and I went and spoke to him.

'Hello, I'm Geoff Lee, known as Taz.'

'I'm Frank Williams and this is Judy.'

'It's unusual to see a dog in a camp,' I said

'Yes, I know dogs have wandered into camp and been eaten, but Judy is an official prisoner of war. She hates the Japs. I'm afraid she might bite one of them and I know what would happen then.'

Thankful for the care Andy and his mates had shown me, I felt I must return to work to earn full rations. This entailed laying a siding for one group, and with others I was fetching gravel for ballast from the river with those silly cane baskets. Thankfully, the river had returned to its normal level.

The sun was setting as we made our way back to camp. We were just passing some loaded wagons in the siding when a commotion broke out at the end of the column. All the guards rushed to see what was happening. Taking advantage of their temporary absence, those nearest the wagons dived underneath and loaded as much rice and dried fish as possible into rice sacks through holes in the bottom of the wagons. Judy, who had come out of the jungle, now gave a low growl as a warning that the guards were coming back and then shot back into the trees. Now I knew where the extra food had come from that had put me back on my feet and appreciated the risks that had been taken on my behalf. I could foresee that all hell would be let loose when those wagons were unloaded.

The bridge had now been rebuilt and the first task was to retrieve the rails from the riverbed. This was not too difficult now the water was at a very low level. Native divers tied ropes to them while we dragged them clear. Some were badly bent whilst others still had sleepers attached to them, which had to be removed from the reusable rails. It was announced that the new deadline for the completion of the line was 18 August 1945.

We began laying the line across the bridge, which we completed without any serious delays. A steam engine with just a Jap driver aboard set off slowly to cross the bridge, which was visibly shaking. Even the sound of the engine did not drown the creaking of the timbers. The cheers from the guards as it reached the far bank were short-lived. The engine cleared the bridge and then suddenly disappeared down the embankment. Our laughter soon subsided. The guards started lashing out at us, driving us to where the engine was lying upside down and half submerged in mud. There was no sign of the driver. His body was brought out after much frantic digging, accompanied by screaming, shouting and blows from the guards. We were then expected to get the engine back up the embankment, a job equal to a thousand ants carrying a dead elephant up the 12-foot slope. We spent many hours sweating, pulling and pushing without being able to move it a fraction. Using poles and fulcrum we were unable to get purchase in the mud. The recovery of the engine had to be abandoned.

Soon after this section was repaired a diesel engine pulling three wagons passed us with about a hundred men on board. I thought I recognised some who must have survived the bridge collapse. We moved forward across the bridge to another camp, which was occupied by those who had passed us earlier. They were survivors of the disaster, and had been sent back down the line afterwards to put ballast between the sleepers. Others there had escaped on the wrong side of the river. Ron Thompson managed to climb up the sleepers, still attached to the rails and hanging into the water. No one had any idea of the death toll. Near the camp a white post had been put up by the Japs to mark the Equator.

It was quite a surprise when we moved to a new site for tree felling. In a clearing the ground was covered with yellow fungi. I smelt and tasted one, and found it quite palatable but, still dubious as to their nutritional value, we only took a few back to camp. I showed them to Hank, who was with us again. He was very excited.

'Before the war these were highly prized as a delicacy when brought into the towns,' he told me.

'Well, there's plenty there,' I replied.

They were delicious when cooked. One problem was how to get so many back to the camp. This was solved when the group fetching our trees from the jungle came for the second one. The guard whose job it was to count them had fallen asleep.

'That's good,' I said. 'Don't take one out yet, go and pick some mushrooms. Here are some rice sacks. If he asks how many you have brought out, tell him *san* [three].'

This ruse gave us more time to pick some, having one less tree to fell. In the following days we brought to the cookhouse pounds and pounds of this welcome additional food, which made it possible to give the sick extra rations. No matter how many we picked, there was no decrease in the amount available. The cooks took Hank's advice and dried some in the sun for future use. On our next move forward to keep up with the railhead, there was no sign of fungi within our restricted area.

Moving to a new camp, we found it partially occupied by other British and Dutch prisoners but we had no chance to mix with them. Two working parties were lined up in the morning, one group being

Above: Members of 84 Squadron on the SS *Yoma*, January 1942. Inscribed on the back of the photo is: 'Ginger Norton, John Ramsden, Joe Holden, Tich Oldfield, Len Rough, Ernest Mortimer, all sent to Haruku and Sumatra.'

Right: The only photo of Geoff taken in Singapore after his release in September 1945 shows him sitting on the left showing his bare back.

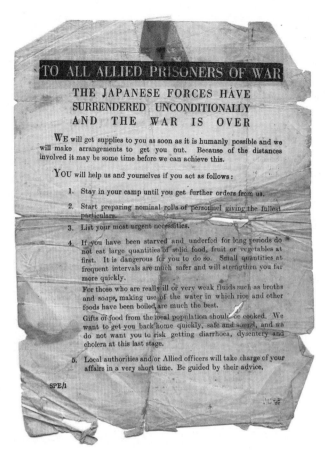

TO ALL ALLIED PRISONERS OF WAR

THE JAPANESE FORCES HAVE SURRENDERED UNCONDITIONALLY AND THE WAR IS OVER

WE will get supplies to you as soon as it is humanly possible and we will make arrangements to get you out. Because of the distances involved it may be some time before we can achieve this.

YOU will help us and yourselves if you act as follows:

1. Stay in your camp until you get further orders from us.

2. Start preparing nominal rolls of personnel giving the fullest particulars.

3. List your most urgent necessities.

4. If you have been starved and underfed for long periods do not eat large quantities of solid food, fruit or vegetables at first. It is dangerous for you to do so. Small quantities at frequent intervals are much safer and will strengthen you far more quickly.

   For those who are really ill or very weak fluids such as broths and soups, making use of the water in which rice and other foods have been boiled, are much the best.

   Gifts of food from the local population should be cooked. We want to get you back home quickly, safe and sound, and we do not want you to risk getting diarrhoea, dysentery and cholera at this last stage.

5. Local authorities and/or Allied officers will take charge of your affairs in a very short time. Be guided by their advice.

SPE/1

Left: Leaflets dropped into the camps when Japan surrendered.

Below: Geoff's identity release book, which states that he was captured in Tasikmalaya, Java on 18 March 1942 and was released from Logas, Pakan Baroe, Sumatra, on 20 September 1945.

PARTICULARS OF RECOVERED PRISONER OF WAR.	PARTICULARS OF RECOVERED CIVILIAN INTERNEE.
1. Names in full.... **LEE, JOHN GEOFFREY** (Surname first in capitals)	1. Names in full........ (Surname first in capitals)
2. Nationality.... **BRITISH**	2. Nationality........
3. Rank.... **L.A.C. I.**	3. Designation........ (Mr., Mrs., Miss, Dr., etc.)
4. Service number.... **157565O**	4. Internee number........
5. P. W. number.... **56. 543. 870. ect ect.**	5. Civil occupation........
6. Service.... **RAF** (i. e. British Army, A. B. R. O., R. N. Z. A. F., etc.)	6. Address at time of internment........
7. Unit, formation, ship, etc.... **84 Squadron**	7. Religious denomination........
8. Religious denomination.... **C of E**	
9. Date and place of capture.... **TASIKMALAYA Java 18. 3. 42**	8. Date and place of internment........
10. Date and place of recovery.... **LOGAS - PAKAN BAROE Sumatra 20.9.4**	
11. Signature or thumb print of holder.... **J. G. Lee**	9. Date and place of recovery........

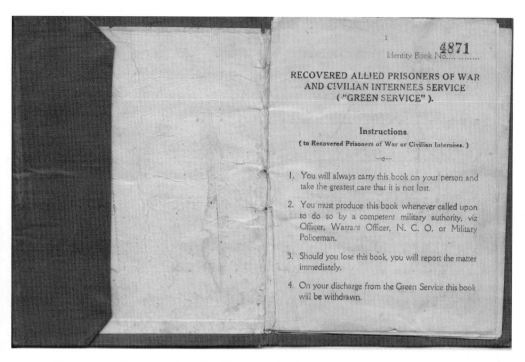

Above: Instructions page from Geoff's release book.

Below: An RAF squadron leader guards a trio of handcuffed war criminals, left to right: Lt Soni, the officer in charge of the camp at Ambon and Haruku, and the vicious Japanese guards Gunso Mori (far right) and his interpreter Kasiyama (centre), the notorious 'Blood' and 'Slime'.

Any one who was on Haruka will reconise this trio. The Jap Officer in charge of the camp was chaerged with War Crimes and hung in Singapore. Kasiama, the English speaking horror, was sententenced to 10 years, but the Americans needed an interpretor and he was released. Gunso Mori was hung for War Crimes. They were called Blood and Slime. Some will remember his greeting when we arrived on Haruku. "You are here to die".

WARNING

GUARD YOUR TONGUE

YOU are free now. Anything you say in public or to the press is liable to be published throughout the whole world.

You have direct or indirect knowledge of the fate of many of your comrades who died in enemy hands as a result of brutality or neglect.

Your story, if published in the more sensational press, would cause much unnecessary unhappiness to relatives and friends.

If you had not been lucky enough to have survived and had died an unpleasant death at the hands of the Japanese, you would not have wished your family and friends to have been harrowed by lurid details of your death

That is just what will happen to the families of your comrades who did die in that way if you start talking too freely about your experience.

It is felt certain that now you know the reason for this order you will take pains to spare the feelings of others.

Arrangements have been made for you to tell your story to interrogating officers who will then ask you to write it down.

You are not to say anything to anyone until after you have written out your statement and handed it in.

SPE/U/2

Above left: A leaflet issued by the government to all returning FEPOWS.

Above right: Betty and Geoff Lee, in about 1946.

Left: First letter from the MOD, 6 April 1976.

Ministry of Defence Whitehall Library

MINISTRY OF DEFENCE
Old War Office Building Whitehall London SW1A 2EU

Telephone (Direct Dialling) 01-218
(Switchboard) 01-218 9000 } ext 0016

J.G. Lee Esq.,
14 Carmel Gardens
Arnold, Nottingham.

Your reference

Our reference

Date 6th April 1976

Dear Sir

Thank you for your letter of 31st March.

I regret that this library holds no material relating to the Sumatra railway and I would suggest that you contact the Imperial War Museum, Lambeth Road, London SE1 and the Commonwealth War Graves Commission, 2 Marlow Road, Maidenhead, Berks. SL6 7DX; either or both of these organizations may well be able to assist you.

Yours faithfully,

Chief Librarian

Commonwealth War Graves Commission
2 Marlow Road Maidenhead Berkshire SL6 7DX

Telegrams Comgraves Maidenhead   Telephone Maidenhead 34221

J G Lee Esq
14 Carmel Gardens
Arnold
NOTTINGHAM

Your reference

Our reference
ENQ 8   (Mrs B Walton)
Date
15 April 1976

Dear Mr Lee

Thank you for your letter of 12 April 1976 about the railway in Sumatra built by
prisoners-of-war of the Japanese.

Unfortunately, I cannot help you as we have no information in our records about this
particular railway. However, our Librarian has made enquiries of the Imperial War
Museum and I think you may well find that a visit to carry out a little research in
their library will prove most useful. The address you require is as follows:

> Imperial War Museum
> Lambeth Road
> Lambeth
> London SE1

I am sorry I cannot be more helpful.

Yours sincerely

B. Walton (mrs)
Director-General

Commonwealth War Graves Commission
2 Marlow Road Maidenhead Berkshire SL6 7DX

Telegrams Comgraves Maidenhead   Telephone Maidenhead 34221

J G Lee Esq
14 Carmel Gardens
Arnold
NOTTINGHAM

Your reference

Our reference
REC 1/7   (Mrs B Walton)
Date
15 June 1976

Dear Mr Lee

I am writing again about the railway in Sumatra built by prisoners-of-war of the
Japanese.

It occurs to me you may be interested to know that the graves of the prisoners who
lost their lives and were originally buried at Pakan Baru (or Pakan Baroe Camp 11)
and from surrounding camps were moved firstly into Medan Dutch War Cemetery in
1950 by the Army Graves Service. In 1961 at the request of the Indonesian
Government the Commonwealth dead from the cemeteries in Sourabaya, Palembang, Medan
and Muntok were brought into Djakarta War Cemetery which, with the 474 Commonwealth
war graves already there, brought the total to 1,181. There are 271 Air Force
graves, including those of 26 unknown airmen, in the cemetery which is under the care
of this Commission. The cemetery is in the suburb of Menteng Poeloe about 7 miles
outside the city.

We would very much like to know a little more about the specific route the railway
took, therefore I have taken the liberty of enclosing 2 photocopy maps of Sumatra
and we would be most grateful if you could mark on either one of the sheets the
line of the railway. We would also like to know where Logas is.

I am enclosing a stamped addressed envelope and look forward to hearing from you
again.

Yours sincerely

B. Walton (mrs)
Director-General

Second letter from CWGC,
15 June 1976, asking for a
map of the Sumatra Railway.

ENCS

```
Route of The Sumatra Railway. Started at Pakenbaru March 1944.
Started at Moearo September 1944.
Completed August 15th 1945.
Overall Length 260Km.                              Siak River.
Rails, Trucks and Steam Engines were transported      Packenbaru
from Singapore, via the Siak River     River
Rails for the Moearo start from        Kampa
dismantled lines North of Padang.
```

Map of the route of
the Sumatra Railway,
similar to the one
sent to the CWGC in
1976.

```
                                    Kampa  Two.
                               Lipatkain
                                 Equator
                                    Kotabaru
        .. Spur Line To
           Coal Mine.
                                   Logas
                            Rengat    Palembang

    Mountain
                              Moearo
        Existing Line
        to Padang.
Indian
Ocean    Padang.
```

Imperial War Museum
Lambeth Road London SE1 6HZ

Telephone 01-735 8922

J G Lee Esq   Your reference
14 Carmel Gardens
Arnold   Our reference
NOTTINGHAM   CMR/PH/045987
                                     Date
                                     26 January 1978

Dear Mr Lee

Thank you for your very interesting letter of
22 November and for the loan of the enclosed
photocopies.

I am glad that you were able to make some progress
in your enquiry on the basis of my letter of
28 April and regret that this library can provide
you with no more detailed information than that
which I was then able to give.

May I express the hope that the diligence with which
you have undertaken your research will shortly be
rewarded.

Yours sincerely

Caroline M Reed
Dept of Printed Books

Enc: Photocopies

Letter from IWM, 26
January 1978.

HEAD OFFICE
Kebon Sirih 52, Jakarta, JAVA
Phone: 348107– 348108– 351465
Cable: CALPACEM

OPERATING OFFICE
Rumbai, Pekanbaru, SUMATRA
Phone : Pekanbaru 338–339
Cable : CALPACEM

Jakarta, 6 December 1979

Mr. J.G. Lee
14 Carmel Gardens
Arnold, Nottingham
UK.

Dear Mr. Lee:

      I refer to your letter of 17 October 1979 on your plans to visit Pekanbaru in February 1980. It just happened that I assisted Mr. C.G. Thompson during his visit to Pekanbaru in April 1972. I am now stationed in Jakarta, and met the Thompsons when they stopped at Jakarta on their way to London early this year.

      With regard to hotel accomodation, Pekanbaru has indeed a good "Riau Hotel", in which the Thompsons were also staying. We will be happy to assist you in making the necessary hotel reservation and taxi arrangement, if you wish us to do so. As far as your journey is concerned, I suggest that you fly direct by GA-945 from Singapore to Pekanbaru in Garuda Indonesia Airways (40 minutes by Fokker-28), and then proceed to Jakarta (also Garuda) enroute to New Zealand or other places in Indonesia.

      Brig. Gen. Nugroho Notosusanto, Director of the Center of Armed Forces History has indicated his interest in meeting you, perhaps during your visit to Jakarta, the Indonesian capital. Gen. Nugroho (48) who studied also at London University in the early sixties, seems to know the "Far East P.O.W. Association" quite well. It is generally felt in Indonesia, that a "missing link" exists in the recorded data of the Japanese occupation in Central Sumatra. The experience of P.O.W.s, for instance, is another significant source to fill the mystery. The only book about this period is published in the Netherlands a few years ago entitled "De doodenspoorweg van Pekanbaru" (The Pekanbaru railroad of death). It is for this reason that Indonesian historians are eager to obtain more data of that period in the Pekanbaru area.

Yours sincerely,

Wisaksono Noeradi

Letter dated 6 December 1979 to Geoff from the Caltex Pacific Indonesia oil company about his forthcoming trip to Sumatra.

Commonwealth War Graves Commission
2 Marlow Road Maidenhead Berkshire SL6 7DX

Telegrams Comgraves Maidenhead

Telephone Maidenhead 34221

J G Lee Esq
14 Carmel Gardens
Arnold
Nottingham

Your reference

Our reference
PUR 9/3
Date
20 May 1980

Dear Mr Lee

Thank you very much for your letter and the most interesting account of your journey through Sumatra and photographs.

I believe I had heard something of the continued existence of parts of this railway before but this is the first time that I have seen photographic evidence.

You are correct in saying that some of those who died in Sumatra have graves in Indonesia and these are now located in the two war cemeteries at Djakarta and Ambon, the graves previously in Palem Bang, Medan and Muntok in Sumatra having been reconcentrated into Djakarta War Cemetery.

Although attempts were made to locate graves at the end of the war it is true that many others were not found. All of those who have no known grave are however commemorated by name on memorials and most of those who died in captivity in Sumatra are commemorated on the Singapore Memorial in Kranji War Cemetery. With regard to those whose bodies may still rest in the jungle I think you would agree that it is better that after so many years they remain undisturbed.

If you do wish to trace the burial place, or place of commemoration where there is no known grave, of any individuals I will be pleased to help you do this if you can give me the name, rank, number, unit etc of those concerned. In the meantime I am enclosing your photos and also a copy of our 60th Annual Report which I hope you will find of interest.

Yours sincerely,
David Parker

David Parker
Information Officer

ENCS

Letter from CWGC, 20 May 1980, received after Geoff's journey to Sumatra.

RIAU HUIA...
PEKAN BARU.
SUMATRA.

A letter sent by Geoff to his family when he arrived in Sumatra in 1980.

DEAR ALL, I AM SHATTERED. AFTER TRAVELLING FOR 28 HOURS WITH ONLY A 1½ BREAK FOR SLEEP AT 4.30. AM. THE CALTEX OIL COMPANY HAVE BEEN WONDERFUL; LETTING ME HAVE A CAR AND DRIVER - INTERPRETER WHEN EVER I WANTED, AND THEN, HIRING ME A LAND ROVER FOR MY TRIP INTO THE JUNGLE. WE LEFT THE HOTEL A 8 AM TO GO ALONG 150 MILES OF DIRT TRACK, WHICH BECAME HARD GOING AFTER THE MANY SHORT SHARP STORMS, TO REACH LOGAS, PLANNED. TIME WAS 5 HOURS EACH WAY TO COMPLETE IN THE 12 HOURS DAYLIGHT, BUT IT TOOK 9 HOURS TO GET THERE, AND BECAUSE OF THE DANGERS FROM TIGERS BLACK PANTHERS AND ELEPHANTS IT WAS NOT POSSIBLE TO RETURN THE SAME WAY, SO WE HAD TO TRAVEL 300 MILES, FARTHER TO RETURN TO PEKAHBARU, AND THE FIRST 100 MILES OF THE RETURN WAS STILL VERY DANGEROUS SHOULD WE HAVE STOPPED FOR ANY REASON IN THE DARK, BUT THE TRACK WAS NOT AS BAD AND THERE WAS MORE CAMPONGS. WHICH THE ANIMALS ONLY RARELY VISITED. (GOING OUT) → AFTER CROSSING THE FIRST FERRY WE STOPPED FOR LUNCH, AND IF YOU DIN'NT EAT THE NATIVE WAY WITH YOUR FINGERS YOU WENT HUNGRY, THEN A FEW MILES ON WE CROSSED THE EQUATOR, BUT WHILE WAITING AT THE NEXT FERRY A BOY WAS INJURED SO WE TOOK HIM BACK TO THE FIRST FERRY, CROSSING THE EQUATOR TWICE MORE. NOW HOW DID THAT RAILWAY TRUCK. ARRIVED IN THE MIDDLE OF JUNGLE 300 MILES FROM THE NEAREST RAILWAY, AND WHO WROTE IN ENGLISH. "OCTOBER" THEN A WORD WE COULD NOT READ, 'THUNDER' MORE LATER. LOVE TO THE YOUNGSTERS, DAD.

Geoff Lee in Sumatra 1980.

Kunjungan Kembali Bekas Tawanan Perang

Sungguhpun telah lama berlalu, Perang Dunia II masih meninggalkan kenangan pahit terutama bagi mereka yang pernah mengalami sendiri. Di sekitar Pekanbaru ini ribuan tentara Sekutu dan romusha, semasa pendudukan Jepang, gugur dalam kerja-paksa membangun jalan kereta api. Beberapa bekas tawanan Jepang (POW) yang masih hidup tidak melupakan pengalaman pahit ini. Salah seorang diantaranya adalah J.G. Lee yang pertengahan Pebruari lalu berkunjung ke Pekanbaru dan melihat kembali daerah-daerah lokasi kerja paksa itu.

Pada tahun 1940, sebagai pra jurit I pada Skuadron 84 Angkatan Udara Inggris (RAF), Lee yang berusia 21 tahun bersama pasukannya Skuadron 84 Angkatan Udara Inggris (RAF) diterbangkan dari Cairo ke Singapura. Maksudnya untuk memperkuat angkatan perang Sekutu terhadap kemungkinan serangan tentara Jepang. Namun mereka datang terlambat, karena ketika itu Jepang sudah mendesak maju sehingga pasukan tadi terpaksa mendarat di salah satu tempat di Sumatra Selatan. Lee bersama-sama kawan-kawannya kemudian bergerak menuju Pulau Jawa. Ketika Jepang mendarat, mereka lari ke Bandung dan Yogyakarta tetapi tertangkap di Tasikmalaya. Sejak itu mulailah penderitaan mereka sebagai tawanan perang. Bersama-sama dengan tawanan lainnya yang berkebangsaan Belanda, Australia, Selandia Baru dan Indonesia, Lee diangkut ke Ambon. Di sana mereka dipekerjakan dalam pembangunan lapangan terbang di Pulau Haruku. Beribu-ribu rekannya mati akibat menderita, kekurangan gizi, penyakit-penyakit biri-biri, malaria dan disentri. Dari Ambon mereka diangkut ke Singapura dan terus ke Pekanbaru. Di sini mereka melakukan kerja paksa untuk membangun jalan ke reta api antara Pekanbaru dan Muara.

Nottingham

Jalan kereta itu mula-mula direncanakan oleh Belanda untuk memudahkan hubungan antara Selat Malaka dan Samudra Hindia. Jepang membangunnya untuk mengangkut batu bara dari Ombilin ke Pekanbaru dan mengapalkannya lewat Sungai Siak ke Singapura. Sepanjang jalur rel kereta api yang akan dilalui ini didirikan kamp tawanan. Lee ditawan dalam kamp di Logas. Ia masih ingat bagaimana para ta-

<u>Atas</u>: Lee (x) bersama rekan-rekannya pada saat pembebasan si Singapura (1945). <u>Bawah</u>: Lee di muka sisa lokomotip di Tanjung Rhu (1980)

wanan bekerja mengangkat batang-batang rel itu dan menebang hutan dalam penderitaan yang menyedihkan. Ribuan kawan kawannya terkubur sepanjang jalur jalan kereta api itu. Ketika Jepang kalah akibat bom atom tawanan perang mereka dibebaskan dan dipulangkan ke negeri masing-masing. Lee kembali ke Inggris dan menetap di Nottingham. Ia kemudian membangun keluarga dan karirnya di bidang perdagangan tekstil. Kini ia telah mempunyai dua orang anak yang sudah dewasa, namun kenangan pahit yang dialaminya di tengah rimba Sumatra tetap membekas. Itu pula yang membawanya datang kembali bulan lalu. Dengan diantar oleh karyawan Bagian Hubungan Masyarakat CPI, Lee berkesempatan menelusuri kembali tempat-tempat dimana ia pernah menderita dahulu ***

apa & Siapa

* Pengurus Persatuan orangtua Murid "Cendana" untuk periode 1980/1981, terpilih pada akhir bulan Pebruari. Mereka terdiri dari: L.Purbodiningrat (Ketua) K. Sundramurti (Wakil Ketua), J.B. Noer (Sekretaris), R. Manurung (Bendahara) dan Ny. R. Djamaoeddin (Anggota).

* PEGAWAI BARU:

- Adam Le Roy Breth, Koordinator Konstruksi Senior pada Bagian CRG, Duri.
- Edward Lawrence Cole, Ahli Teknik Perminyakan pada Bagian Teknik Perminyakan, Rumbai.
- Wilson Scott Young, Ahli Teknik Senior pada Bagian Teknik Umum, Rumbai.

Geoff's visit made the local news in Sumatra.

Geoff's photographs of the remains of trains found in Pakenbaru, Sumatra in 1980.

Geoff (centre) and fellow ex-RAF POWs on the 1986 trip to Java, Ambon and Haruku.

Photographs of the cemetery at Ambon taken during the 1986 visit.

FEPOW wreath left at the Ambon cemetery.

Right: Memorial at Antjol (Ancol) cemetery in Jakarta, Java, photographed during the 1986 visit.

HERE ARE COMMEMORATED
FIFTY EIGHT OFFICERS AND MEN
OF THE COMMONWEALTH
WHO PERISHED IN CAPTIVITY
IN FEBRUARY AND MARCH 1942

WITH SEVENTY TWO OF THEIR COMRADES
WHOSE NAMES ARE NOT KNOWN
THEY LIE BURIED AT ANTJOL

Below: Geoff (far right) with six fellow RAF FEPOWs during their visit to Ambon cemetery.

A FEPOW memorial at Oosterbeek, Holland, which was unveiled in 1988.

Bogey and wheels of the Oosterbeek memorial.

Right: Geoff Lee (left) with a fellow FEPOW survivor.

Below: Invitation to a reception at the Guildhall in 1992.

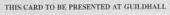

THIS CARD TO BE PRESENTED AT GUILDHALL

GREAT HALL   No. 338

CORPORATION OF LONDON

In the presence of
Her Majesty Queen Elizabeth The Queen Mother
Reception at the Guildhall for the
National Federation of Far Eastern Prisoners of
War Clubs and Associations
on Tuesday, 8th December 1992, from 11.30 am to 2 pm

ADMIT BEARER

NOT TRANSFERABLE   BRIGADIER JOHN PACKARD
Lounge Suit or Blazer   Chairman of the Reception Committee

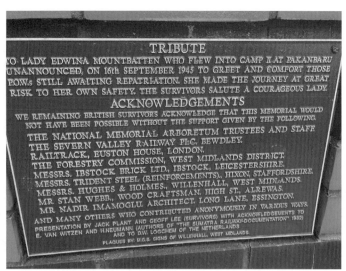

Above left: The Sumatra Railway memorial monument pyramid at the National Memorial Arboretum, Alrewas, Staffordshire.

Above right: Monument plaque naming Geoff Lee as a contributor.

Below: Monument plaque giving information about the Sumatra Railway.

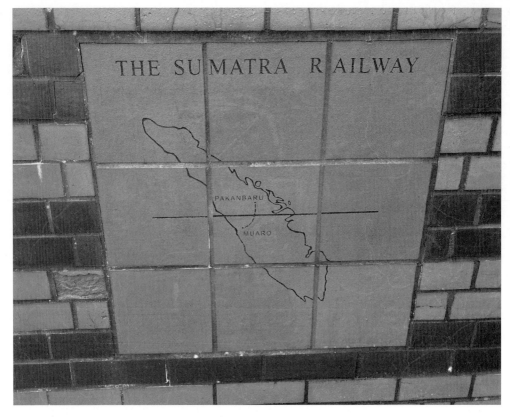

Above: Map of Sumatra on the monument.

Below left: The memorial plaque mounted at one end of the rail track exhibit at the NMA, which was dedicated on 14 May 2002 by Prince Charles.

Below right: Replica of the Equator signpost in Sumatra at National Memorial Arboretum.

those who had been there when we arrived, while our section stayed together. Before we moved off in opposite directions, I thought I saw Bill Woodhouse, but again, no chance of us meeting. After the evening meal, which was now just basic rations, I walked through the huts, in the dark, calling for Bill. In the third hut he replied, 'Is that you, Taz?'

'Yes, Bill. I'm pleased to find you again. I have often wondered what became of you. Have you seen anything of Reg?'

'No, I'm afraid not,' he told me.

'How did you come here?' I asked.

'We were put aboard a riverboat, the *White Lady*, at Singapore, and sailed up the Siak River to Pakenbaru,[1] then moved forward to where the line was being laid,' he said. I outlined my movements since seeing him last in Singapore.

'We crossed a large bridge, which seemed in danger of collapse during the floods, but it stayed up with just a bend in the middle,' he continued. 'The steam engines have to negotiate it very slowly.' His treatment by the guards and the standard of food seemed to be on a par with my experience.

A pregnant sow was brought to the Jap camp, to make use of any waste food. In their eagerness to keep it well fed, they gave it a lot of good food several times a day. Had they wasted this much food during the past months, while we were kept on starvation rations? It was easy for us to arrange a lookout throughout the day by those unable to work. As soon as food was put into the sow's trough, someone collected it. This was boiled up and shared out at the end of the day. The poor pig did manage to eat some food before it could be removed, as sometimes the guard stayed with it for a while. Even so, it got thinner as the days passed. Finally it gave birth to a little runt, which soon died. From then on, the Japs completely ignored it and stopped its food supply. We failed to understand why they didn't kill and eat it, as it was clear it would soon die of starvation. Hank told me: 'I've asked the Jap officer if we can have the pig, but only got a clout for my trouble. He told me he couldn't kill it, or give to us, because it belongs to the Emperor and it was a bad pig for not producing a litter and must be left to die.'

The question was, how to get our hands on it knowing there was not much time left. Our chance came the following night. A violent tropical storm put out the perimeter fires. We knew a tiger had been prowling nearby for several nights, probably attracted by the scent of the pig. Now it was a race between us and the tiger. Half a dozen of us rushed to the pig pen, broke down the fence, and grabbed the half-dead animal. As fast as possible we hurried to the cookhouse, where it was killed. Some of its blood was put into a tin and spread around the pen after the rain stopped. The initial commotion when the guards saw the pig was missing soon died down. As we had hoped, they blamed the loss on the tiger, without realising the blood would have been washed away in the heavy rain, or apparently being aware of the absence of the tiger's spoor. The meals next day were a real treat. I can't remember when I had last tasted pork.

Meanwhile, the line advanced steadily without any major hold-up, apart from occasional derailments due to the splitting of the green sleepers. Nothing much changed except that the guards now had fixed bayonets, which made it more difficult for them to hit us with their rifle butts. Each night a burial party had to muster, sometimes for just a single burial, at other times for several. The line was now running parallel with a large river. In the distance could be seen another rail-laying group coming towards us. Did this mean it was getting close to 18 August, the date by which the line had to be completed? As the days passed and we got closer together, it became obvious that the other group's banking was several feet higher than ours, and somewhat to the right. After a great deal of coming and going by Jap officers and engineers it was finally decided that we should raise our banking, starting some distance back. I thought it was a miracle that the two sections had met with so small an error.

The two groups were now housed in a new camp in order to work on rebuilding our section of banking. I was now able to bed down alongside Bill. A group of about a hundred, including Bill, Hank and me, were put aboard three wagons to go back down the line. We travelled until late afternoon, passing several of our former camps, pointing out to Bill where we had picked the yellow fungi.

'I wish we could stop and gather some,' I said, 'they're delicious.' The shaky bridge was crossed very slowly. 'This is the bridge that collapsed,' I told Bill.

'The way it's trembling, I doubt if it could stand another flood,' he replied.

We finally arrived at our destination camp as it was getting dark and I was unable to tell if it was a camp I had previously been in as most of them looked just the same. A much-needed meal was provided as no provision had been made to supply food for us on the journey.

The following day we were put to work moving lumps of rock in native-style handcarts, which was extremely difficult over the rough ground. The guard, indicating that I wasn't pushing hard enough, shouted, *'Kura-kura, Speedo-speedo.'* If he heard the single word I uttered I doubt if he understood its meaning. He continued shouting, then, without warning, he stuck his bayonet through my left foot. He threatened my three mates, who had stopped pushing on hearing my yell of pain. The language I used is unfit to be recorded here. A more senior guard came over. On seeing what had happened he slapped the offending guard but offered no assistance to me. I got the impression that the guard was disciplined for halting the work rather than for injuring me. Although there was no means of stopping the bleeding, I had to carry on working for the rest of the day. My foot was badly swollen the next morning and I could only hobble about with the aid of a stick. This meant I would only qualify for half rations. Bill was very concerned for me but had nothing that could be used as a bandage. He washed my foot, and then wrapped some rice sacking round it to keep out the dirt.

When Bill returned from work in the evening he told me, 'I made contact with a native today. He will exchange a chicken for any clothing.'

'I've got nothing, only my blanket,' I replied.

When Bill was leaving for work the next morning, I gave him my precious blanket. He brought back a small chicken and some bananas. Bill insisted on cooking the chicken himself while I rested my foot. Soon he came back, having boiled it over an open fire, and we shared it. I couldn't see his portion but felt he had given me the larger share. It was good. It was not the pangs of hunger that prevented me from sleeping, but an invasion of what seemed to be hordes of parasites, eager to sample a fresh supply of blood. The only time I had been without the protection of my blanket before was when Bill went down with malaria.

Because of the discomfort, and the throbbing of my foot, I decided to take a walk in the dark. Hobbling out of the hut I was stopped by the dreaded sound of 'Oi!' I had passed a guard without bowing and fully expected to receive a clout. Turning around, I said, *'Banjo'* (toilet) and bowed. He waved me on. When I returned, he was still there and called me to him. This is it, I thought. From his pocket he took some photographs and showed them to me by the light of his torch. They were of his mother, father, brothers and sisters. He also had a little dolly charm. Although neither could speak the other's language, I learnt he was 17 years old and wanted to go home. By hand signals he asked if I had any photographs, which I had not. He showed concern about my foot but did not understand how it happened until I demonstrated with his bayonet, telling him it was done by a Korean guard. He understood 'Korean' and said something in Japanese. I fetched my last possession, my cigarette case, and insisted he keep it. I could perceive his pleasure when he saw the picture of Mount Fujiama on the case. He indicated that he would leave some food just inside the hut. With a bow to each other, we parted. Over the next few days several packs of native-style food – rice with fish or meat, wrapped in a banana leaf – were placed in that certain spot.

My foot was causing me some concern, it was festering badly. I then tried the maggot treatment – a few maggots, placed on the injury and held in place with a leaf. After a short time I could see an improvement.

One morning we were all called out on parade and told there wouldn't be any working party that day. A train would pass through to mark the official opening of the now complete line. We must all bow to the officers as it passed. After standing for what seemed like hours, the train at last arrived, travelling from the south towards Pakenbaru.

'Bill,' I said, 'you'd better pray they get across those two bridges safely or there's no telling what will happen to us.' We heard nothing, so took it for granted that there had not been any mishap. 'One thing they have not told us: was the line completed on time? Was today 18 August 1945?' I pondered.

All days were alike to us.

Chapter 13

Is This the End?

Dawn was breaking the next morning as I woke up. I sat for a while listening. Something was different. I shook Bill until he awoke.

'What's the matter?' he asked.

'Sit up and listen,' I said.

'I can't hear anything.' He was puzzled.

'That's the point. There's no shouting or yelling from the guards as on normal mornings.'

'You're right. They should be around by now. I wonder what's the matter?'

By now everyone was curious and came out of their huts. There wasn't a guard to be seen anywhere, just a few turbaned Indians in Jap uniforms. The Japs must have pulled out overnight. Did this mean the war was over? An RAF sergeant was the most senior rank in our group, and took charge.

'I'll see if I can get any information from the Indians,' he told us. Hank went with him, but they soon returned and reported, 'They wouldn't tell us anything. In fact, they refused to speak to us. I hope they understood when we told them we wouldn't stand any interference from them.'

Sergeant Brown outlined two options open to us. The first was that we could set off for Pakenbaru with the steam engine and trucks. The drawback to this was we were not certain the war was over, and the Japs may have set up an ambush further up the line. We all knew that the punishment for attempting to escape was death. The second option was to clear an area of jungle and keep a fire going day and night, hopefully to attract the attention of any Allied aircraft. The only snag to this plan was that during our time in Sumatra, we had not seen any aircraft.

The fittest men set about clearing a patch behind the camp and started a fire while others made an assessment of the quantity of food that was available. There were two skinny cows in the guards' camp, a sack of good rice and some large tins. These looked like they contained the type of seaweed that made us sick when we first landed in Sumatra. A further four sacks of rice were in one of the wagons, but nothing else. We knew we could supplement our food supply with roots and fruit from the jungle, but this had its drawbacks. In the past we'd relied on the sound of the work on the railway to guide us back from the dense jungle. Here there were no such sounds. I was given the job of thumping an oil drum to prevent anyone getting lost. Meanwhile, one of the cows had been killed and the smell of cooking meat wafted through the camp. It had been decided to have a good meal now and revert to rationing tomorrow, having no idea as to when and from where relief would arrive, or if it would come at all. This was something we dared not talk about.

Several days passed without a sight or even the sound of aircraft, and our spirits, which had been raised in the first few days, began to flag. Several deaths had occurred since the Japs had left and others seemed to have lost the will to live, including Bill. This I thought was due to the newfound freedom – no parades or working parties under Jap orders. If one wanted to work, one could find plenty to do. Those who chose not to work hung around listlessly, contemplating the plight they were in. I was concerned over Bill's condition. He wasn't so much ill as lethargic; he had no diarrhoea or malaria, just a slight swelling of his ankles due to beriberi. It even seemed too much trouble for him to eat.

'Bill, you've got to snap out of it or you won't make it,' I told him.

'What's the use?' he answered. 'If the war's over why haven't we heard from the outside world?'

'Hang on, relief will come soon,' I went on. 'Have you still got those photos you showed me while on the *Yoma*?'

'Yes, they are in my pack.'

I took them out. They were very tatty but still discernible.

'Bill, this is your wife, Helen, and your son Simon. He will be about 6 years old, now won't he?'

'If this is August 1945, then he was 6 last month. Helen's birthday is in October.'

'Just remember, Bill, they are living for the day you return.'

'Perhaps Helen thinks I'm already dead, not having any news of me, apart from the card I was able to send from Jaar Mart, if that reached her.'

'Look, Bill, I'm not going to let Gunso Mori's prediction come true. I'm going back home, and so are you.'

In the morning I was pleased Bill didn't lie down again after he had been to the latrine. He also showed concern as I uttered 'Ouch' as my foot touched the ground. 'Is it painful, Taz?' he asked.

'Yes, but it's my own fault. I was on my feet too long yesterday, and I forgot to replace the maggots.'

'Let me see it,' he said.

It was badly inflamed. Bill washed it and fetched fresh maggots. After he had wrapped rice sacks around my foot, he told me to stay put while he fetched my breakfast.

It was no longer ongle-ongle for the morning meal; now it was soft boiled rice, and the sago was used to thicken the stew. The other cow had to be killed; otherwise it would have died from starvation with there being no grass in its compound. This meant there would be two large meals that day, as there was no way meat could be kept with the temperature over 80 degrees. It was about midday when someone shouted: 'Aircraft approaching!' Everyone rushed to the clearing.

As a single-engine plane came towards us we all waved our arms and shouted. Then … silence! It was a Jap fighter plane. We tried to reach the shelter of the trees, fully expecting a burst of gunfire. It passed over, and then turned, and coming down lower, it circled the clearing several times before flying off. This raised the question, was the war over or not? The answer came the next morning, in the form of two twin-engine planes coming towards us. We didn't rush to the clearing this time until we saw the American markings. Soon chutes began drifting down. Eagerly we set about collecting the containers that were attached but the contents were disappointing. There was no food or medical supplies, just shirts, shorts, underwear, socks and some bars of soap. While the soap was very welcome, we had been without clothes for so long that a little time longer wouldn't make much difference.

Sergeant Brown called us together and said, 'I'd have thought some news about the progress of the war would have been included in the containers. It would seem it's finished in this area, but we know nothing about the rest of the world.' He continued, 'You will all get some clothing and the soap will be shared. If you exchange clothing for chickens, meat or fish, bring it to the cookhouse so all will get a fair share. Any fruit you obtain, share it with the sick. Contact has been made with some natives.'

Again, I'd done too much and my foot was very painful. Bill did his first-aid job, bandaging it with strips of torn-up undervest and then covering it with a sock to keep it clean. He then set off for the nearby kampong to barter his shirt and shorts. He returned with a large hand of small bananas, several papayas, some pink fruit with prickly skins and blocks of gula jawa. His contribution to the cookhouse was a quantity of dried fish. As most men had traded their clothing, there was quite a party atmosphere, with plenty of fruit for all. This was followed by a substantial meal.

'I learnt that the name of the kampong is Logas,' Bill told me. 'The natives are fetching supplies from across the river, using the contents of two containers that dropped into the river, as currency.'

As the sun rose above the trees, the sound of aircraft could be heard. Soon a single-engine plane approached and circled the clearing before dropping some leaflets. Eagerly they were picked up, but they conveyed little to us other than that Japan had capitulated on 15 August 1945 and we were to make our way northwards to Pakenbaru. Sergeant Brown called us together, saying, 'It would seem our only chance of reaching Pakenbaru is with the engine and three wagons standing in the siding. Is there anyone who can drive a steam engine?' There was no answer. He went on: 'I reckon it to be a journey of over 60 miles, so walking with so many sick is out of the question. Can I have some volunteers willing to learn to drive? It's a British engine so all the controls are clearly marked.'

A number of hands went up; the sergeant chose six and took them to start their training. Bill, in a much better state of mind than a few days ago, had gone to find something to do. Thanks to him having seen to my foot earlier, it was now less painful. I decided to go to the kampong with my shirt and walked along the now worn track. Suddenly, to my horror, a Jap came around a bend in the track riding a bicycle, his rifle slung over his shoulder. He must have been just as shocked at seeing me as I was at seeing him. He fell off his bike as he tried to free his rifle, almost knocking me over. I grabbed his rifle and, with strength generated by fear, brought the butt end down onto his head. He was still alive but bleeding badly. I slung his empty rifle into the undergrowth and, taking his bike, carried on to the kampong. With much gesticulation, I was able to convey to them what had occurred. I gathered they had seen the Jap ride by. Two men agreed to return with me. It would be unwise to leave the Jap there, whether alive or dead. The smell of blood might attract a tiger, making the area unsafe. Reaching the spot, the only evidence of what had taken place was a pool of blood. Of the Jap there was no sign. A search through the undergrowth came to nothing. We returned to the kampong, where I collected bananas, coconuts and two chickens in exchange for the bike and shirt. Telling Bill later what had happened, he posed some unanswerable questions: 'I wonder where he came from. Someone must have forgotten to tell him the war was over. Then again, are there other Japs down the line who don't know it's over? Or even prisoners?'

'What puzzles me,' I said, 'is where did he go after I left him? He was too badly injured to help himself. Could there be other Japs close by who assisted him? Or did a tiger get him?'

The learner drivers seemed to be handling the engines well, running backwards and forwards, starting and stopping. Further supplies were dropped the next morning. This time it was all medical goods and food. The cooks prepared the best meal we had had in ages: thick soup, followed by meat and vegetable stew, with tinned potatoes, rounded off with rice pudding made with condensed milk. There was no rationing, so we ate until we could eat no more. Our stomachs could not cope with such a large meal and we paid for our gluttony with bouts of sickness and diarrhoea during the night. We did not have any medical orderlies with us, and we had no knowledge about most of the medical supplies and what they were to be used for. The bandages and dressings were a blessing, not only to me, but for all those suffering from tropical ulcers, which had developed from comparatively small cuts. Also, the medicines were too late for two men who died during the night.

Not many had an interest in breakfast and for a change there was no queue. A special dish was prepared for the sick who had been unable to eat much of the evening meal, consisting of soft boiled rice sweetened with jam, with butter added. To prepare for the big move planned for the following day, firewood had to be cut and loaded onto the tender to feed the boiler on the journey. A bamboo frame was erected on one wagon and a parachute lashed to it to provide protection from the sun for the prostrate sick. Fewer men would be leaving Logas than arrived there and the wagons would still be overcrowded. The covered one carried the sick, some sitting, others lying down. The rest had to stand in the other two wagons. Finally, we got under way, going slowly northwards, stopping at intervals for the call of nature. Two men died on the journey and were buried alongside the track.

Late in the afternoon we reached the camp with the natural spring. The bamboo pipe was still operating. Not wishing to travel during darkness in case of breakdown, we stayed the night. Protection fires were lit around the camp. There wasn't time to cook a meal, so we made do with canned potatoes and corned beef. We occupied just one hut and found that the bugs and lice had somehow managed to survive without food since it was last occupied at the time of the bridge collapse. How I missed my protective blanket.

Setting off again just after dawn, we soon reached that large shaky bridge. Having no faith in the structure, the engine was uncoupled and driven across slowly. A cheer went up when it reached the far side without mishap. Then the wagons were pushed across. Further along, we passed the white post marking the Equator. Soon afterwards, we saw a board with Japanese ciphers painted on it. This I took to be where the line from the south joined the one from Pakenbaru. Rounding a long curve, we came to another large bridge, which had a distinct bend in the centre. This didn't look any sturdier than the previous bridge, so we crossed it in the same manner.

At last, the end of the line. Here at Pakenbaru there was a semblance of organisation. We found a list of our names, number, rank and unit. Medical officers, orderlies and Red Cross personnel had been flown in from Singapore. They took charge of the sick. Some concern was shown over the state of my foot, but it was much easier after the professional treatment I soon received. We were informed that this was No. 2 camp Pakenbaru, alongside the airfield, and the date was 12 September 1945.

It was not until Bill and I went through the huts looking for sleeping space that we realised just how grossly overcrowded the camp was. All ten huts were occupied by the sick, many grotesquely swollen with beriberi. Others were gaunt, breathing skeletons covered with skin. Every bone in their bodies could be seen. We, like the large number walking around, would have to sleep in the open. After queuing for quite a while, we were served with a strict ration of meat and potato stew, which still left us feeling hungry. One could join the queue again, which Bill did, but I had been too long on my feet and had to rest.

A nursing orderly, seeing the tattered state of my bandage, came over to dress my foot again. I asked him, 'How are we going to be taken away from here?'

'Some of the serious cases have already been taken to Singapore,' he replied. 'Some by boat, others by the only Dakota plane we have at our disposal, and more are leaving today.'

'Having seen the condition of those in the huts, a good many won't make it unless they can get hospital treatment soon,' I said.

'Yes, that's true,' he agreed. 'Deaths occur every day. There is a large burial ground just outside the camp. It wasn't until a week ago that we knew you were here. Some women internees had been brought out from Palembang, while a POW camp near the airfield was cleared. The biggest threat to life for so many here is they had fought to stay alive for three and half years but now they seem to have lost the will to live.'

It was on 15 September that we got our biggest surprise. A silver twin-engine plane landed and a lady in army uniform arrived. She climbed onto a railway wagon and told us: 'I am Lady Mountbatten. The war with Japan ended after the Americans dropped atom bombs on two Japanese cities – the first on Hiroshima, on 6 August, followed on 9 August by another on Nagasaki. Both cities were completely destroyed.'

There were murmurs from the men. 'Atom bombs? What are they? Capable of destroying cities?'

Lady Mountbatten continued: 'The war in Europe ended in May this year after France had been invaded in June 1944. Dakota aircraft are being prepared to take you all to Singapore in the next few days.' She then walked among the sick. Her talk with them probably did more good than any medication.

The evacuation of the sick was vastly speeded up. More planes were landing and ambulances were dashing to and fro. Soon there was room in the huts for those who had been sleeping outside. At last, the time for which I had hoped and prayed for the past three and half years had arrived. The date was 20 September 1945. My name was on the list to board the next plane.

'Is Bill Woodhouse on the list?' I asked.

'No. Only those needing medical treatment are listed, but don't worry, everyone will be away in a few days,' the orderly replied.

'Cheerio, Bill. See you in Singapore,' I said as we parted.

I boarded the Dakota with about thirty or forty others. It was devoid of seats to allow more to be transported each trip. My thankfulness to be on my way was tinged with sadness as I thought of the many comrades who would not be coming with us. It was only a short flight to Singapore. A very bumpy landing threw us about, but no one was hurt. Disembarking as quickly as possible, an Australian reporter arranged us in the shadow of the plane to take photographs of our final release. He had taken pictures in the camp, and naturally, he had concentrated his interviews on his fellow Australians. Over the tannoy, the sound of a male singer drifted across the runway. The words were very distinct: 'Don't fence me in ...' Very apt. We were each issued with a released prisoner's pay book and asked to fill in the details: name, number, rank, and place and date of release.

'Your name is on the Logas list, so your place of release is Logas, Pakenbaru, Sumatra,' the young lady in charge told me.

After the paperwork was completed, I was taken to hospital. There I was put in the care of a nursing orderly named Ron. Taking me to a bathroom, he removed the dressing from my foot while the bath was filling and then left me to indulge in the luxury of the hot water. He looked in on me from time to time as I wallowed, telling me to stay as long as I liked. 'You won't need these again,' he said, picking up my sacking shorts. 'Put those new clothes on when you are ready.'

After drying off with the soft white towel, I had a shave with the kit by the wash basin, and then donned the new underwear, white shirt and shorts. Sheer bliss and joy. The nightmare was over. Ron returned with a dressing gown and took me to a bed in a ward. 'Sit there. The MO will come shortly to look at your foot,' he told me.

The MO duly arrived and asked, 'How did this happen?' I told him. 'When was this?'

'It must have been two or three weeks before the Japs left.'

'What treatment did you get at the time?'

'There were no medical supplies. I did as a Dutch doctor had done while on the island of Haruku. I placed maggots on the wound, held in place with leaves. When the first medical supplies were dropped to us, I used pink lint and zinc ointment.'

'Had you got footwear?' he queried.

'No,' I replied.

'I'm amazed. Under those conditions gangrene could have set in after a few days. You were fortunate; any further delay may have meant losing your foot.'

Ron returned and they spoke together before the MO left. After wrapping a bandage around my foot, he took me to the scales: '6 stone, 10 pounds,' he declared. Now I had to get undressed and put on the dressing gown. It was time for the process of delousing. This meant removing all my body hair. When that was over Ron dressed my wound; this time the whole foot and ankle were bandaged.

'Now put on your pyjamas and get into bed while I fetch you some food and drink.' I climbed into bed, between the cool, crisp white sheets, on a firm mattress. Sheer luxury!

'Is that all?' I asked, when Ron returned with my meal – just a small piece of fish and a small portion of mashed potatoes.

'Yes, I'm afraid so. You've got to take some pills to de-worm you.'

A thorough examination by an MO followed. Ron brought me two telegram forms; messages had to be limited to ten words. To my sister, I wrote: 'Norah, I'm safe and well, be home soon. Love Geoff.' Having no record of my brother's army number, I was unable to send the other to him.

It was daylight when I awoke. 'Where am I?' was the first thought that flashed through my mind. Then came a sense of relief as I realised that the war was over. I had slept soundly through the night and felt refreshed. As I lay in the comfortable bed, the true meaning came to me: no more bowing to the guards, no more beatings, no more working in the sweltering heat, no more bugs and lice, no more disturbance from the men sleeping so close, and no more hunger pains. Well, not quite – I was hungry now!

Ron soon arrived with my breakfast – a poached egg on toast and a strong cup of sweet tea. He also brought a news-sheet dated Monday, 17 September 1945, the South East Asia Command newspaper, which reported:

LIVING DEAD RAIL SLAVES

A story of war prisoner slave labour, exceeding in callousness that of the building of the Bangkok-Moulmein railway, is expected to come out of Sumatra, says Alan Humphreys, Reuters correspondent in Singapore.

News of Japanese brutality towards British, Australian and Dutch war prisoners set to work on building the central Sumatra railway was radioed from Sumatra by South African Major Jacobs, a member of the Mastiff Organisation, which dealt with parachute supplies of medical requirements, food and clothing for released prisoners. Major Jacobs was the first to visit war prisoner and internee camps in Sumatra, flying in a Japanese plane, piloted by a Japanese. He described as living dead those who had worked on the railway. Major Jacobs also reported shocking conditions and appalling atrocities at Rantauprapat camp, housing 6,000 internees, including 500 British women and children, and said that at the Allied POW camp at Palembang, 249 died in three months from illnesses and malnutrition.

So, another railway had been built by prisoners. But where? Reading further, an article referred to the Siam-Burma Railway. Was this a third railway? Then I recalled that Bangkok was the capital of Siam. If Moulmein is in Burma, then both articles were referring to the same railway.

'Can I get up, Ron?' I asked.

'Only to go to the bathroom. Take these two pills now.' As he removed my bandages ready for the MO's inspection, he went on: 'They'll clear your system, so you'll be able to cope with more wholesome food.'

The MO arrived, accompanied by two others, who poked and prodded my foot.

'You say it was a Dutch doctor who used maggots on open wounds. What was his name?' asked one.

'Sorry, Sir, I can't remember.'

So as not to put my foot to the ground I would have to use crutches, I was told. I was to get plenty of practice with them during the next twenty-four hours … to and from the toilet! So far, I had been kept isolated and had no idea where Bill and the others were. Now I had to take my pay book to the foyer and was paid forty-three Straits dollars.[1] I had not seen so much money since the pay parade in Batavia in March 1942. There was no one that I recognised in the foyer, and no one knew Bill Woodhouse. After buying some personal items, writing paper and envelopes, a wallet and wristwatch, I wrote a long letter to Norah.

Lying on the bed reading accounts by men from other camps, I realised that the treatment meted out to us was not unique but had occurred in most other camps. We were fortunate not to have contracted cholera, as they had in Burma. It was a surprise to learn that they had had concerts in Changi camp.

My foot was healing nicely, and I was now eating full meals. Apart from some nights when I relived some fearsome incident in a dream, waking in a hot sweat, life was pleasant. Walking now without crutches, I went into the hospital grounds, where some kit was being issued, and passed a Jap weeding a flower bed. I could not resist putting my toe behind him and tipping him forward. My action did not meet with the approval of a young naval officer who was passing. He told me: 'You can't treat prisoners of war in that manner.' I was speechless. Well, almost. I told him a few Jap POW facts. He made a note of my name and number, but I heard no more.

There was no RAF kit available so I had to settle for white naval shorts, shirts, socks and underwear, to which we could help ourselves. So, I filled two kitbags. Others had received telegrams from home but I was somewhat disappointed that I'd heard nothing from my sister.

Thursday, 4 October was the day I had waited so long for … I embarked for England.[2]

Chapter 14

My Homecoming

It was as if I'd woken from a deep, dreamless sleep. There was no doubt I was standing on Liverpool Central station platform, properly dressed in RAF blue, complete with greatcoat and leather shoes. My last recollection was being driven to Singapore docks in a Bedford bus, dressed in white shorts and shirt, wearing canvas shoes.

'What date is it?' I asked the man standing next to me.

'December 18th,' he replied, looking at me askance as if I should have known.

'Oh, so we're home for Christmas.' A useless statement that didn't provoke a reply.

Then I realised that I was grossly overweight, in fact, bloated. An officer called out my name and number and told me my twelve kitbags had been put in the guard's van.

'But I've only got two, sir.'

'There's twelve with your name and number on them.'

When had I filled those extra kitbags? With what … and from where? I could not recall anything of the journey. By which route did we come? Did we call at any ports? Not wishing to be thought mad, I didn't ask anyone. We boarded the train, our destination RAF Cosford, near Wolverhampton. Looking at my pay book, I saw I was paid £2 on 4 October, the day I left Singapore hospital, a further £2 on 10 October and £2 on 18 October. All three entries were signed by D.J. Copley.

There was no one I knew in the carriage and my inquiries about Bill had drawn a blank. In fact, there was not one person from Pakenbaru. At Cosford I was taken straight to hospital. My weight was 14 stone 5 pounds! The MO diagnosed my complaint as wet beriberi, brought on by eating too much of the wrong food. My body had been unable to assimilate it, causing me to fill with water. He put me on a strict diet and vitamin B pills. During the next three days I was not able to rest, day or night, as the water drained away. My weight dropped to about 7 stone, leaving me awfully weak.

'Hello Geoff. You've lost some weight. How are things going?' an airman asked. I was puzzled. He knew me, but I couldn't place him.

'I'm going home for Christmas,' he went on. 'Don't you remember me? I was in the next bunk to you on the boat.'

'Oh! I'm sorry, I can't recall your name,' I replied.

'I'm Phil Rogers.'

'The truth is, Phil, I can't remember anything about the journey. I don't even know which way we came home.' It was mystifying.

'We called at Colombo, where we were allowed a few hours ashore, although you were down with an attack of malaria. The next call was Port Said, after passing through the Suez Canal. There was mail waiting for us at Gibraltar. I received a letter from home, but there was nothing for you.'

'I can't understand why my sister hasn't written,' I mused. 'Phil, can you tell me how I managed to fill ten kitbags while on board?'

'Well I filled three from Red Cross and ship's stores. No questions were asked. Food was available day and night and you always seemed to be eating.'

After a few moments' silence he said, 'I'll have to be going now, Geoff, I've got a train to catch. Look after yourself.'

'Cheers, Phil, thanks for talking to me. Have a good time.'

Now came another setback – malaria, again. It was hardly the Christmas I had hoped to come home to. Christmas … the word took my thoughts back to March 1942, when it became obvious there was no means of escape from Java. We had to accept we would be prisoners of the Japs. Meanwhile, we tried to convince ourselves that the war would be over by Christmas. Yet three had passed virtually unnoticed – just a normal day in the harsh environment of a Jap prison camp: no festive fare, only the usual few grains of poor rice. And work. Always work.

I shrugged myself back into the present. Now there was plenty of food for those able to eat it. Ironically, I was on a strict diet. Everything was good. But I fretted for news of my sister Norah. Why hadn't I heard from her?

My strength was beginning to return with the coming of the new year, although I had lost a further four pounds. Soon, well wrapped up against the cold, I was allowed to walk round the grounds. Early in February

I was allowed to go out of the base with Steve Green, a survivor of the Borneo Death March, which I had read about in Singapore. We went to a nearby village, where, in the local public house we met a group of RAF men who had been prisoners of war in Germany. 'How did you get on?' they wanted to know. 'What were the conditions like?' We told them. They looked at us in amazement, which quickly turned to disbelief and contempt. 'Don't give us that. It's against the Geneva Convention. No country dare treat their prisoners like that. We were prisoners, okay, but we could always get extra food from the camp shop, and we had Red Cross parcels.'

They were so openly derisive that I swore, there and then, never to speak again about the Japs' atrocities and brutality. Steve remarked as we walked back to the hospital: 'If they've read any of the reports from the Far East, they must think it's all lies.' We were both very upset by the experience.

There was a heavy fall of snow overnight, the first I had seen since 1941. It had a certain appeal looking through the window, but I wasn't tempted to go outside. The start of a new course of medication meant I couldn't wander far from my bed. To pass the time I began writing about my experiences as a prisoner of the Japs while incidents were still clear in my mind. March came in like a lion. Then the good news: I was granted a weekend leave. Now I might find the reason why I hadn't heard from Norah.

I was issued with a new uniform to fit my present size and collected £3 pay, a travel warrant and a ration card. A sealed letter, addressed to RAF hospital Watnall, Nottingham, was handed to me with the instructions that I phone the number on the envelope should I get ill, also that I must catch the 9.45 am train from Nottingham on Monday morning. Now I was on my way, being driven to Wolverhampton station to catch the 5.30 pm train to Birmingham New Street. Shortly after arriving at New Street, there was an announcement: 'The next train to arrive at platform 3 is to Sheffield via Derby. Passengers for Nottingham change at Derby. Delays may occur, due to flooding on the line in Nottingham.'

It was 11.05 pm when I finally arrived at the Midland station. Hope Drive, where my sister lived, was only a short distance away, near the castle, so I set about walking at a steady pace. My thoughts were in turmoil. During the last six months I hadn't received any reply from 30 Hope Drive. Would I now find out why?

A light came on in the house after my second knock. A man came to the door and asked, 'Yes?'

'Does Mrs Miller live here?'

'No. I don't know anyone of that name.' I briefly explained my reason for asking.

'We've lived here for the past two years, and the previous occupier wasn't Mrs Miller. I think it was last October that a telegram arrived for her, then some letters arrived, which we returned as unknown.'

'They must have been from me. Sorry to have troubled you and thank you for listening to me so late at night.'

'Good luck in finding your sister. Cheerio.'

I was in a sombre mood as I made my way to the city centre. All I had achieved was to establish that Norah had not lived at 30 Hope Drive for more than two years. Where to now? During my seven-day embarkation leave in 1941, I had stayed at the NAAFI Club, Bridlesmith Gate. Maybe I could find accommodation there. I was five minutes too late; it closed at midnight. Utterly dejected, having no idea what to do or where to go, I wandered over to the bus station. Sitting in a bus shelter, I tried to visualise the address on the only letter I had received from Norah in 1941. It was in the wallet taken from me by the Japs. Had I memorised the wrong address? I woke up with a start as a policeman spoke to me. Sorry, lad, you can't stay here.' I explained my predicament.

'Do you know where Goldsmith Street is?' He asked.

'Yes,' I replied.

'See the policeman there. He will find you some accommodation that we use in emergencies such as yours,' he said.

'Thank you, officer,' I replied as I set off walking again.

There was no one about on Goldsmith Street, not even a policeman. Back at the bus station, another policeman directed me to an all-night service canteen on Broad Street. By now I was almost dead on my feet through fatigue and hunger and gave a sigh of relief on reaching the canteen. After a cup of tea and a sandwich I fell asleep across the table and it was six o'clock when I awoke. For a few moments my thoughts were disjointed and then I recalled the happenings of the night. As I got a cup of tea, I realised that my wallet was missing. 'Has anyone handed a wallet in that I may have dropped during the night?' I asked the lady behind the counter.

'No, I'm sorry,' she replied.

I had enough change to pay for my breakfast. Later I must go to the NAAFI to ask the almoner to replace the £2 that was in my wallet to enable me to book accommodation for the next two nights, but it was still dark, and too early to do anything yet. As I sat, I wondered if Bill and Sis Wilford still kept the King of the French public house on Woolpack Lane, Hockley. Cyril and I had known Mr and Mrs Wilford and their three teenage daughters, Joan, Doreen and Betty, when they lived on Eltham Road, West Bridgford, before moving to the public house, where we made frequent calls. At eight o'clock I walked to Woolpack Lane.

'Hello, Doreen,' I said as she opened the door.

'Geoff? Aah …' and she fell to the floor in a faint.

Joan rushed to help Doreen, and Betty called out, 'Dad, it's Geoff.'

'Geoff who?' came the reply from the kitchen. Bill came to the door. 'Come in, Geoff, it's good to see you.' I explained I was unable to contact my sister since my release from the Japanese prison camp and had only arrived in Nottingham for the first time late last night.

'Why did Doreen faint when she saw me at the door?'

'Let me tell you what's happened since you and Cyril visited us on the last day of your leave,' said Bill. 'A few weeks after you left, the RAF police called, telling us you were absent without leave. This we didn't believe but heard no more until Cyril came home on sick leave. He had been taken ill in the Middle East and was flown home. He told us the police had called at his home, too. He notified the RAF that you had been on board the *Empress of Asia* with him at the time of their enquiries. They in turn told him that you had since been posted as missing, believed killed, when the *Empress of Asia* was sunk in Singapore harbour. You had both left the *Empress* at Durban and the last time he saw you was when you landed in Egypt. We heard nothing more until August 1944, when Cyril's sister told us he had been killed in Normandy.'

Tears welled up and I had to leave the room to cry alone. With my composure returned I went back in and thanked Bill. I now understood why Doreen had fainted.

'You're welcome here at any time, Geoff. We didn't know your sister, but I remember you cycled to North Wales over a bank holiday weekend to see her,' Bill recalled.

'Yes. The last letter I received from her told me she was moving to an address in Nottingham after the death of her husband. That letter was lost while I was a prisoner,' I told him. Bidding them farewell, I made my way to the NAAFI. The almoner advanced me £3. The NAAFI was fully booked, so I was given the address of a Mrs Harris of Goldsmith Street, who could provide bed and breakfast. After explaining my situation, a lady representative of the Red Cross said she would help me trace Norah.

'You know she could have remarried in the four years since her husband died,' she remarked.

I stayed at the NAAFI for lunch and then strolled through Old Market Square on my way to Goldsmith Street. Passing the Elite cinema, I was tempted by the display in the window of Watmough's sweet shop. Inside I asked the young lady for a quarter of chocolate caramels.

'Sweet coupons, please,' she said.

'Oh, I'm sorry, I didn't know they were rationed,' I told her.

She answered sharply: 'Where have you been, on the moon?' I left.

Mrs Harris, a very pleasant lady, made a cup of tea. We sat talking for a while. She was curious as to where I had been. I outlined my movements without graphic details. Later, in my room, the realisation of the traumatic revelations of the past eighteen hours came home to me. I sobbed uncontrollably. There was a knock on my door, and I woke with a start. Mrs Harris called: 'Mr Lee, it's eight o'clock and your breakfast is almost ready.'

'Thanks, I'll be down soon,' I said.

I enjoyed that breakfast. A real sunny-side-up fried egg, a rasher of bacon, fried bread and potatoes. The only egg I had seen so far was the powdery scrambled sort. The next hour or so I spent in my room jotting down notes. Then I decided to take a walk, but I was at something of a loss. Where should I go? What should I do?

A brass plate outside the house next door read 'Mr Hammond. Dental Surgeon'. He had been my dentist for some time before I joined up. My teeth had caused some concern to the RAF dental officers and they had delayed treatment until my health improved. I got the impression they wanted to remove them all. As it was Sunday, I wouldn't be able to see Mr Hammond this trip, being obliged to return to Cosford the following morning. My first thought was to visit Cyril's parents, but I didn't know the frequency of the buses to West Bridgford. As I intended taking lunch in the NAAFI, I spent the time wandering around the city centre instead.

There were no delays on the return journey, and transport was waiting at Wolverhampton to take me back to Cosford. A full medical examination followed. The MO told me the course of injections for preventing recurring malaria seemed to have been successful. My weight had increased by 6½ pounds. Now the time I'd been dreading had arrived, the final verdict of a group of dental officers: 'All out' was their answer. After explaining how Mr Hammond had cared for my teeth since schooldays, I asked if I could seek his opinion. They made a note of his address and said I would be told later. The following morning, one of the officers gave me the news: 'I have spoken to Mr Hammond and made an appointment for you to see him at 2.00 pm on Thursday.'

Good, I thought, an extra day in Nottingham. Although I had only booked a room with Mrs Harris for the three days from Friday, she was able to put me up on Thursday.

Mr Hammond greeted me. 'Ah, yes, I remember you. You lived in Clifton village when you first came to see me.'

'Yes,' I replied, and told him what the RAF dental officers had said.

'Sit down and let me take a look.' He made notes as he prodded and poked my teeth. 'They are in a terrible state. I can understand why it was suggested that they all come out, but don't worry, I believe I can save most of them. It will take some time, and may be painful. I've got to phone your dental officer for his permission to carry out the treatment. Come back at ten o'clock tomorrow.' This better report cheered me somewhat, as I hadn't fancied the idea of dentures at my age.

As Thursday was half-day closing in West Bridgford, Cyril's father, who owned a shop on Central Avenue, was likely to be at home. I caught a No. 14 bus to Abbey Road and walked to his home. Mr Whitehead answered the door.

'Hello, Mr Whitehead. I'm awfully sorry to …'

Without a word he slammed the door. Utterly dejected, I returned to my digs. I realised it would have been better to have written a letter before meeting him. The last word he had heard of me was of my death on the *Empress of Asia*. But why slam the door in my face? It was a very fitful night. I dreamt of the collapse of the bridge in Sumatra and being dragged from the water. Cyril came into my dream, dressed in full army uniform, as I had seen him that last time in Egypt. Even after I'd awakened, I couldn't seem to shake off my dreams.

Mr Hammond had received permission to carry out the necessary treatment to my teeth. 'The same time tomorrow,' he said, when the first session ended. Weary through lack of sleep and discomfort of the treatment, I had to rest for the remainder of the day.

Refreshed after a good night's sleep, I kept my appointment with Mr Hammond. In the afternoon I went to Central Avenue in the hope of seeing Cyril's sister, Margaret, who I knew had worked in her father's shop. I walked past several times before I saw her, and then went in.

'Hello, Geoff, I'm pleased to see you. Dad told me you had been to our house. He still believes you were absent without leave.'

'Mr Wilford told me the sad news about Cyril, and I'm sorry.' I told her of the sequence of events after I last saw Cyril, and as I hadn't been able to contact my sister, I was unaware, until Mr Wilford told me, that I had been reported killed.

'It was a shock to the Wilford family when I arrived at their door, as it must have been for your father. I should have written to him first,' I told Margaret, and said she would explain to her dad what had taken place.

On Sunday, I caught a South Notts bus to Clifton. Nothing seemed to have changed as I passed the village school, facing the green, where the dovecote stood, and then past Green Cottage, where I was born, opposite the white vicarage. The name 'Allen' was still above the small shop. While resting on the stile that led to Clifton Grove, I recalled the carefree times we boys were caught by Mr Moss scrumping apples in the orchard opposite. In St Mary's churchyard I went to the grave of my parents. There was no headstone, but there was on that of my grandparents, which was alongside.

Alone in church, I said a prayer: 'Our father …' I remembered my happy schooldays when I was a choirboy here. Everything changed so dramatically when Dad gave up working and later became ill. I cried. Calling at Green Cottage, I found the Elliott family still lived there. They had moved from next door, after my parents had died. The eldest daughter, Evelyn, answered my knock, with Mabel and Olive close by.

'Come in, Geoff. It's good to see you returned safely.'

'Did you get my letter?' asked Mabel.

'Letter, what letter?' I asked.

'A list of prisoners of war held by the Japanese in Java was read out on the wireless. Your name was included, and I wrote to the address given,' Mabel explained.

'When was this?' I asked.

'About March or April 1944,' she replied.

'No, I didn't receive your letter. Thank you for the thought.'

After telling them how I became a prisoner, I told them of the reception from others who knew me, and how, so far, I had been unable to trace Norah. 'Have you seen Jim?' I asked.

'No, but someone saw him, still in uniform, at Ruddington,' said Evelyn.

Returning to Goldsmith Street, I made some notes on the unexpected news of the broadcast. Maybe Norah or Jim had heard it.

On Monday I was back in Cosford, where I went to see the adjutant to ask him to get the Service Police to write to all who had been contacted when I had been reported absent without leave, stating it was untrue. He agreed it should be done. I gave him all the details. The question of my kitbags now arose. Flying Officer Peters asked me: 'What do you intend doing with them?'

'I don't even know what's inside ten of them,' I replied.

'Shall we go and have a look?'

'Yes, certainly, sir.'

'Have you got the keys?'

'No, I'm afraid I've lost them.'

He sent for two airmen to cut the locks. I recognised those I had packed in Singapore, full of naval gear. The next was full of tins of vacuum-packed Player's cigarettes, another contained Australian tinned fruit and bully beef. Others were packed with winter weight clothing, pullovers, socks, sheets and blankets. There were the contents from Red Cross parcels … the list was endless.

The officer laughed. 'You didn't mean going short again, did you?'

'It certainly looks that way, but it's odd, I can't recall packing this lot.'

'Well, it's all yours,' he told me. 'Have you an address where I can send the kitbags to?'

'No, I'm afraid not. There's too much for me to handle. I'll pack one bag to take with me on Thursday. The tropical kit is no use to me. The remainder of the food can go the hospital kitchen, and the chaps in the ward would appreciate some cigarettes.'

'Just as you please,' he said.

It took some time to sort everything out, but finally I was left with four kitbags full of sheets, blankets, towels, socks, underwear and cigarettes, apart from the one I was taking with me.

'I'll have these sent to the Midland station left luggage office,' said FO Peters. The two airmen who had taken the food to the kitchen were sent to get new locks, and were rewarded with two tins of cigarettes each.

Returning to the ward, the WAAF nurse was cross with me. 'I should have been off duty half an hour ago, but couldn't go until you'd had your injections.'

'I'm so sorry. If you don't smoke give them to your boyfriend,' I said as I handed her a tin of cigarettes.

The morning brought a surprise. Another kitbag arrived. This had 'Bombay' written on it, as well as my name and number. It was locked, and my new keys wouldn't fit, so I asked for someone to cut the lock. It contained RAF issue tropical kit and a full blue uniform, including greatcoat, shirts, socks and shoes. But the most precious thing was the contents of an envelope – the filigree silver trinkets I had bought in Cairo in January 1942. These could now go to Norah, as I had intended. But when? And where?

This was the kitbag I had left on board the *Yoma* when I disembarked at Oosthaven, Sumatra, the one I had tried to retrieve while the *Yoma* was in Batavia dock. So the *Yoma* must have been one of the few ships to escape from the Far East. What would have been the outcome if I had found something useful to do, as the naval officer had suggested, while I was on board looking for this kitbag? I would have missed three and half years of terror, starvation and sickness. But what then?

My thoughts turned to my four mates on the *Yoma*. I knew the fate of Ginger and Jock and presumed, having had no news to the contrary, that Reg had died when the boat was sunk returning from Haruku. I'd last seen Bill Woodhouse the day last September when I was flown to Singapore from Pakenbaru, and heard nothing of him since. I prayed that he had arrived home safely to his wife in Sheffield.

Mrs Harris was pleased with the tins of food I brought for her, as was Mrs Wilford when I called at the King of the French. I was only just beginning to realise how severe the rationing was, having been protected from its effects by the adequate meals in hospital and the low-cost meals at the NAAFI. Mrs Harris told me the four-day ration cards I brought with me were very generous. The dental treatment was going well, and there was a vast improvement already. Mr Hammond told me I was fortunate there was no disease of the gums, otherwise it would have been impossible to rebuild most of my teeth.

Over the next few weekends I visited friends in Ruddington, and met more people I knew in Clifton. Arthur Roberts, whose mother kept a newsagent's shop on Bromley Road, West Bridgford, and who had often made a threesome with Cyril and me, had just been demobbed from the navy, and we talked about old times. It seemed ironic that he had never left England. Mr Wilford had shown me the letter he had received from the Service Police. They regretted their error, which was brought about by me being put on the draft from the reserve at the last moment, and apologised for any distress their visit had caused.

I visited Margaret Whitehead at the shop. She answered my question: 'Yes, Dad did receive a letter from the RAF, but it hasn't convinced him you didn't desert. There was no explanation as to how you got to the Far East if you weren't on the *Empress of Asia*. I've told him the sequence of events as you explained to me, but he refuses to talk about it.' I said a sad goodbye to Margaret, realising there was nothing now I could do to change her father's mind about me.

Central Avenue hadn't changed. The Tudor cinema, where I had been on firewatch duty before I left Nottingham, was still open. The high-class grocery shop, Parish's, and the billiard hall above the garage were as I remembered them. I had a sandwich and cup of tea at the small café. I was passing time until the Test Match, the only public house in West Bridgford, opened at six o'clock.

Before I joined the RAF I had worked several evenings as a waiter in the men only bar, where only spirits were served, ninepence a tot. As I served each order, the customers bought me a drink and I'd raise my glass on the bar without drinking any. Later they insisted I drink with them. This was serious; I wouldn't last long if I had to drink with each round. The landlord came to my rescue. He put a bottle of cold tea at the back of the bar and served it to me in a special glass. The customers marvelled at the amount of 'whisky' I could consume without being drunk. On my embarkation leave I called in one evening and everyone shouted for me to serve them. 'Come on, Geoff, we haven't had a waiter since you left.' Foolishly I relented. It was alright at first, with my glass on the bar. Then they insisted I drink with them, despite my explanation that I hadn't drunk whisky since I last served them. There was no cold tea and soon they were without a waiter. This bar was no longer men only and I did have a drink, but not whisky.

It was Wednesday and I was back in Cosford when the letter I'd been waiting so long for came from the Red Cross. Norah was in Nottingham General Hospital. They understood she was not seriously ill and they would send a representative to let her know I had arrived home safely.

Eager to see Norah at the earliest moment, I asked Mr Hammond, when I arrived at Nottingham, if I could postpone my dental appointment until Friday. He agreed, and I walked to the General Hospital. I was shown into a ward where Norah was sitting on her bed reading a book. She didn't see me until I said, 'Norah'.

'Geoff?'

'Yes, it's me.'

She slumped sideways onto her bed, in a dead faint. Her book fell to the floor. A nurse soon revived her and she looked at me closely. 'Geoff, it is you. But how?' We hugged each other, unable to speak as the tears flowed freely. Composure returned, and we began to talk calmly.

'The last news from the RAF was a telegram telling me you were missing, believed killed. With no word from you over the years, I feared the worst,' she told me.

I told her what had happened. 'It was March when I was allowed out of hospital for my first weekend leave. It was late at night when I went to Hope Drive. The fellow who had lived there for two years didn't know you.'

'What number Hope Drive, Geoff?

'Number 30,' I replied.

'My address is 33, the other side of the road.'

'I'd got No. 30 etched on my mind since the guards took my wallet, which contained your last letter. I would have thought the postman would have known where Mrs Miller lived and be able to deliver my telegram and letters.

A lady joined us. 'I'm Mrs Chambers, from the Red Cross. I was asked this morning to come and tell you your brother had returned home safely, but I see you have already met.'

'Yes. It was quite a shock after being informed four years ago he was missing, believed killed, and no word since. But bless him, he's back safe and sound now,' Norah told her, giving me another hug.

'That's enough about me. What are you doing here?' I asked.

'Oh, just a little tummy trouble. I think I will be going home soon.'

Mrs Chambers wished us both well and left. Lunch was brought for us and we talked through the afternoon. Norah told me she had only seen our brother Jim on one occasion, when he was on embarkation leave, although he had written intermittently from overseas. His last letter, a few weeks ago, said he had now been demobbed and was staying in

Leicester. I told her about the radio broadcast announcing the returning servicemen and the letter Mabel Elliott had sent. A nurse interrupted our conversation. It was time for Norah's medication, and I must leave.

'I've a dental appointment tomorrow morning, so I'll see you later in the day. Bye for now.'

Friday, and Mr Hammond told me: 'All that remains is to polish your teeth and your treatment is finished. You are minus just two teeth. The RAF have arranged to cover the cost of periodic examinations, even after you have left.'

During the next two days I spent several hours with Norah. She asked: 'How did the Japs treat you? What was it like?'

I didn't wish to go into details about these questions, and replied, 'Bad. Rough,' refusing to explain further, apart from telling her it was impossible to say how many malaria attacks I had suffered. 'The treatment at Cosford is to stop it recurring.'

A surprise awaited me at Cosford: a letter from Jim. He had been to Clifton and was told where I was. He would be at Green Cottage next Saturday.

The dental officers were extremely pleased with the work of Mr Hammond, and the MO told me the course of injections was now complete. Having forgotten to take the filigree trinkets for Norah last week, I made certain I had them with me when I left for Nottingham on Thursday. Norah had been discharged from hospital the previous day, so I took a steady walk to Hope Drive. A letter from Jim was waiting for her when she arrived home, telling her what he had learnt at Clifton, which she now knew direct from me. She found the story of the filigree silver fascinating.

'It's amazing that your kitbag had been unloaded in Bombay and returned to you four years later, intact,' she said. When I told her about the four kitbags at the left luggage office at the Midland station, she told me she would look after them for me.

'I can't carry them all at once, but I will fetch one now.' It was only a ten-minute stroll to the station but it took much longer on the return journey, struggling with the kitbag. The cigarettes were of no interest to Norah, but she gladly accepted a pair of sheets, pillow cases and towels when we unpacked the bag. We shared a tin of peaches for tea.

On Saturday, after lunch at the NAAFI, I caught a bus to Clifton. Jim and I greeted each other like the long-lost brothers we were, not having met since he was called up in 1939. A young lady I hadn't met before was introduced as Kathleen, a relative of the Elliott family. Jim talked of his war service. His unit left Egypt sometime after I had sailed on the *Yoma*, reaching Ceylon as Singapore fell. He then went to India, and later to Burma. Because our dad hadn't contracted malaria during his army service, Jim had the idea that the frequent bouts throughout his life had rendered him immune, but he dismissed that theory when I told him of the countless number of attacks I had endured. In recounting my experiences I avoided details of life in the prison camps, telling only of the places I had been to. Jim was surprised when I told him how I had missed seeing him in Cairo. We talked until it was time to catch my bus back to Nottingham.

During the night I suffered the most severe bout of malaria since returning to England. Mrs Harris was concerned when I didn't get up for breakfast and she knocked on my door. Lacking the strength to raise myself, I murmured, 'Come in.' She had an awful shock when she entered. I had been sick several times and was shivering with cold one moment, and burning up with fever the next. I asked her to phone the number on the envelope beside my bed and ask for an ambulance. Soon I was in the sick bay at Watnall. A young Polish MO examined me but failed to locate my swollen spleen, a prime symptom of malaria. He diagnosed flu. 'It is malaria,' I told him, 'and I need quinine or Mephaquin tablets.'

'No, it's flu,' he insisted.

'Have you read the letter that came with me?' I asked.

'I have not seen a letter.'

During the next few days the flu medication did nothing to improve my condition and my repeated requests for quinine were refused, as was my plea to be returned to Cosford. Finally it was decided to send me to Rauceby in Lincolnshire, where, thankfully, they had knowledge of malaria, and I was at last given quinine. The fever soon began to subside and I was able to eat small quantities of food without vomiting. After a week, with my strength returning I was taken back to Cosford, where the MO gave me thorough examination. 'I fully expected you would have another bout of malaria; that was the reason for the letter you had with you,' he told me.

'It must have got mislaid when I was taken to Watnall,' I said.

'In the next few days you will be going to Sunningdale Park for recuperation, prior to your discharge from the RAF,' he informed me.

PART TWO

Chapter 15

A Review

I returned to Nottingham, dressed in my new navy suit, having been discharged from the RAF with a small war pension. My priority was to find some digs. Mrs Harris regretted she had no vacancies and Norah only lived in a bedsit, so she had no room for me. My only choice was to stay at the NAAFI for the time being. Luckily, I soon found some digs in West Bridgford. After living on back pay for several weeks it was necessary to think about employment, so I enrolled on a training course in joinery.

The year was 1946 and it proved to be matrimonial season for many people as everyone seemed to be making up for lost time. Jim, my brother, married Kathleen Ketton in October, the relative of the Elliott family, and they went to live in Leicester. In December, I also got married, to Betty, the youngest of the Wilford sisters. Tommy, their tousle-haired 10-year-old brother, managed to get into the wedding photographs. Both Joan and Doreen had married during the war.

The King of the French pub was now closed and my new in-laws took over the management of Colwick Hall, near Nottingham Racecourse. There was no electricity or gas, just oil lamps and coal fires, and it was reputed to be haunted. Betty and I took over two rooms for our own use, the remainder being occupied only during race meetings to house racing apprentices.

The first real home of our own was a rented sales shop on Commercial Road in Bulwell, where we traded in second-hand furniture and crockery. We stood on Sneinton market on Saturdays, selling offcuts of upholstery leather cloth, and I was soon able to give up my job as a joiner with Nottingham Council. We worked hard but life was good. To enable me to stand more markets, we bought a second-hand car and my brother-in-law taught me how to drive.

An empty shop premises on Bloomsgrove Street, Radford, was being offered for sale. It was built in 1937 by Shipstone's as a beer-off but had remained closed throughout the war. There were three bedrooms, living room, kitchen, bathroom and garden. The shop was fully fitted with counter and shelves. With the aid of an £800 mortgage, we bought it for £950. The sale of the Bulwell business provided us with the capital to open it as a grocery shop. As the business became established, I gave up the markets. Then our lovely auburn-haired daughter Christine was born. Life was very good.

There was still control on the sale of eggs; they had to be stamped with the lion mark, unless they were home produced. I went to Melton market and bought a dozen day-old Rhode Island Red chicks and kept them in a run in the garden. When they began to lay, about ten a day, our customers had to be rationed. The long hours that we worked in our back-street shop were made even more intense when we started selling fruit and vegetables. I had to be down at the wholesale market by five o'clock in the morning, and with my wife having to run the home and care for Christine, as well as serve in the shop, we had no time for leisure.

During these years my health had been somewhat of a problem. The mild attacks of malaria only lasted a day or two and were quite manageable, but the worst drawback was my back, which sometimes locked, forcing me to lie flat for several days. Thankfully, the nightmares, which had alarmed Betty in the early days, were now few and far between. I still had not managed to eat a large meal, but my weight did remain constant.

I joined the Nottingham and District Far East POW Association and received £76 compensation from the Japanese assets in England. I rarely attended meetings, to avoid the usual question 'Did you work on the railway?' Knowing they meant the Burma Railway and not wishing to discuss what I was trying to forget, my answer was 'Yes'. No one knew of the notes I had written while at Cosford.

We decided to sell the grocery business, while retaining the property. Mr and Mrs Newman bought the stock at cost plus £150, and we agreed to a rent of twenty-five shillings a week, which would cover our mortgage. For our next business venture, we took over an empty council shop, designated to sell drapery, at Meering Avenue, Newark. This meant that Betty could manage the shop while I stood four markets a week to provide us with a living and, hopefully, profit from the shop would cover the rent and rates. Life was now less hectic and with the shop trading only five and a half days a week, we had time for outings.

Just a few months after moving, it came as a shock when Nottingham City Council notified us that they intended to build high-rise flats on Bloomsgrove Street and all existing property was to be demolished. They offered us £850 for our shop, and alternative housing for our tenant. As our property was modern compared with the houses around it, an independent valuer suggested a fair price would be £1,600 and alternative shop premises to enable our tenant to carry on his business. Two years elapsed before the council agreed to pay our asking price and offered Mr Newman a council shop on St Ann's Well Road, Nottingham. Meanwhile, we had given up the tenancy of the shop at Newark as it failed to make a profit because the residents of the estate could catch a bus from outside our shop and, for one penny, ride into Newark town centre. I also refused to sell imported goods, mostly Japanese, which were flooding the markets.

We moved again, this time to a terraced house on Northgate, New Basford, opposite what must have been a high-class gent's outfitters and pawnshop before the war, owned by Mr Pearson, who still opened each day without any saleable stock. We took it over to sell second-hand furniture and advertised to clear houses. Trade was good, but I had to employ men to move heavy goods so as to protect my back. It was then I met Ernest Smith, who dealt in second-hand clothing. This meant that any clothing in the houses we cleared was sold to him. He, in turn, passed any furniture he came across to us. Sometime later, Ernest began buying overmakes and surplus stock from local textile factories and we needed premises from which to sell to market traders.

The furniture in our shop was cleared and a partnership was formed, creating Northgate Wholesale Supplies, dealing only in British-made goods and selling the factory seconds to market traders. As trade expanded, Ernest had to travel further afield to maintain supplies, and so needed a decent car. Also it was necessary to buy a new van for me to collect and deliver goods. Our son Derek was born, and Christine started at Claremont Primary School. Nottingham City Council had plans to redevelop Northgate, so we bought the former premises of the Co-op on Sandon Street, New Basford, from where we carried on our business. Betty and I bought a large house on Beech Avenue, just around the corner from Sandon Street.

After forming Lee, Smith and Lee (Nottm.) Ltd., we purchased Calverton Lido, a 5-acre site in Calverton, Nottinghamshire, which included an outdoor swimming pool, changing rooms, games room, a bungalow, the Springwater Social Club and a restaurant. I was licensee and Mr and Mrs Bromyard were employed to manage the social club, and they lived in the bungalow on the site. At weekends our family stayed in a caravan there to be easily on hand to work in the club, which was very popular, and also be ready for hot summer days when the lido would be full of local coal miners and their families. During the 1960s, hardly anyone had their own cars and the locals would walk the 2 miles to the lido from the village with their picnic baskets and swimming costumes to spend the day there. I looked after the grounds and pool, which was filled from a local spring and was very cold.

The years passed quickly and in 1969 we lived on Carmel Gardens, Arnold, in a modern bungalow. Christine left school and worked on the lido site during the summer. Eddie and June Bridges took over the management of the restaurant at Calverton Lido. When their son, Eddie, came home on leave from his Grenadier Guards regiment and met Christine, it didn't seem long before wedding bells were ringing from Woodborough church. Son-in-law Eddie left the army and joined the police force.

Planning permission had been obtained to build a modern hotel on the lido site, at an estimated cost of £100,000. Our hoped-for backing from a brewery did not materialise and having suffered a financial loss due to inclement weather over the previous two years, we decided to sell the site to the highest bidder over £40,000. Our agent told us the sale seemed set for success as a number of bids had been submitted, some over the reserve price.

Then came the bombshell. Just a few days before the sale, my wife and Ernest told me they had cancelled the sale as they wanted to build the hotel themselves. I was absolutely shattered. That they could make such a major decision without asking my opinion was beyond my comprehension. The agent was equally upset but had to obey the instructions of the majority of shareholders. He had now to inform all prospective purchasers that the sale was off and he expected some claims for compensation to be submitted.

My only option was to resign from Lee, Smith and Lee (Nottm.) Ltd.

Chapter 16

Research

Some time had elapsed since I resigned from the lido company, during which time I worked in the wholesale business. My wife had gone to live in the caravan at the lido and I was now granddad to Christine and Eddie's children, Darren and Dawn.

Although I had not let anyone read them, I now had time to type out the notes I had written at Cosford. Meanwhile it occurred to me that at no time had I seen any reference to the Sumatra Railway. I re-joined the Nottingham FEPOW Association and was curious to know if others had heard about the Sumatra Railway. All my enquiries were met with scepticism. As one man put it: 'That must have been just a siding.' I decided to read the history of the war in the Far East at the local library but found no reference to Sumatra. The Burma Railway was well documented, as was Changi jail, Singapore. There were reports about life in prison camps throughout the Far East, including Java, Ambon and Haruku, but not a word about Sumatra. In an effort to obtain some information I wrote to the Imperial War Museum, the Commonwealth War Graves Commission and the Army Records, receiving almost identical replies from each: 'There is no record of a railway being built by prisoners of the Japanese in Sumatra.' A query to a local newspaper produced the same reply.

Did this mean I was wrong? Had I in fact worked on the Burma Railway? But no, I still had my released prisoner's pay book, which gave the place of my release as Logas, Pakenbaru, Sumatra. The Japs had erected a white post marking the Equator and I had seen Orang-utans, which only live in Sumatra or Borneo. Surely there must be others who had worked on that railway? Also, where was the record of Lady Mountbatten's visit to Pakenbaru on 15 September 1945?

My immediate task was to trace others who had been transported from Java and Singapore to build this line, and it was with this in mind that I accepted the job of Public Relations Officer for the Nottingham Association.

Through a more detailed application form, I found four others in Nottingham who had worked on Haruku and had then been taken to Sumatra from Singapore to Pakenbaru via the Siak River, including Ernest Mortimer, a Nottingham member who lived in Doncaster. He was one of the 738 survivors from the Jap ship *Juno Maru*, which was sunk by the submarine HMS *Trade Wind* off the west coast of Sumatra on 18 September 1944. The survivors from the *Juno Maru* were landed at Padang and then taken to Pakenbaru. Two thousand prisoners and an unknown number of natives had sailed from Batavia (Jakarta) and the ship carried no sign that prisoners were on board. By writing to other POW associations throughout the country, I contacted many more of those I was seeking. One former RAF sergeant, Ron Thompson, from Cheadle, had picked up a piece of paper at Pakenbaru after the Japs had left and it listed the names of 132 men who were in hut No. 4 at Kotabaru, Sumatra, in March 1945. My name was on the list. Ron, who had been in charge of a contingent being transported from Singapore to Pakenbaru on the riverboat the *White Lady* on 16/17 July 1944, had managed to retain a list of fifty names who were on board. He, like me, also survived the collapse of the bridge in Sumatra in March 1945 by climbing out of the river up the sleepers.

I then received a letter from John Swanney of Scarborough, who invited me to meet him at the Rancliffe Arms, Bunny, near Nottingham, while he was visiting relatives in the area. He had brought with him a book written by Edwin Varley about Frank Williams – *The Judy Story: The Dog with Six Lives*.[1] In a chapter near the end, Frank describes life on the Sumatra Railway.

'I was with Frank and Judy for a short time,' I told John.

'Yes, I also met them,' he said, 'although I can't recall which camp it was.'

The book contained a poem, written at Pakenbaru, Sumatra, in 1944, which includes the lines: 'Every sleeper claimed a body / every rail a dozen more'.

'Those lines have been used in reference to the Burma Railway,' I said.

'But there couldn't have been any contact between men in Burma and Sumatra,' John replied.

'No, but maybe some reporters didn't know their geography.'

Judy was awarded the Dickin Medal, the animal VC, for her wartime service, before she died in Africa, where Frank had taken her when he went to work on a groundnut scheme.[2]

John and I talked at length and realised our paths had crossed several times. Mary, John's wife, who was present while we talked, said she had learnt more about life in Jap camps that day than she had at any time before. Along with the others I had contacted, John had become frustrated in his efforts to convince people that a railway had been built in Sumatra and was pleased the truth may at last be told. Before we parted, I promised to send him addresses of others who were with us and we agreed to meet at the forthcoming reunion in Blackpool.

In due course, a coach and hotel accommodation was booked for the fifty or so Nottingham members attending the reunion. While sitting in the hotel lounge, one of our members came to me and said, 'Geoff, I want to apologise. I always thought you were mistaken when you mentioned the Sumatra Railway. I've been talking to a fellow from Doncaster; he knows you and he worked there.'

'Oh, you mean Ernest Mortimer?'

'Yes. He's a Nottingham member and came up with his wife by car.'

'I've been in touch with him, but so far I haven't met him. Tomorrow I'll introduce you to several more who helped to build it.'

During the reunion, I was satisfied that our group had set others pondering why the records were incomplete, although some were not convinced and thought we were making everything up.

Oliver Greenwood gave me the address of Mr Neumann of Amsterdam, who had worked in Sumatra before the war and had returned twice to trace the railway. The story of his experience as a prisoner of the Japs and his journeys since were published in a Dutch TV magazine, which I had had translated. Each year, a reunion was held in The Hague for the former railway workers. I attended on several occasions.

The Judy Story was now published in paperback and I bought copies by the dozen to distribute amongst other associations and individuals. One of the subscribers to the book was Hilton Stanton, of Sydney, Australia, who gave me the address of Claude Thompson, who lived in Auckland, New Zealand. Claude was one of a small group of sick men who were returned to Java after only a short time on Haruku. In March 1944, he was in the first batch of prisoners sent to Pakenbaru to start building the railway. The following March he saw the bridge collapse but had managed to get off the debris unnoticed and was resting in a native hut. In 1978, he and his wife flew back to Pakenbaru in the hope of finding evidence of the railway. All they found were the derelict engines by the side of the Siak River and were unable to go further without suitable transport. They went on to Ambon and Haruku, later sending me photographs taken on their journey.

Feeling I had enough evidence to convince the Imperial War Museum that this railway had been built by prisoners of war of the Japanese, I sent a list of names and addresses, a copy of the Reuters news report by Major Jacobs (*see* Chapter 13) and a copy of the Judy book. A few days later, everything was returned, with the comment: 'We have heard something of this railway, but there is no official recognition.' What did they expect me to do? Go back and find the railway? While the idea appealed to me, it seemed impossible, knowing the line could not still be in use. Meanwhile, further evidence came to me, first from Holland: a letter written from Medan Prison, Sumatra, by the Jap officer who was in charge of the railway, pleading for his life after being sentenced to death for crimes against prisoners of war in Sumatra. Translated to Dutch and then English, this is a verbatim copy:

Medan, 17th June 1948
To Maj J.J.A. van de Lande

Dear Sir,

I would like to offer my hearty congratulations for you on your activity with best health in your new place and would like my cordial thanks for your kindness to me while you were in Medan. I was sentenced to death by the Temporary Military Tribunal, Medan on 30th May 1948, and now spending lonesome days in a solitary cell waiting for the last moment. I reproach myself, not others. I gave up myself as my destiny given by the God.

The verdict announced at the court for me was quite reasonable which I understood very well with my appreciation. I was sentenced by the charge of high mortality in the camps and my insufficient supervision towards my Korean subordinates who ill-treated the POWs without my knowledge. Charge 1, 2, and 3 of my accusation were the matter connecting with the accused DO1 Isamu. The charge about my responsibility of issuing foods, clothing and so on to the camps have been duly acquitted at the court by the President on the reason of insufficient evidence. It is really my great regret that I newly came to know the fact of maltreatments inflicted by my Korean subordinates upon the POWs when I was examined at Medan in the time of preliminary hearing after the capitulation, except the cases which were duly sent to the Japanese Tribunal without delay. I would never tolerate any illicit conduct in the camps, if I were aware of. I took all my possible steps within my competence to prevent them. The verdict announced that I should be punished to the most severe sentence because of my violation of Hague Treaty.

I frankly admit the high mortality in my camps. But as previously mentioned, the President has acquitted the supplying responsibilities such as foods, clothes and so on to the camps, and admitted other causes of the high mortality in favour of me. I am deeply convinced that it must have been difficult to get better results because of my poor position at the lower end of the line of command. Furthermore, bad natural features of Pakenbaru area made me much disadvantage. I dare say, no POW has died because of a personal misconduct, whole through my tenure. Contrary to my expectation, Maj Asami of Atjeh case[3] has been sentenced to 15 years, and myself to death, which I can hardly understand. On the other hand, I am quite happy to report you that none of my subordinates has been sentenced to death, viz. DO1 Isamu to life, NAGAI Susumu 8 years and ISHII Haruyoshi 4 years respectively. My last and best hope whole through the time was attend the funeral of my old mother in Japan, but all came to impossible at present. I would break my heart, if I think over my old mother, wife and 4 children in Japan who are supposed to be in extreme poverty without any financial support. Every minute and every second, I am only waiting for the warm merciful mitigation by His Excellence the Governor-General to whom I submitted my petition in due way. I would be very much obliged, if you will be so kind, to bring forward the petition from you in favour of me to His Excellency, by taking my miserable situation into your consideration.

At last, I have honour to report you that I have always been treated very kindly and I could have the chance to correspond with you by the profound kindness of Mr P. Rozendaal here.

Hoping your safe and success with good health.

Your most grateful, I remain
[signed by]
MIYAZAKI Ryohei
c/o Medan Prison, Sumatra.

His plea was unsuccessful. We had been told the Imperial Japanese soldiers would commit hara-kiri rather than be taken prisoner. Gunso Mori and Kasiyama were advocates of hara-kiri, but lived to be tried by the War Crimes Commission in Singapore.

In a letter in the London Association news-sheet, Colonel L. Robinson, the former CO of an Australian regiment, sought information. He had written the regimental history of the war, only to receive many complaints from his former soldiers that he had missed out the part they took in building the Sumatra Railway and wanted to contact anyone in England who had worked on the project. I sent him the results of my research and an outline of my time there. He was grateful for my help but was at a loss as to why there was no official record, as it could affect the history of other units. Some of what I had written was confirmed by his own men.

I decided to look into the possibility of returning to Sumatra, as Claude Thompson had done. He had contacted the Caltex oil company in Jakarta, Java, so I did likewise. The reply, in December 1979, from Mr Wisaksono Noeradi, was extremely helpful, offering to assist me should I wish to visit Sumatra. They were interested in the probability of building a road between Pakenbaru and Palembang oil fields. Thomas Cook Ltd. formulated the itinerary.

Chapter 17

The Return Journey

Concorde flight 065, scheduled to depart from Heathrow at 2.30 pm on 3 February 1980, was delayed. A steward told us: 'We regret that due to a strike in Paris, your plane will not now leave until 16.30. Help yourselves to the buffet and champagne.'

Most of the seventy passengers were not unduly concerned. Soon a party atmosphere prevailed, although a few kept aloof. Again, the steward made an announcement: 'Concorde is now on its way from Paris. Your departure time will be 22.30. A Boeing 747 is due to leave shortly for Bahrain, where connections can be made for Singapore and Hong Kong. Anyone wishing to board this plane will receive a refund. Dinner will be served at 19.30.'

Most took this option; only twenty-seven sat down to the sumptuous meal, to which I was unable to do justice. Away at last, the captain informed us we were flying at 46,000 feet, at 700 mph. With champagne flowing freely, the party spirit was maintained, with the stewardesses joining in. Then, another announcement: 'This is the captain again. You sound as if you are all enjoying yourselves. We are now passing over the Alps, and soon we'll be above the open water of the Adriatic, when our speed will increase to the maximum 1,400 mph at 62,000 feet. Put your watches forward one hour.' Even at the speed shown on the indicator in the cabin, there was no awareness of movement, and through the portholes bright stars could be seen both above and below us, in the black sky.

Our speed dropped back to 700 mph as we neared the coast of Egypt and soon Concorde landed gently at Bahrain, just four hours after leaving London. In the only room that was lit, our group joined those who, having missed their connection, had travelled on the Boeing 747. They were rather annoyed at having had to wait for hours in that cold room, with free cups of tea the only refreshment. The hour stopover, when the plane was refuelled, soon passed and we all boarded Concorde to find that the seat covers had been changed to the colours of Singapore Airlines. The stewardesses were now brown-skinned, dark-haired Malay girls, who had a friendly chat with us all before take-off. With a roar, we were airborne again, soon reaching maximum speed, as shown on the indicator. We flew south over the Red Sea, turning east to cross the Indian Ocean. The captain kept us informed of our progress. Now we passed south of Sri Lanka, almost directly above the Equator. A typical Oriental meal was served, which I knew as Nasi goreng, with fried rice and individual portions of fish, meat and sauces. The champagne still flowed freely.

Soon the party spirit died down as many took the opportunity to get some much-needed sleep. I contemplated my journey ahead. After three days in Singapore, there would be a week in Sumatra. What would this achieve? Was I on a wild goose chase? Jakarta, Java, was the next call, then three days later on to Bali for one day only. Then we'd be calling at Ujung Pandang, Celebes, to catch a plane to Ambon, to stay a week, visiting the War Graves cemetery and, hopefully, arranging a boat trip to the island of Haruku. To continue my itinerary, I would return to Bali and then fly direct to Sydney, Australia, to stay with Hilton Stanton for a week before flying to Auckland, New Zealand, to visit Claude Thompson before the long flight back to London. I had paid all my air fares before setting out and for hotel accommodation as far as Jakarta; thereafter, I must book as required.

This review of my journey brought back some sad memories and I was unable to conceal an occasional tear. The man in the next seat was now awake and said, 'I could see you marking lines on your map, and saw you were upset at times. Would you like to talk about it?' I outlined the reason for my journey.

'My name is John. What is yours?'

'Geoff Lee,' I replied.

'While I thought I had a reasonable knowledge of war with Japan having worked out here for a number of years, I have never heard of a railway being built by prisoners of war in Sumatra,' he continued.

Our conversation was interrupted by the voice of the captain: 'As you can see, our speed has reduced to 700 mph, at 30,000 feet, as we approach the northern tip of Sumatra. We will land at Singapore in thirty minutes.'

Nine hours after leaving Heathrow, Concorde circled Singapore several times before it began to slowly, almost silently, drift down to Changi Airport. Coming in from the seaward end of the runway, it touched down gently and, with a final burst of power, came to a halt. The local time was 3.30 pm. As we prepared to disembark, John said, 'Geoff, I wish you luck in your quest. Maybe, in the future, I will read about it.'

As we left the plane we were each given a framed colour photograph of Concorde standing near to palm trees, along with other Concorde trinkets. After passing through customs and collecting my luggage, I joined others who were staying for three days at the stopover price of £5, and then boarded a coach to travel the short distance to the Holiday Inn. With the temperature in the nineties, I needed to fit myself up with suitable clothing. After a shower I went to one of the many tailors in a shopping arcade to be measured for two linen suits. These were delivered four hours later. They cost £4 each.

Following an excellent dinner, the lack of sleep caught up with me. I retired to my well-appointed rooms and slept soundly until dawn. Fully refreshed, in the cool of the morning before breakfast I took a walk around this beautiful city, with its high-rise hotels and clean, tree-lined streets.

Booking a taxi for the day, my first visit was to Krangi[1] War Cemetery. Here the neat rows of white headstones in the well-cared-for grounds marked the resting place of 4,463 Allied soldiers and sailors who died before and after the fall of Singapore in 1942. There were 24,346 names of those who have no known graves, which were recorded on rows of panels. These were from many parts of the Far East. Hundreds had died while being transported by sea as prisoners – many who had perished from disease and many more from the result of Allied submarine action throughout the war zone. The following inscription appears on the memorial:

1939–1945

On the walls of this memorial are recorded the names of twenty-four thousand soldiers and airmen of many races united in service to the British Crown who gave their lives in Malaya and neighbouring lands and seas and in the air over Southern and Eastern Asia and the Pacific but to whom the fortune of war denied the customary rites accorded to their comrades in death.

They Died for All Free Men.

129

A separate memorial records the names of 107 men – 94 British, 2 Australians, 5 Indian and 6 Malays – who died in the Singapore Civil Hospital, with the inscription:

> The soldiers whose memory is honoured here, perished in captivity in February 1942, who were buried in one grave in the grounds of Singapore Civil General Hospital.

I studied the memorial registers, making a note of any names with relatives in the Nottingham area, hopefully to send them photographs of the graves on my return home. My taxi driver helped me locate the graves. With that task complete, I spent some time alone in the chapel of rest, where my emotions took over. Leaving Krangi, we passed Bukit Timah Hill, the site of the last Battle of Singapore. The driver advised: 'It wouldn't be wise to visit there. The Japanese erected a memorial, to which pilgrims come at this time of year.'

Not having been in Singapore before the Japs took over, I wanted to see the causeway, a road connecting the island of Singapore and Malaya. Having no visa, I was unable to cross into Malaya and had to be content with looking at the skyline on the far side. Making our way back to the hotel, we passed Changi jail, now occupied by civilian prisoners.

I took my evening meal – consisting of sweet and sour pork, bean shoots and fried rice – in the Malayan restaurant and then retired to my room to write some letters and make notes of this emotional day. Then it was early to bed, as I'd booked my taxi for 8.30 the following morning. My driver arrived exactly on time. I wanted to see as much as possible of this beautiful city and I asked him to include the Raffles Hotel, the docks and the site of River Valley camp. Otherwise I left the route to him. At the docks, the mast of the *Empress of Asia* was still visible in the harbour, just as I remembered it during my short stay in 1944. My mind went back to those days, in particular to the discomfort from the heat of the concrete as I worked barefoot. As a test, I removed my shoes and socks. There was no way I could now walk unshod. The taxi driver took me to the site of the River Valley camp, now replaced with modern hotels. Gone were the vermin-ridden atap huts. I told him of the music that drifted in the still night air at that time. 'That was most likely from the night club, the Great World, just across the way,' he told me.

We stopped outside Raffles; the facade was the same, although the square in front appeared smaller than I remembered. How I had longed to be able to go inside as we passed on the way to the docks each morning. Now I could. To finish the day, I ate alone in the luxurious surroundings, with a superb first-class service. Tomorrow I would begin the primary task of my journey, so I asked my driver to collect me at 8.30 am to catch the 10.30 flight to Pakenbaru, Sumatra.

Chapter 18

The Railway

After a forty-five-minute flight, the Fokker Friendship landed at Pakenbaru. The few passengers were met by a host of immigration officers, who soon began going through their luggage. Before my turn, a voice from the back of the room called out: 'Mr Lee, come this way please.' I went forward, to be met by a small, well-dressed gentleman.

'Hello. I am Mr Wowo. The Caltex oil company have asked me to look after you during your stay in Sumatra,' he told me in perfect English.

'Hello. I am pleased to meet you,' I replied.

A car was waiting, and Mr Wowo drove me to the Riu Hotel. After booking in and leaving my luggage in my room, he said, 'I must first take you to the immigration office, where you will have to leave a photograph of yourself.' I had been told this by my travel agent before leaving England and had brought a dozen photos with me. That duty carried out, we returned to the hotel for lunch, native style.

'Is there anything you want to do this afternoon?' asked Mr Wowo.

'No, I'll take a walk in the town. I can't buy much until I change some travellers' cheques, as I was only allowed to bring 3,250 rupiahs (£2.50) with me.'

'As it's Sunday, you will have to wait until tomorrow,' he advised.

I walked around the locality of the hotel. There was very little traffic, apart from numerous cyclists carrying large bundles. At once I attracted quite a crowd of curious, brown-skinned children, who most likely had ever seen only a few white men. By taking my camera from its case, I caused a ripple of excitement among the children, all eager to get into the picture, jostling each other for position. After numerous calls of *'Nanti'* (wait), they were finally lined up. Stepping back two paces and raising my camera, I found the children had followed me. I rearranged them, this time behind a line drawn in the dust, using the only words I knew may be appropriate: *'Teda jallan'* (don't walk). Success at last.

As the children drifted away, satisfied they were in the picture, I decided to return to my air-conditioned hotel room, away from the stifling heat, which was more oppressive than in Singapore. A gentle slosh down with cold water from a large brick tank in the 'bathroom', using a plastic ladle and the water draining away down a hole in the concrete floor, had the desired cooling effect. I lay on the bed until it was time for tea. Was the bread and butter with jam a concession to an Englishman? It was welcome anyway, as was the papaya and banana salad. Later, in the lounge, a football match was being shown on television. It was from the City Ground, Nottingham – Forest versus an eleven whose name I cannot recall. I didn't know which team a group of youths supported, but they became extremely excited as the game progressed.

When the bar opened, I had difficulty finding out the price of a bottle of beer. After much gesticulation, the barman wrote down r1,400 (£1).[1] It seemed from their glances that the half a dozen young men at the far end of the bar were talking about me and one of them came over. Although neither of us could speak the other's language, it soon became clear he thought I needed female company. Meanwhile, one of the other young men had left the bar and now returned with a young lady, who came and sat beside me. Under these circumstances, how does one convey that what she is offering is not included in my plans? After some gestures, she seemed to get the message and left, only to be followed by a second lady, then three more, all being dismissed in turn. Thankfully alone at last, and having just enough money for one final bottle of beer, it came as a shock when the barman asked for r7,500, which I gathered, after much sign language, was drinks for the ladies. I was confident he would not report the debt to the management as it would show him to be a conspirator with the ladies. Before going to bed, I made some notes and wrote several letters home, then relaxed, watching a couple of geckos chasing flies on the walls and ceiling.

Waking as dawn was breaking at six o'clock, I went for a cup of tea. Considering Sumatra was so close to Java, where fine quality tea comes from, what was served was disappointing: a beaker of warm water with a small Twinings teabag, which barely coloured the water. Mr Wowo arrived as I finished breakfast. 'Our first call must be to a bank to change your travellers' cheques,' he told me. It was strange to see armed guards standing at the bank door. However, this bank could not change my travellers' cheques. Mr Wowo saw my concern. 'Don't worry, another bank will,' he reassured. Thankfully, the next bank changed £300 into rupiahs and I came out with a case full of notes.

Now the search for the railway began in earnest. Driving along a wide road with very little traffic, we turned into a lesser road, in the native quarters, and followed it until we reached the Siak River. It was here, in those far-off terrifying POW days, that most of the equipment for the railway was unloaded from coasters from Singapore. Close by were ten or twelve steam engines. Some had native huts built alongside. Nearby was a red-roofed school room, and our arrival caused the lessons to cease abruptly. All the children came rushing out, eager to have their photographs taken. For a while it was not possible to see the engines because of the attention of the happy, well-dressed children. To overcome this I turned my camera on the school and started to take photographs. This brought them down off the engines. After taking a few shots of them as a group, I was able to get clear pictures of the engines.

The position of the locomotives caused me to wonder what method had been used to unload them. The derricks on the coasters may have been capable of putting them ashore, but if a land-based crane had been used, surely they would have been placed on prepared tracks and all facing the same way? But there was nothing orderly here. This gave me the impression that they had been manhandled into those positions and I could visualise the prisoners who had had to undertake this work, and the shouting and the beatings from the guards as they strained to move these monsters.

Leaving what I presumed to be Camp No. 1 (I had not been here as a prisoner), we made our way to the airfield, in the hope of finding evidence as to the position of Camp No. 2, which I recall was within sight of it. This was the last camp I had been in before flying to Singapore on 20 September 1945. I thought finding this camp, with the airfield as a guide, would be simple, but it was not so. We drove around the airfield perimeter, stopping now and again to search for signs that might indicate the position of the camp. It was only after an hour that we saw some rails being used as fencing in a kampong. Mr Wowo enquired of some of the older inhabitants, who pointed in the general direction of where the camp had been. We were told that after the last prisoners were taken away, the huts were burnt down. Some years later, soldiers came to carry out work at the burial ground. Today there was no sign of the hundreds of graves that I knew from my research would have been there.

While making my notes that evening, my thoughts flashed back to those last few weeks at Camp No. 2 … to after the war was over, when so many of my fellow prisoners had died having fought to stay alive for three and a half years in the appalling conditions, suffering the lack of food and sheer brutality of the guards, only to die with freedom just days away. I shed a tear for them.

Tuesday dawned with the usual clear blue sky, which foretold of another very hot day. At 8.00 am, Mr Wowo arrived with a map of the locality, explaining: 'Camp 3 may be difficult to locate, but by drawing a line south from Camp 1, through Camp 2, we may get somewhere near, although we don't know the distance between the camps.'

'I never stayed at Camp 3, but must have passed by it on the way to 2, and I can't recall anything outstanding that would help,' I replied. The 'straight line' theory couldn't work, as the railway line would have crossed the middle of the runway. Which way was the diversion made, east or west? We decided on the east, being somewhat in shorter distance than the route to the west, to skirt the airfield.

If finding Camp No. 3 seemed difficult before, it now proved to be impossible. For several hours we searched without success and there was no kampong nearby where we may have got information. Abandoning the search for Camp No. 3, it was essential now to find the jungle track we needed to follow the next day in the hope of finding more conclusive evidence of the railway line. Mr Wowo was driving slowly along the road, flanked by tall trees and undergrowth, when I called out: 'Is this it?' He stopped the car. There was a narrow opening, just a dirt track, without any indication as to where it led.

'Yes,' he said, 'this seems to be what we are looking for. It is heading south. We'll drive a little way along it to have a look.'

Leaving the bright sunlight, we drove into semi-darkness between the towering trees and there was a distinct drop in temperature. We returned to the road and arranged some pieces of wood to mark the entrance to save time the following day. The next morning, I had an early breakfast as we intended to set off at 6.00 am, hopefully to reach Logas and return to Pakenbaru during the twelve hours of daylight. From somewhere behind me, a lady's voice said: 'I do not eat rice.' When I asked the waiter if the lady was English, I received a negative answer. He added that she was Javanese. A few moments later, a diminutive lady passed my table, most certainly not Javanese. I hurried to the door, but she was gone. Having no time to enquire further, I joined Mr Wowo, who was waiting in the foyer. He had come this time in a Land Rover and with him were a driver and a mechanic.

We set off, making for the jungle track we had marked the previous day. Although there were signs of other vehicular traffic having used this route, we did not see anyone. There were no kampongs, only thick, impenetrable undergrowth, like a green wall on each side. Due to the dense vegetation, there was no way of knowing if any remnants of the railway were in the vicinity. Three hours had passed, and nothing had been achieved. Were we on a wild goose chase? The going became even slower when a violent thunderstorm broke: a solid sheet of rain, vivid flashes of lightning and earth-shaking crashes of thunder. The track turned to mud and I was thankful we were in a four-wheel drive Land Rover with a good driver.

The storm passed ... or had we passed the storm? Just a short distance beyond the mud, the track was dry, without a sign of rain. Pressing on, we soon ran into another storm. Here we encountered a blue van bogged down in the mud. Mr Wowo offered assistance. He explained to me they could cope – they had a winch on the front of their van and by attaching a rope to a tree they could pull themselves free. The storm was soon over and were back on the dry track. Several times a rustling could be heard in the undergrowth; sometimes just a spasmodic sound, like a monkey jumping from tree to tree. Other times it was much noisier, maybe made by larger animals ... orang-utan, black panther, or tiger? We didn't know as we were unable to see them. There were strange-sounding calls from unseen birds, audible even above the sound of the engine. The impenetrable jungle now gave way to more open ground, dominated by coconut palms, interspersed with banana plants.

'We are nearing Lipat Kain. That's just over 40 miles from Pakenbaru and it is almost midday,' Mr Wowo observed.

'That is not very good is it? We have just time to reach Pakenbaru before dark,' I remarked.

Lipat Kain was a bustling community, situated on the Kampar River, which judging by the numbers of floating craft, was their highway. There was a native eating house, and Mr Wowo suggested that he, the driver and mechanic should have a meal there while I ate my prepared sandwiches. 'I don't think the kind of food and the service would suit you,' he told me.

'You know that I'm not a stranger to the local food and customs. If you eat there, I will also,' I said.

The four of us sat down at a table. There were plates, a finger bowl and a beaker of water, but no cutlery. The proprietor brought in a large steaming bowl of white boiled rice, which he placed in the centre of the table, followed by a dozen or so smaller dishes, each containing four items of food. There were things like boiled eggs, small fish, bamboo shoots, smoked fish, slices of some kind of meat, chicken drumsticks, with mango and chilli sambal. Now I must eat in the proper manner, I told myself, picking the food up with the fingers of my right hand and then rinsing them before taking a portion from another dish. Curious glances from others in the room soon turned to smiles of approval when I was seen to be eating correctly.

'Don't drink the water,' warned Mr Wowo.

When the meal was over I insisted on paying. The proprietor came in with a sheet of paper, making a note of what we had left: half the rice, one or two portions on some dishes, none on others. He charged me for only the food we had eaten. What would happen to the remainder, I wondered. Would it be served to the next customers?

In the interest of safety, I asked my companions if they thought we should return to Pakenbaru while we had a chance of arriving before dark. This would mean admitting failure, not having found any sign of the railway. Before replying, Mr Wowo decided to enquire if any of the local people knew about the railway. Meanwhile, I walked down to the riverside. The water level was at its lowest and the ferry was able to dock directly on the riverbank. Nearby, a wooden structure provided three further landing stages, at various heights to suit the rising levels of the river, the highest being 25 feet above the present water level. There were several accumulations of coconut husks floating in the water, held in place by nets, which indicated their chief trading commodity was copra, for the production of coconut oil, while the husks would be used for matting.

Mr Wowo had some success, and told me: 'We are very close to the route of the railway. A short distance to the east, a large bridge was washed away many years ago. It had been built at the confluence of the Kampar and Sebajang rivers to carry the railway. The line followed the south bank of the river, crossing the jungle track a short distance beyond the river.'

After a discussion we decided to go on, at least until we found some evidence of the railway. We boarded the ferry for the short crossing of the Kampar River. The track was much better here and was in regular use. We met women carrying bundles on their heads, one man struggling with a large bundle tied to his bicycle and others pulling handcarts. We passed the granite pillar erected by the Dutch that marked the Equator, a few miles north of the Sebajang River.

The ferry was waiting when we reached the river, so we drove straight on board. A small kampong occupied both banks of the river, and seemed to be a suburb of Lipat Kain. A cool refreshing drink of milk from the green coconuts we bought was very welcome, as we dared not drink the local water. Our enjoyment was cut short by an agonising scream. A motor scooter, which had been parked on the highest landing stage, had fallen and injured a boy of about 10 years old. Mr Wowo rendered first aid from our medical kit, but there were more serious injuries than the cuts and bruises he treated. As ours was the only vehicle available, we were asked to take the boy to the clinic at Lipat Kain. The boy was made comfortable in the back of the Land Rover, and with his parents, we set off back to Lipat Kain.

I was surprised how well the clinic was equipped, being in such an outlandish place. Even so, I saw little hope of the boy surviving. Realising now there was no possibility of reaching Pakenbaru before nightfall, we carried on south, crossing the Equator three times in a couple of hours. Beyond the Sebajang River the terrain was more open – still a lot of scrub, but not as dense as earlier in the day. Then I saw it, and gave a shout of glee. Just visible through the bushes was a railway wagon. Vegetation was growing through the rotting floor. On the side was a stencilled number, still readable after all these years: 1603. True to the report from Lipat Kain, the railway had crossed the jungle track as this wagon was on our right-hand side, whereas the Kampar bridge had been on our left. The next find was a slab of sandstone, on which were Japanese symbols – a Japs' grave, according to Mr Wowo. Nearby was a rail carrying truck. A few miles further along was another truck, No. 1606. Stencilled alongside was a square, with Jap writing, which Mr Wowo translated as 'October 1944'. Did the Englishman who stencilled the square somehow find out the meaning? It would seem likely, as he had painted alongside, in freehand, 'October, bloody thunder'.

We crossed the Singingi River by ferry. Was this where the bridge was washed away in March 1945? Yes, it must be, because the place we arrived at was Kotabaru. It was from this camp that I was forced to go to the doomed bridge. My presence at Kotabaru camp in March 1945 was confirmed by the piece of paper Ron Thompson had picked up after the Japs withdrew at the end of the war. There was no sign of the camp, only what must have been one of the largest steam locomotives used on the railway. It was now standing in front of the local school as a permanent monument of the days past. The schoolmaster was head of the kampong and invited us in for a cup of tea.

As Mr Wowo and the schoolmaster talked, I took a walk by the river. My thoughts went back to that unforgettable night of terror. Over the years I've found it impossible to estimate the number of deaths that were caused by that calamity. Those who escaped were sent to different camps. I came across a line of what were obviously graves – mounds of earth without any form of identification, most likely prisoners who had died in the camp but sadly could not now be named. I stood in silence, thinking about those far-off days with a tear in my eye. Had I been on a burial party when some of these were interred? Were any my personal friends? Alas, there was no way of knowing. Pressing on, we saw a derelict truck almost alongside the track, an ideal position for a photograph.

Now the terrain changed to swamp. Again we were thankful for the four-wheel drive Land Rover. This area brought back memories of the almost hopeless task of building a sound foundation for the railway line amidst the constant bawling and lashing out by the merciless guards, and of the ever-hungry, blood-sucking leeches. Leaving the swamp behind, the rising track narrowed between thicker undergrowth until we reached an outcrop of rock on our right-hand side. This rose to a point some distance away beyond the tops of tall trees. It was too far to walk to the rock and there was no way to drive, but I believe this was possibly where I encountered the tiger at the spring, as the camp was under the tall trees close to the river. We passed a branch-line junction. I realised that this must have been the line to the coal mine that the Australians had been working on before we met them and after the bridge tragedy. Another truck came into view on the right-hand side, engine No. 1607. A short distance beyond that was a steam locomotive, which was almost hidden by undergrowth and banana plants. This indicated to Mr Wowo that we were nearing habitation – Logas, in fact.

Now nearly 90 miles from Pakenbaru, with only one hour of daylight remaining, the thought of driving through the jungle for twelve hours in the darkness was somewhat daunting. From the time I had first contemplated my journey to Sumatra, I had a secret desire to reach Logas. It was the place named on my released prisoner's pay book, but I thought I had little hope of achieving this ambition: here I was, at last.

News of our impending arrival had reached Logas before us, via the river, and we were greeted by the entire populace, led by their headman. The kampong, which I remember had been located some way from our prison camp, now included part of the camp site. There were many indications that this was the camp. Scattered all around were pieces of rusting iron, wheels, springs, axles and the like. The headman told us that this had been a major depot, receiving supplies from Singapore and Java via the Indigiri River to Rengat. Goods were also brought into the port of Padang and transported to Logas by rail. The headman told us he had supervised the reinterment of the prisoners who had died at the camp. A special place had been set aside for this where no one may go, not even me. All I could do was take a photograph of the general direction.

He next took us to meet a man who had been forced to work on the railway, having been shipped from Java. He lived just outside the kampong, in a native-style hut but on stilts, along with his wife, son, daughter-in-law and grandson – just one room for them all to live in. At my request to take his photograph, he went to a corner of the hut and brought out what must have once been a white shirt, now discoloured with age. I asked, through Mr Wowo, where he had got this from and he replied that he had exchanged food for it after supplies were dropped into the camp. Maybe he got it from me. He wanted to wear it, possibly for the first time, but I wanted to photograph him in his native dress. Later I regretted that I hadn't ask him to wear the shirt while I took the photograph. With the light fading, I could only pray that the photographs would turn out alright. Bidding the man and his family farewell, I looked at the plants growing at the edge of the jungle. There were the yellow tomato-like fruit and various leaves and berries that had helped to sustain me during those horrendous days in 1945.

Darkness descended with the speed one expects in the tropics. Now twelve hours since we had left Pakenbaru, it was time to consider the return journey. One thing was certain: there were no hotels in Logas, so we couldn't stay there. The formidable prospect of our journey was not made easier with the knowledge that tigers had been seen in the locality and fires had to be kept going throughout the night around the kampong. Mr Wowo's suggestion to carry on travelling south made some sense. We did not know if the ferries we had used earlier would be in operation through the night. According to the map, there were no rivers to cross on the southern route until reaching the Koeantan River at Moearo, where we would at last come to proper roads. We did not know what conditions we would encounter, but hoped it would be no worse than the journey had been so far. This route would add many more miles to return to Pakenbaru, taking us close to Rengat, where we would turn west towards Padang. Then we would have to go through the mountains on the west coast.

There was a delay before setting off while the mechanic checked the vehicle, knowing full well how serious a breakdown could be in the next few hours. During this time I was once again surrounded by children, curious at seeing a white man, as visiting strangers must have been a rarity in this remote place. I wished I had thought to bring some sweets or baubles to give them. Under way once more, the full moon was, for the most part, hidden by tall overhanging trees. Overall, the track was not too hazardous, with just short stretches of mud to contend with after the frequent showers. Thankfully we didn't encounter such violent storms as we had earlier in the day. It took us five hours to reach Moearo, yet we did not see any kampongs or other vehicles along the route.

While waiting for the ferry, a check showed a rear tyre was punctured, which we hadn't noticed before due to the rough track. With the wheel changed, we were soon on our way again, now on proper roads. We made for Sawah-Loento, the first town where it might be possible to get accommodation for the night. Mr Wowo made enquiries. My three companions could be put up but they were unable to cater for an Englishman. I insisted that I could stay in the Land Rover, but they would not leave me. So, after a much-needed meal, we headed for Padang Pandjang.[2] When we arrived, even though it was two o'clock in the morning, the place was extremely busy, with vehicles of all shapes and sizes hurrying about. We had another meal while a new tyre was being fitted to the spare wheel. When we left, Mr Wowo took a turn at driving to give the driver a break as he had been steering for many hours along rough track in the dark.

An hour later, we arrived at Boekit Tinggi,[3] a total contrast to Padang Pandjang. The town was in total darkness. There was no point stopping here, so we decided to carry on towards Payakoemoeh.[4] On the new highway, built by Caltex, running between Padang and Pakenbaru, the Land Rover's engine began to misfire. The mechanic diagnosed points failure and he did not have a spare set. We went slowly, still in total darkness, until we reached a garage. The lights came on in answer to the sound of our horn. Soon the parts were supplied and fitted, and we were on our way again.

Payakoemoeh was eerily quiet. With his sound logic, Mr Wowo said, 'This is the last town before we reach the mountains. With the driver tired it would be better if we wait until dawn before we tackle the winding mountain passes.' Knowing how weary I was myself after some twenty-two hours of travelling, I agreed we should try to get some sleep in the Land Rover.

We awoke after what seemed to be just a few minutes as all hell broke loose. The town woke up, as if roused by some communal alarm, at exactly 5.00 am. Motor vehicles started up and street vendors set out their wide variety of goods for sale, each proclaiming their wares, and children with baskets were selling ready prepared food. But, without doubt, the most noise came from the top of the mosque, where the priest called the faithful to prayer with the aid of a loudhailer. Vying with the priest, the cinema manager, on the opposite side of the road, proclaimed the merits of his current feature, interspersed with dialogue from the film, also using a loudhailer. With no prospect of further sleep, we bought some packs of food, satisfied our hunger, and waited for dawn.

As the sun rose, the outline of the mountain range could be seen in the east. We came to the rising ground soon after leaving the town. Although very warm, there were patches of mist where the sun had not yet reached. As the gradient increased, the road followed a zigzag course, with ever-increasing sharper angles, sometimes on the edge of a sheer drop. I now fully understood why the driver had not wished to tackle this road in the dark. Finally we reached the summit, under a clear blue sky with the temperature many degrees cooler than in the lowlands. We stopped to look at the panoramic view of the road snaking down through lush green vegetation before starting the descent.

Every few miles a lay-by allowed coming vehicles, of which there were quite a number, to pass in safety. Surprisingly, it was an uneventful journey down. After some time we stopped alongside a large globe which depicted the world. This marked the Equator. Now we continued on a wider, straight road and without further stops we reached Pakenbaru by midday – thirty hours after we had left and with only one hour's sleep! I was extremely pleased with the outcome and deeply thankful to my companions for making it possible. I offered a gratuity, which I felt was due to them, but they refused to take it. Mr Wowo explained: 'They are on the Caltex payroll, and their pay will include the last thirty hours.' Back in my hotel, my first thought was about the English lady I had caught a glimpse of before the journey. 'She left for Jakarta yesterday,' I was told by the receptionist. Now for that much-needed washdown and change of clothes before sitting down for a meal, this time with a knife and fork. Even the customary glass of warm water containing the small teabag was welcome. Bed at last … no need to count sheep, or watch the geckos on the ceiling.

It was early morning when I woke, having slept soundly for sixteen hours. Before breakfast I took a walk in the clear, cool morning air, passing groups of papaya palms, their marrow-like fruit hanging from the centre crowns of leaves, similar to the way coconuts grow on taller palm trees. I spotted durian trees with their pleasant-tasting but vile-smelling fruit. Then I saw breadfruit hanging from the thick branches of a large tree, and there were also plantations of bananas – each long, fruit-bearing stem hanging from the centre of the plant, showing various stages growth from purple flower to green and yellow fruit.

Mr Wowo arrived in a car as I finished my breakfast. He was to take me to the Caltex oilfields at Rumbia, at the invitation of the management. There I spent an interesting morning being shown around, amongst the numerous 'nodding donkeys' that pumped oil from deep down in the earth. I was shown a unique type of solid oil that had been discovered here, which had to be heated to a high temperature and conveyed through electrically heated pipes. It could also be transported in solid blocks. Caltex had used it to build roads, and even with the local temperature around 100 degrees, there was no sign of it melting. Then I had an excellent lunch with the management in the executive dining room.

Back at the hotel, I made some notes about the journey along the route of the railway in preparation for a meeting with the press, which was arranged for six o'clock at a restaurant in Pakenbaru. It soon became clear during the meal that not everyone had a fluent knowledge of English. With my inability to understand Malay, I was glad to have Mr Wowo by my side, but even he seemed unable to convince them that not all men in the RAF were pilots. Another misunderstanding arose when I answered questions about my feelings while visiting the former camp sites. I said: 'I could not keep back the tears on seeing the unmarked graves of my mates.'

One reporter asked: 'Did you have women in the camps?' I looked at him in astonishment. Apparently, my use of the word 'mates' had brought the confusion. One reporter thought I said 'I had missed my maids'.

Mr Wowo soon cleared up the misinterpretation.

Chapter 19

Surprises

At 2.30 pm, Mr Wowo came to collect me for the last time, to take me to the airport to catch the 3.30 Geruda flight G105 to Jakarta, Java. Although I had only known him for a week it was like saying farewell to an old friend. There was no way I could fully express my thanks for all the assistance he had given me. Again he refused a gratuity, but wished me Godspeed and good fortune in the future. He had brought with him two news-sheets, in Malay. One had reproduced the two photographs,[1] while the other printed a pencil drawing that looked somewhat like me. He also provided me with translations of both sheets.

On my arrival at Jakarta, I took a taxi to the Indonesian Hotel, where I was booked to stay for three days. Sheer luxury! After a real bath, I dined in one of the five restaurants. That was a proper English meal in comparison to the Eastern fare of the past week. This was followed by a pot of Java tea, hot and strong, with milk and sugar – a total contrast to the drowned teabags in Pakenbaru. I ended the evening in one of the several bars, where a variety of entertainment was provided.

As usual I rose early to take a walk in the cool morning air, but even at this early hour on a Sunday morning, the traffic was frightening. Seven roads converged onto a large water tank or reservoir, which was surrounded by a brick wall and formed a traffic island. The roads approaching were controlled by just red and green traffic lights, and you took your life in your hands crossing the four lanes. Everyone was in a hurry, sounding their horns and weaving from lane to lane. I finally reached the far side in one piece. I doubt if any vehicle in Jakarta is without a dent or scratch.

After breakfast, I took a taxi to the Commonwealth War Graves Commission cemetery at Menteng Poeloe. By mistake the driver took me to the Netherlands' cemetery. Apparently he didn't know where the British section was, so I had no option but to return to the hotel, where

I had lunch. Afterwards I took a walk through the native quarter, where the main means of travel was the trishaw, which I used to return to the hotel after a pleasant afternoon.

On Monday morning, my first task was to report to the immigration office to leave a passport photograph with them. Next, I rang the Caltex office, hoping to speak to Mr Neoradi, the director, who had authorised the assistance that had been given to me. I was told he had been called to Sumatra. I was very disappointed as I wanted to be able to thank him personally. My next call was the British Embassy, which I had seen on my Sunday morning walk. Mr McArthur met me and I explained the reason for my visit, to which he replied: 'This is the first I have heard of a railway being built by prisoners of war of the Japanese in Sumatra. I've heard of the Burma Railway, but not a word about the Sumatra one, and it's virtually under my nose.'

'I have had the same trouble in England,' I told him. 'No one would believe me, but they will in future with the photographs I have taken.'

'Let me have some copies when you return to England,' he said.

I showed him the two news-sheets and also a copy of Major Jacobs' report to Singapore in September 1945. When I told him the taxi driver had been unable to take me to the British section of the war cemetery, he offered to take me himself. We set off in his chauffeur-driven Rolls-Royce. I had to smile when Mr McArthur said, 'This chauffeur thinks everyone should jump out of the way quickly when they see this car coming. His language is not exactly polite.'

The British section was at the rear of the Netherlands' cemetery, which was the most beautifully kept resting place, with neat rows of white headstones. The white memorial chapel is shared by the British and Netherlandish visitors. After looking through the cemetery register, I took photographs of those graves with Nottingham connections in the hope of tracing relatives when I returned home. I said a prayer in the chapel. Mr McArthur asked me to stay for lunch, which gave me time to tell him more about the Sumatra Railway. After lunch, as I was leaving, having thanked him for his assistance, he said: 'It's been a pleasure meeting you, Mr Lee. Not every day do I meet such a person as you; usually it's businessmen needing assistance.'

Back in my hotel room, making notes of the morning's events, the telephone rang. It was Mr McArthur. 'As I told you, I have heard nothing of the Sumatra Railway in all these years. Now, on the same day, I receive

146

two enquiries regarding it. Mrs Jarvis from Dorset has been to Pakenbaru in the hope of tracing the movements of her cousin, who died there on 21 August 1945, six days after the end of the war. His grave is in Jakarta cemetery. She is due to return home tomorrow. Would it be convenient for you to see her?' Naturally, I said I would be glad to meet her.

When Mrs Jarvis came into the hotel foyer, I recognised her as the petite lady I had caught a glimpse of in the Riu Hotel. I greeted her with: 'I saw you in Pakenbaru, but didn't have time to speak to you.'

'Yes, I caught a glimpse of you too, but didn't know you were English,' she replied. 'It's a long story. My cousin was in the Royal Signals and his mother was informed that he was missing, believed killed, in March 1942. Later they confirmed that he had died. A year later, she received a prisoner-of-war letter from him and two further cards arrived a year after that.

'His pay book, containing some jottings, was returned to his mother after the war was over. In it was an entry by J. Wyatt, who recorded his death on 21 August 1945, at Logas, Sumatra. In February 1954, the War Office notified her that he had been reinterred in Medan, Cemetery, Sumatra. In April 1962, she received a letter from the Commonwealth War Graves Commission telling her he was now buried at Mentang Poeloe, Jakarta, Java. I have seen his grave.'

'Well, I was in Logas when the war ended,' I told her, 'but moved to Pakenbaru before release. I thought everyone had left Logas on that last train.'

'Failing to get any information in England, I came to look myself,' she responded. 'Even so, I have learnt nothing here either, until meeting you.'

'On my return to England, I will send you some copies of the photographs I have taken along the line as far as Logas, and details of the building of it,' I promised. 'Mr Neumann of Amsterdam has written a documentary account of the railway, but it has not yet been translated into English.' Then I added: 'You have not yet told me his name apart from Raymond. Although I'm not very good at remembering names, it may ring a bell.'

'His name is Raymond Darrall, Royal Engineers,' she replied.

'Sorry, but I can't recall that name, although we were in the same camp when the war ended. He must have been too ill even to board that last train.'

Time went so quickly and there was so much I wanted to tell her, but she had to leave to prepare for the early morning flight to Singapore, on her way back home. I suggested she should endeavour to attend the London Reunion of the Far East Prisoners of War, to be held in October, where I may be able to introduce her to others who had worked on the Sumatra Railway. After exchanging addresses, we bade each other farewell.

On Tuesday morning I asked the hotel receptionist to book a hotel on Ambon Island for three days, from Thursday. She read 'John Lee' from my passport. As she wrote down the hotel address for me, she said: 'Don't expect too much when you arrive, but I have booked, as far as I know, the best there is on Ambon. There are very few visitors to that island.'

Not having spent much time in Jakarta (then Batavia) as a prisoner, there was nothing I was familiar with as I toured the city by taxi. Nor was there a landmark that I could recall from my first visit in 1942, almost thirty-eight years ago to the day. As my flight to Denpasar, Bali, was due to leave at 5.00 am, I retired early to my room in order to pack.

The DC-3, at 30,000 feet, flew over smoking volcanos along the length of Java. At this height the sun rose earlier than at ground level, and revealed the tiered paddy fields down the mountainsides. It all made for a very pleasant flight. After landing, I had a surprise when I left the customs hall. A local gentleman addressed me by name. Immaculately dressed in a cream suit, complete with buttonhole, he asked: 'Have you booked accommodation for tonight?'

'No,' I replied.

'Excuse me, sir, but are you connected with Caltex or the British Embassy?'

'No, neither,' I said.

'Don't worry, Mr Lee, I am here to look after you while you are in Bali. I will take you to the Kota Beach Hotel, where a room is kept for ex-servicemen of any nationality at a special rate.'

He took me to his large American car, where his chauffeur was waiting. It seemed strange to see the locals bowing their heads as the car passed through Denpasar. This made me curious as to his name, but his reply to my question was: 'It wouldn't convey anything to you if you knew.' By his precise English I came to the conclusion he had been educated in England.

It was the usual procedure, after booking in at the hotel, to leave another passport photograph with the immigration office. Having left

Jakarta so early, I had not yet had breakfast. When my gentleman told me he would collect me at 10.30 am, I remedied this with nothing more exotic than scrambled egg on toast. I had some time to spare before 10.30, so I took a walk along the beach. The number of adults and children begging came as quite a surprise to me. I had seen it in Cairo, but this was the first time in Indonesia. At 10.30, the car arrived and my escort took me first to a batik factory, where I watched the complicated process of printing colourful designs onto sarongs. Next we walked round a twenty-four-hour market, where practically anything one would need could be bought, including fruit and vegetables, radios and car parts, and even spurs for cock fighting, although that is illegal in Indonesia.

Now we drove out of Denpasar, passing exotic flowering trees and wonderful scenery, including tiered paddy fields on the hill slopes, which, I was told, produced three crops a year. In the valleys, groves of coconut palms occupied both sides of gentle streams, located close to kampongs. The day was ended with a high-class meal at the Bali Hyatt hotel.

Next morning, after a comfortable night's sleep, I awoke at dawn and took a leisurely walk around the town. Even at that early hour, the streets were thronging with various types of transport and locals carrying heavy bundles of bamboo across their shoulders. The one thing I hadn't noticed the previous day was that all the prices in the shops were marked up in US dollars. This implied that most of the tourists were American.

My flight to Ujung Pandang, the capital of the island of Sulawesi (formerly Makassar and Celebes respectively), was booked for 11.30 am. My host arrived in good time and we drove to the airport. While waiting for the boarding call he showed interest in my past. Where was I held as a prisoner? What work was I forced to do? I gave him an outline of those three and a half years. Still he would not tell me who he was. It was time to part so I bade him farewell and thanked him for the assistance he had given me.

It was only a short flight to Ujung Pandang. There I was met by an army of porters, all with large numbers on their backs. Number 5 took my cases, saw me through customs and then called a taxi, at my request. He deposited my cases in a locker and gave me the key. With nearly two hours to wait until my flight to Ambon, I wanted to visit Ujung Pandang, but a storm broke before the taxi reached there, so I returned to the airport. Number 5 saw me arrive and took charge again. Taking me to a café, he kept close by until it was time to depart. Having collected the key from me, he carried my cases to the plane but sadly I had to obey the large notices saying 'No tipping allowed'.

It was a pleasant flight in the Fokker Friendship. At just over 20,000 feet, the islands we flew over could be clearly seen. Passing through customs at Ambon, I boarded a taxi, giving the driver the name and address of the hotel in town. We made quite good going until we reached the ferry. The road beyond was narrow, with native houses built close to the edge. A constant stream of vehicles moved in both directions.

After a long and dusty journey, I was met at the hotel by a large Chinese gentleman. He introduced himself as the proprietor, then looked down a list and shook his head. 'There is no booking for John Lee,' he told me in his best English. I looked over his shoulder and there, plain to see, was the name Lee. He politely explained: 'That is Chung Lee, a Chinese gentleman who is due later this afternoon, and I'm afraid the hotel is full up.' My taxi driver, who had fortunately stayed with me, took me to another hotel, where my entrance caused quite a stir. The proprietor also said he had no vacancies, which my driver did not believe. During the ensuing conversation I heard the word *'maken'* (food). So the trouble appeared to be that they could not cater for a European. Notwithstanding my efforts to convince them that I would eat as they did, it was to no avail. So, on we went to the next hotel, the last one on the island.

At the Josiba Hotel, the driver indicated that I stay in the car while he went in first. A few moments later he returned and announced that they had rooms. But when I walked in I got the same reaction as I had at the previous hotels. However, after much talking and gesticulation they decided I could stay. Thankfully, there was air conditioning in my room. The bed had a wooden base and a palliasse covered by a clean sheet, but without over sheets; there was just a straw-filled bolster, known as a 'Dutch wife' (its purpose to absorb the sweat during the humid nights). The washing and toilet facilities were as one would expect in a native hotel. After a much-needed washdown, it was the usual duty to report to the immigration office to leave a passport photograph. The proprietor gave instructions to the driver of the cycle trishaw and told me not to pay him more than 50 rupiahs.

We threaded our way through the streets, which were crowded with Japanese cars and motorbikes, with drivers seemingly attempting to knock others off the road. A hazard to the trishaw drivers were the large open storm drains. The journey to the immigration office took about fifteen minutes but soon we were on our way back. Then I was in for a surprise, as my driver turned into a square where a group of other trishaw drivers were congregated. He indicated that I dismount and *'jalan-jalan'* (walk). For a few moments I refused to pay him, until a few of his mates advanced in a threatening manner. So I set off to the hotel, where the proprietor was waiting for my return. He was furious that I had had to walk back. This was the first time I had encountered animosity on my travels. When the driver returned, the proprietor vented his wrath on him, ordering him away from his pitch outside his hotel.

I sat down to a typical native meal – rice, of course, with the usual side dishes. A few touches of refinement put the service above the level of the roadside café. There was a white tablecloth, decorated china serving dishes, and porcelain spoons. The proprietress looked several times round the door, obviously curious to see if I was eating what was set before me. It came as a surprise when I asked her for some *'kichi-pesang'* (small banana). These had a very distinct and delicious flavour, and as they were only 3–4 inches in length, one could eat several at a time. After a short time she produced a 'hand' and she was still further surprised when I thanked her in her language: *'Trema-casi banya.'*

After a hot and sticky night, being kept awake by the sound of torrential rain, I welcomed the dawn. The rain stopped, but the road was still flooded as I went out for a walk as even the storm drains had been unable to cope with the deluge. After breakfast I ordered a taxi to take me to the Ambon War Cemetery. It was a slow and tedious journey as the overnight rain had created deep potholes, so the busy traffic could only crawl between them. A large boulder had been placed in one of the holes, presumably to stop water splashing onto the building alongside the road, and this had almost brought the traffic to a standstill.

We finally arrived at the ornamental bronze gates of the cemetery. This site had been a former prisoner-of-war camp and was laid out by the Commonwealth War Graves Commission. I asked my driver to wait. Passing through the gate, I walked to the Ambon Memorial, which is in the form of a shelter and dedicated to 460 Australian soldiers and airmen who have no known grave. Beyond is the Cross of Sacrifice and the neat rows of low headstones surmounted by bronze plaques, on which the names are engraved. The total number of British, Australian and Dutch graves is 2,137. The cemetery is beautifully maintained by a local father and son. Tropical trees and shrubs are planted throughout the site, with mature trees around the perimeter, creating an atmosphere of peace and tranquillity. While the visits to Krangi and Jakarta war cemeteries were heartrending, the Ambon cemetery is more personal and was the saddest part of my journey. I had to look through the cemetery registers for the names and grave numbers of my personal friends who died on the island of Haruku and have been reinterred at Ambon. I was unable to hold back the tears as I read the details of those I had known, usually by nicknames, such as Nobby, Taffy, Jock, Geordie and more, but now saw their proper names for the first time.

My thoughts went back to that time of sheer brutality when these young men died from dysentery, beriberi or malaria, without any medication that may have saved their lives or at least eased their suffering. The inadequate supply of food, both in quantity and quality, together with the long hours working on the airstrip in the oppressive heat, took a toll on health and lives. Most prisoners were without footwear and, in many cases, with only a piece of sacking to maintain a degree of decency. I recalled the selfless assistance some of them offered me when I was down with malaria, such as collecting the obligatory 100 flies to qualify me for half rations and sharing any extra food they might have come by. My tears were for them: they died, I survived. Thankfully, I was alone while scanning the registers. My list complete, I set about taking photographs. It is not easy to focus a camera with your eyes streaming … there lies little Geordie; I remembered when I washed away the maggots and filth of dysentery shortly before he died.

Now with my painful task complete, I returned to my taxi. The driver, unable to speak English, must have seen I had been crying and placed a consoling hand on my shoulder. He took me on an unscheduled and much appreciated tour of the island. We called at a model native village, built under the supervision of a World Aid Organisation,[2] the English-speaking schoolmistress told me. Here new techniques had been demonstrated with the better use of available materials for house building and sanitation. A stream rose from the base of a sheer cliff, flowing through a deep, clear basin in which swam numerous large fish. No one was allowed to interfere with them. A bamboo screen prevented them from swimming downstream. The next section was for drinking water only, while the next was for personal cleanliness, and the washing of clothes could only be done in the last section. Water was diverted from the stream into a trench to provide toilet facilities, beneath an atap and bamboo shelter. Periodically, the position of the trenches was changed, while the former ones were filled in, ensuring there was no pollution of the water for villages further along the stream.

There was an Anglican and a Roman Catholic church, as well as a Moslem mosque, built alongside each other, and I wanted to know if there was any isolation between the three groups. No, I was told; they apparently lived in complete harmony. As there were no regular preachers, when one of any of the denominations came to give a service, all would attend. I was invited into the school, where the pupils rose as I entered and said in unison what sounded very much like 'Good morning, sir'. The happy, well-dressed children indicated they would like me to photograph them, which was not possible inside without a flash, so I took them outside.

After I had said goodbye to the schoolmistress, my driver took me straight back to the Josiba Hotel, where a pleasant surprise awaited me. A Javanese couple, Jan and Sue, had come to stay there. They spoke perfect English. Now I was able to convey to the proprietor my desire to visit Haruku. I learnt that he was born there and would look forward to a visit himself. So, without further ado, he left to make arrangements.

Walking in the town later, I came across two hoardings advertising Rinso and Sunlight soap. As I prepared to photograph them, a soldier approached, shouting and gesturing. I became alarmed as he tried to grab my camera. I couldn't understand what I had done wrong until I looked to where he was pointing. Just behind the hoarding, some children were doing PT in the schoolyard, but beyond them was a military barracks. Now I understood, but I was finally able to convince him that I had no interest in the barracks, only the hoardings. 'English!' I told him. 'Rinso, Sunlight – English.' He seemed satisfied and walked away. In the nearby river, women were washing their clothes. The flow of the brackish water was sluggish due to debris being piled up by the tide at the mouth of the river. Under those conditions it was doubtful – even with the use of Rinso and Sunlight soap – if the clothes could be washed clean.

Next morning, I rose early. The proprietor told me he had arranged for a motor boat to take us to Haruku. The rendezvous was to be at ten o'clock that day on the south-west coast of Haruku, the nearest point from Ambon. We must make an early start. Our group set off in the proprietor's car – Jan and Sue, along with the proprietor and his wife, who had closed the hotel for the day, and me. After leaving the crowded airport road, it was a pleasant journey through the lush vegetation of a South Sea island. The boat owner was waiting when we arrived. According to Jan and Sue, there was some misunderstanding about the number who would be travelling. Although the boat could carry all of us, the owner wanted extra payment to take five passengers. After a little friendly bartering, we got under way. The view of the Ambon coastline was as one would imagine, with tall coconut palms and flowering bushes down to the edge of the sandy beach, standing out against the calm blue sea. Soon we passed a small island, the home, I was told, of a rare bird of the pigeon family. It was here also, in the raid on Haruku, that the first bomb was dropped by Allied planes on the nearly completed runway. The remaining bombs, as I have recorded earlier, did little damage to the rock-hard runway. The boat owner asked if I had been on Haruku at the time of the bombing. When I said that I had, he started to chant: 'Brrr, brrr, brrr, boom, boom!' with significant gestures.

As we came closer to the island, beneath the scorching sun shining from a cloudless sky, the landing stage came into view. It was a strong wooden structure reaching out into the sea, unlike the flimsy rig we had worked on unloading the *Amagi Maru* on that dark and stormy night thirty years ago. Here now was a peaceful and beautiful tropical island, with the lush vegetation beyond the white sandy beach mirrored in the azure sea. It would seem that the whole populace of the nearby kampong had heard of our intended visit and had turned out to greet us, led by the headman. He shook each of us by the hand, and then took us to his house for tea. A tour of the kampong followed, accompanied by the happy residents, the children taking a particular interest in me. It was evident that the kampong had also benefitted from the expertise of the World Aid Organisation.

We were then taken to the airstrip past where the prison camp had been situated. The huts had been burnt down long ago to eliminate the noxious parasites living within the bamboo and atap. The last time I had seen the airstrip it was an expanse of dazzling white coral and the chances of anything growing on it looked extremely remote, but now it was covered with long grass, shrubs and small trees. There was a well-worn track across, leading to a neighbouring kampong. The concrete gun emplacements could still be seen along one side of the runway, while on the other side, gaps between the tall coconut palms were intended as plane dispersal points. The headman pointed out the area that had been the burial ground. In 1962, the bodies of those young men who had died had been transferred to the Ambon War Cemetery, where I had found the graves of some I had known.

At my request, everyone withdrew, leaving me alone with my thoughts. I recalled Gunso Mori's speech, on that first working party assembly: 'You are here to die. The Imperial Japanese forces wouldn't have surrendered as you have done, but would have committed hara-kiri, as you should have done.' I visualised the merciless beatings he inflicted on the weak, underfed, overcrowded men, usually on some trumped-up misdeed reported by Kasiyama. He obtained immense satisfaction from his brutality, as I witnessed on a number of occasions when I was on the receiving end. The nicknames for the pair were apt: Blood and Slime. After the war, Mori was hanged in Singapore and Kasiyama received ten years in jail.

My thoughts turned to those grim days, working twelve hours on the airstrip, then on returning to camp being detailed to the burial party. With so many sick with dysentery, malaria and beriberi, the task of burying the prisoners who had died that day could only be carried out by those fit enough for full-time work. At the height of the dysentery outbreak, as many as ten had to be buried each night, in the darkness, with us rarely knowing the names of those we were burying. As in Ambon, I was unable to control my tears but, after regaining my composure, I joined the others. It was a sombre walk back to the kampong, all laughter and chatter having ceased. Although I said nothing about my prisoner-of-war days, it was as if they understood the depth of my feelings.

Before we left Haruku, we were supplied with a typical native meal, wrapped individually in banana leaves. One man chopped the ends off green coconut husks to give us a cool drink of the milk inside. Bidding farewell to the headman, I used one of the few Malay phrases that I knew: *'Trema casi banya'* (thank you very much). That made him smile, probably because of my incorrect pronunciation. The whole of the village wanted to shake my hand.

On the return journey to Ambon I began to feel the effects of the scorching sun on my forehead as I didn't have a hat. It didn't occur to me to wear one, having spent those three and a half years without such a luxury. We landed back on Ambon and I was besieged by the local inhabitants offering hand-crafted articles – wooden statuettes, bead and basketwork – all extremely well made. I bought a few trinkets as souvenirs. On the journey back to Ambon town, I had a lesson in botany courtesy of my Javanese companion. I knew some plants and trees, but he pointed out the pepper tree, turmeric plant and the tree from which cloves are obtained, amongst others. We drove between the lush growth of tall palm trees and the lesser sago palm, interspersed with banana plantations, nutmeg and chilli bushes. There was breadfruit on tall trees, and papayas on palmlike trees, alongside the tall plantain bushes which produced a long, green banana-like fruit, which was used as a vegetable. Further along, the road was blocked. Two men had felled a sago palm, which had fallen across the road. Having split it lengthways, they were busy removing the edible soft centre of the tree with a chuckle – a type of large hoe with a sharp blade. We could have helped to clear the road but instead enjoyed just sitting watching them until only the outer shell of the tree remained. Back at the hotel, I suddenly realised how tired I was after the strenuous journey, so after a washdown and a meal, I wrote my notes then went to bed.

Rising early on my last full day in Ambon, I told the Javanese couple, Jan and Sue, that I would be walking around the town after breakfast and they decided to come with me. They took me to the crowded street market, with its colourful, exotic fruits and vegetables. There was a large display of fish, from small sardine-like ones, fresh and dried, to large silver specimens, with a variety of pink and brown fish completing the display. I said to Jan: 'If we, while prisoners, had been allowed to catch some fish, or some of the fruits and vegetables had been made available, it's likely some lives could have been saved.'

'Yes, that's true,' said Jan. 'With two and three crops a year there is no shortage of food on these islands. Nowadays, surplus produce is exported to Japan, paid for with cars, motorbikes, televisions cameras, etc. My business is spices, which are exported throughout the world. High wages can be earned from the biannual harvest. This, as you can see, has resulted in the congestion of the roads, as all the young men want to own a motorbike or car,' he told me.

Leaving the market, we came to the only petrol station in the area, which had just one pump and a long queue of impatient drivers, all sounding their horns as they waited their turn. In quieter parts of the town, outside most of the homes stood tables covered with spices such as mace, turmeric, cloves and chillies, drying in the sun. We stopped at a roadside teahouse and ordered a glass of what they called tea, but it was lukewarm and bitter.

I told Jan that I was curious about the gentleman who had taken charge of me in Bali. He replied: 'I don't go to Bali often, but have heard about this man. He must have some connection with the airline, as I understand he seeks out English visitors and takes them on sightseeing tours. It is rumoured that he is the son of the last king of Bali, but holds no official position now.'

'That would explain why the people in the streets bowed their heads as his car passed,' I said.

'I never heard his name mentioned,' he told me.

Going further, we came to the quayside, where dozens of new cars and motorbikes had just been unloaded from the Japanese ship that was now at anchor in the harbour. After lunch at the hotel, Jan had to go about his own business, so I booked a taxi to take me to Liang. There had been a prison camp there, I had been told, although I had not been incarcerated there myself and could only look in the general area where it may have been. This place I found to be the most beautiful spot I had ever seen. There was not another soul about, just utter silence as I walked among the tall palm trees bordering the white sandy beach. This had always been, in my mind's eye, my ideal picture of a South Sea island.

With two flights booked for tomorrow, I retired early. It only seemed minutes before I was woken by a violent thunder storm. The rain pounded on the tin roof of the hotel, like a drummer gone berserk. This and the ear-splitting crash of thunder, which seemed to shake the building, made further sleep impossible. I lay on the bed, tossing and turning until the sky began to lighten with the dawn as the storm passed. From the window I could see the road was flooded, with people wading through the water carrying their wares. Again the storm drains had been unable to cope during the deluge, but now the water level was slowly subsiding. Large puddles remained on the uneven road, offering a chance to some youthful car drivers to indulge in what they obviously considered to be fun. Leaving a space between their car and the one in front, they would roar through the water, splashing all and sundry.

While I was having breakfast, the proprietor suggested that an early start to the airport would be wise in case there was any damage to the road. He would take me, and Jan and Sue would come with us. My flight was not until one o'clock but, as it turned out, the early start was good advice. Some sections were difficult to negotiate, but we arrived in good time. It was difficult to express my thanks to the proprietor and Jan and Sue for the assistance they had given me. They had made it possible for me to visit Haruku, something I may not have been able to achieve on my own. They told me that if ever I returned to Ambon, a warm welcome would be assured at the Josiba Hotel. I boarded a Fokker Friendship plane for the short flight to Unjang Pandang.

On my arrival, the numbered porters were ever eager to assist the passengers. Number 7 took my cases as I went through customs, but number 5 remembered me and took them from him. He looked after them while I had a meal, later coming to tell me it was time to board the plane for Bali. Now in Denpasar again, I was surprised to see the anonymous gentleman waiting beyond the customs checkpoint, dressed in a cream suit and sporting a red buttonhole. He greeted me as I approached him: 'Good afternoon, Mr Lee. I have booked a room for you at the Kota Beach hotel.' This greeting gave credence to Jan's theory that he had access to airline passenger lists. Did it also mean that the rumour that he was the son of the former king of Bali was correct?

'Maybe you would like to go to a night club this evening?' he asked.

'As I got no sleep last night due to a thunder storm and I have to catch the six o'clock flight tomorrow morning to Sydney, I'm afraid I'll have to have an early night,' I replied. He agreed that would be best.

After a shower and a proper meal, I took a steady stroll along the beach. The sun was sinking amid a glorious array of colour, which was reflected in the glass-smooth sea. Large waves broke onto the shore, where surfers were taking the opportunity to demonstrate their skills. My enjoyment was marred by child beggars pulling at my clothing while adults tried to sell cheap jewellery in exchange for American dollars. I had noticed on my stay here a few days ago that most goods were priced in dollars, not in rupiahs. This was a phenomenon I hadn't encountered elsewhere in Indonesia.

I had a good night's sleep at the Kota Beach hotel, and was up early the following morning. My gentleman arrived to take me to the airport. I had only to collect my luggage from my room before setting off. It came as a shock to be told, as I was checking in at the airport, that I could not go on this flight. The reason given was that as I had not got a visa to stay in Australia, I could only remain there for seventy-two hours. With my scheduled booking to Auckland, it would mean a stay of seventy-six hours in Sydney. My travel agent had known about this new ruling after my journey had been arranged and changed my stay in Australia from six days to three, as it was too late to get a visa. My gentleman was very annoyed and pleaded that I be allowed to go as my friend, Hilton Stanton, would be expecting me on this flight. He even appealed to the Australian Ambassador to Indonesia, who was travelling on the plane, showing my letter of invitation from Hilton, but even this was to no avail. It was clear nothing could be gained at the airport. We went back to the Kota Beach hotel to book for a further night.

'We'll go and book a seat for you on the 8.00 am flight to Sydney. Your tickets are interchangeable between airlines,' my guide told me. With that settled, I accepted his offer of a further sightseeing tour of Bali. After a pleasant drive through the beautiful countryside, away from the noise and bustle of Denpasar, we arrived at what looked like a private estate. Large wrought-iron gates gave access through the high surrounding wall. We drove through and came to a large stone mansion. The stonework was decorated with elaborate carvings, with strange gargoyles protruding from the eaves.

'This was the home of the Prince of Bali,' said my gentleman. Was this a clue to his identity? Once again, I asked him. Once again, he refused to answer. He took me through a passage. On the walls were garish, grotesque caricatures of mythical creatures – 'to keep away evil spirits', he told me. We then entered what I assumed to be the state room. The only item of furniture was a long low table, with no chairs, just cushions placed around it. The walls were draped with silk and tapestries between life-size statues of women, whose carved, gilded features were superb. They were dressed in rich silks, in typical Balinese style.

Along another passage, again on the walls were grotesque figures similar to those in the first passage. This led to the bridal suite, where a large four-poster bed, intricately carved and gilded, was the dominant feature, draped in multi-coloured silks with a gold lace bedspread. A thick red carpet decorated with gold-coloured dragons covered the entire floor. Throughout our tour of the mansion we didn't see another person.

Leaving this behind, our next stop was a small town. In the centre square was an open-sided building with a golden dome over a larger-than-life statue surrounded by a number of obelisks. The reason we had come here, apparently, was to have lunch at a restaurant that catered for tourists. My offer to pay after finishing our meal was rejected by the manager, who said it was an honour to serve us. That made me all the more curious about my gentleman friend.

Continuing our journey, we drove up a twisting mountain road. The views were spectacular, the driver stopping occasionally for me to take photographs. Then the long downward run, after passing the zenith, back to Denpasar to take tea at the Bali Hyatt hotel. We stayed to watch a Balinese cabaret before returning to my hotel. I thanked my guide for the most wonderful day, fully aware that had I been alone, it wouldn't have been possible.

'I will collect you at six-thirty in the morning, and take you to the airport,' my nameless friend told me.

After taking a shower, I took a quiet walk along the beach in the bright moonlight. Gone were the beggars and hawkers, allowing me to relax before going to bed.

Chapter 20

The Last Lap

My gentleman collected me as promised. As I wouldn't be returning to Bali, this was our last meeting. We set off for the airport. As I waited to board my plane, I asked, once again: 'Please, sir, could you tell me your name? It will seem strange when talking or writing about you to refer to you as my gentleman.'

After some hesitation, he replied, 'Call me Brunei. That is all I can tell you.'

'Thank you, Mr Brunei. You have given me a great deal of pleasure, showing me sights I couldn't have seen without your guidance. I shall be forever indebted to you. Thank you very much.' We shook hands warmly before I passed through customs. It was like leaving a long-established friend. My words of farewell seemed so inadequate.

'Goodbye Mr Brunei, thank you.' I called at the last moment.

'Goodbye Mr Lee. Maybe we will meet again one day,' he replied. With a final wave, Mr Brunei, my immaculate gentleman, had gone. There was no delay in boarding this time, and soon the Boeing 747 took off, flying south-south-east at 28,000 feet, passing over numerous islands, some with plumes of smoke above the highest peaks – a reminder that volcanoes were often active in these parts. The captain announced that we were now passing over the coast of Australia and the town of Darwin. I'd heard of and seen pictures of 'the red heart' of Australia – which I thought only applied to the Ayres Rock and Alice Springs areas – but we were flying over the distinctly red, featureless terrain south of Darwin. The plane approached Sydney after taking a wide sweep out to sea and came in to land from the east, passing over Sydney Harbour Bridge and the Opera House.

Buses were waiting to take us to the reception area, there to be greeted by a large poster, which read: 'It is illegal to bring into Australia plants, fruit or vegetables and animals of any description.' Further along the passage, another poster, above a large container, stated: 'You have been warned. Place any illegal articles into the bin.' I had nothing to dispose of. At the passport checkpoint I was directed into an office, where I was searched. Then followed an endless stream of questions: Why hadn't I got a visa? Had I been to Australia before? Had I got my previous passport? How long was I staying? What was my business in Sumatra? I explained the reason why I hadn't a visa. I explained that I had not been here before and I was travelling with my first passport; my airline ticket was for my flight to Auckland in two days' time; and my visit to Sumatra was to trace the remnants of the railway built by prisoners of war of the Japanese. Accompanied by a security guard, I had to fetch my cases and move into another office, where they were searched, and then move again into another office for more questions, some repeating what I had already answered. The name, address and telephone number of my firm were written down, together with my home number. A second man left the room with these details.

Getting somewhat perturbed by this treatment, I asked to see if my friend, Hilton Stanton, was waiting outside for me. This set off more questions: Who is Hilton Stanton? I showed my letter of invitation. Would I be staying with him? Yes. I was allowed outside, but there was no sign of Hilton. Turning to return, I was confronted with large notices: 'Strictly no admission. Fine for illegal entry 500 dollars.' A policeman let me back in. Alone with one officer, the questions having ceased, he became more friendly. Yes, he had heard of the Sumatra Railway; a large number of Australians had died during its construction. Another officer came into the office and gave a note to the friendly one. He apologised for the delay to which I had been subjected. I could now leave after collecting my passport from the desk near the exit, together with a note for Mr Stanton asking him to phone the immigration office on my arrival at his home. I took a taxi to his address, only to find no one at home. The only course was to be taken to the nearest hotel.

Rising early, after a much-needed good night's sleep, I took a walk along the roads near the hotel. It came as a surprise when a gentleman hailed me: 'I know you are from the council,' he said. 'I'll mend the broken fence as soon as possible.'

'I'm not from the council. I only arrived here last night,' I said, and walked on.

'Please don't report me,' he called after me. 'I'm used to snoops looking round early in the morning.' As I returned along the opposite pavement, he still insisted on calling me a snoop.

After breakfast I phoned Hilton Stanton. He and his wife Betty soon arrived to collect me. We greeted each other like long-lost brothers. There is no doubt we could have passed in the street without recognising each other. The only time our paths had crossed previously was in the atrocious conditions on the Sumatra Railway. For a while we talked about the more pleasant things in life, and then he showed me what he had written about his time as a prisoner of the Japs:

> I was one of the group who, with Frank Williams, Judy and other Australians, had landed in Sumatra from Singapore, sailed up the Singingi River as far as possible, then walked to Padang on the west coast of Sumatra, where they were taken prisoner. Some time was spent building roads near Medan, north Sumatra, then transported by a former Dutch cargo ship, the *Van Waerwijck*, which was sunk on the way to Singapore. This was later taken to Pakenbaru, central Sumatra, via the Siak River, to begin working on the railway.[1]

Hilton was with the group that built the spur line to the coal mine, joining the main line when this was complete.

> Moving into what, at first sight, seemed to be a deserted camp, only to find one solitary fellow, barely conscious, almost at death's door. Every one rallied round to provide food to help him pull through.

I stopped reading. That was me he had written about. Tears came to my eyes as I recalled those grim days in March 1945, and said: 'Hilton, many times during the years I have regretted being unable to thank you and all the others who stole and scrounged food to enable me to live. I knew the extra food could have eased your own hunger pains. So now can I thank you for saving my life and restoring my will to live? Thank you. Please pass on my thanks to any others who were there.'

163

His wife replied: 'He never spoke of this. In fact, he would not speak about those three and half years.' Hilton seemed embarrassed, and remained silent.

Time was pressing and I must replace the laundry I had left at the Indonesian Hilton hotel in Jakarta. Driving to a large department store, I quickly bought the necessary items. Botany Bay was the next stop, then we passed Sydney Harbour Bridge before visiting the Opera House. Hilton told me the original estimated cost had been $2 million, but the actual cost had exceeded $40 million. It was a truly remarkable building. After a tour of the Opera House we had lunch at a nearby restaurant and then drove to a wildlife park north of Sydney to see the indigenous fauna. Now I could tell them back home that I had seen a kangaroo.

We went back to the Stantons' home for tea, where I continued reading Hilton's notes until late. He had, along with Judy and the other Australians, remained at Kota Baru until the war ended, when they finally made their way to Pakenbaru and were then flown to Singapore. For some time, Hilton had been in touch with Derek Stuart, who lived in Perth. Derek had also worked on the Sumatra Railway and belonged to the regiment whose CO was Colonel Robinson. Derek was one of the men from the regiment who had complained about the absence of any reference to the large number who had worked on the Sumatra Railway after Colonel Robinson published the regimental history.

Colonel Robinson had previously given me his name and address and my original plans had been to visit him, but this was my last day in Australia and it was now impossible. Obtaining his phone number, I tried for some time to contact him but I forgot it was only 6.00 am in Perth. We eventually talked for some time. As he and Hilton had been together throughout the three and half years, their experiences were similar. I then made a phone call to Claude Thompson to tell him I would be arriving in Auckland later that day – several days earlier than expected.

There was very little time to see more of the city, after we had a lunch of Nasi goreng – that familiar Malay dish of fried rice with numerous side portions of meat, fish and spices. It was an appropriate meal under the circumstances. Hilton and Betty drove me to the airport, arriving in good time for the 4.30 pm flight. I found it almost impossible to convey my heartfelt thanks to them for their hospitality, and especially to Hilton for his part in saving my life. 'Goodbye, goodbye,' I called as I passed through customs.

The New Zealand Airways Boeing 747 took off on time, travelling east. It soon became dark, with nothing visible apart from the myriad stars in the black sky, at 29,000 feet, until the captain informed us that the lights we could see ahead were Auckland. Landing after an uneventful flight, I passed quickly through customs and immigration to find Claude and Margaret Thompson there to meet me.

'Hello, Geoff, it's good to see you at last,' said Claude. 'We've looked forward to meeting you for so long. In fact, we had thought of visiting you in England.'

They took me to their home, just outside the city, where we talked for a while. I knew from previous correspondence that our paths had crossed many times. Claude was taken prisoner at Tasikmalya, Java, and sailed on the *Amagi Maru* to Haruku, where he worked on the runway until he was badly injured. He was then returned to Java with 183 other sick men and later taken to Singapore, where he worked on the docks. It must have been March 1944 that he was on the riverboat the *White Lady* and taken up the Siak River to Pakenbaru to start work on the Sumatra Railway. Our paths crossed again when I arrived at Kota Baru camp, in early January 1945, although I didn't know this. Claude was already there, he told me.

'During the night, in March 1945,' said Claude, 'the entire camp was turned out in an attempt to save the bridge, which was threatened by rapidly rising floodwater. I was given a flaming torch and forced by the guards onto the debris – tree trunks, branches and sheets of atap from washed-away native houses. As I saw the hundreds of torches stretching across the river, I was petrified. With the bridge shaking alarmingly, it was not possible to guide the debris between the piers. Dropping my torch, I slipped into the water, managed to reach the bank and scrambled ashore, and then laid down in a deserted native hut. I must have dropped to sleep, to be woken by a mighty roar as the bridge collapsed. I looked out but there was no sign of any torches. I made my way back to camp as dawn broke to find so few there.

'Some days later, all the camp was moved to what I believe was Logas, where I stayed until the end. We then went on the only train that was working and returned to Pakenbaru, which was alongside the runway. Lady Edwina Mountbatten arrived in a shiny silver Douglas DC-3, and spent time talking to the sick and dying men lying in the open. She showed no concern for her own well-being moving about among those lousy and disease-ridden men. God bless Her Ladyship.'

'Claude,' I responded, 'you will recall I told you in a letter that I was left behind when your group was moved to Logas and how the group of Australians, including Frank Williams and Judy the dog, moved into Kota Baru and found me alone there. There is no doubt they saved my life. Later I was moved to Logas, and I was also on that train to Pakenbaru.'

Next morning, during breakfast, I told Claude of a puzzle I had been unable to solve. 'Were there any survivors of the bridge collapse on the far side of the river?' I asked. 'Over the years I haven't been able to contact anyone who survived on that side.'

'Sorry, Geoff, I can't help,' he said.

We all set off to see Auckland, where life seemed to proceed at a leisurely pace and no one was in a rush – a city of fine buildings, apart from one place, where a beautiful small church was overshadowed by a high-rise block of flats, almost obscuring it. After a typical English lunch of roast beef and Yorkshire pudding in a café, we carried on our tour, and then returned to the Thompsons' home for tea.

Prior to the planning of my journey to the Far East, I had met Eric Carver, who lived in Levin, a few miles south of Palmerston. He was visiting relatives in Bestwood, Nottingham. He had been taken prisoner in Singapore and worked on the Burma Railway before being taken to Japan. With the few extra days I now had before my flight home, it was an ideal opportunity to visit him and see more of New Zealand. When I told Claude, he suggested I should go to Levin by coach. The first call in the morning was to book a two-day return trip. We then went into the country outside Auckland. Combine harvesters were working on the flatter fields and sheep grazed on the undulating hills. These dome-shaped hills had what looked like man-made steps but Claude told me they had formed perfectly naturally. The bird one saw most was the magpie, but it had more white on it than the British variety.

Returning to Claude's home after a pleasant outing, I phoned Eric to let him know I would be arriving in Levin the following day. Rising early, Claude drove me to the coach station. During the journey we spoke of the time we had spent on Haruku. 'Of course,' I asked, 'you remember Gunso Mori and Kasiyama – "Blood and Slime"? Although I was only there for a short time, I can never forget them. Mori was a sadistic brute, whose main pleasure was beating up any man reported to him by Kasiyama.'

'Here we are, Geoff. I will see you in a couple of days. Enjoy yourself,' said Claude.

On the coach journey we passed through the hills and valleys on twisting narrow roads, without seeing many other vehicles. First stop was the large tidal Lake Taupo, followed by the thermal spring at Rotorua. This seething mass of steaming bubbles provided heat to generate electricity on the island. After lunch, we travelled on to Palmerston, where many of the passengers left the coach. When we reached Levin, Eric and his wife Betty were there to meet me. Eric greeted me like a long-lost brother, although we had only met once before, in Nottingham.

After tea at their home, Eric told me he failed to understand why he had never seen any reference to the Sumatra Railway anywhere. I outlined how I had proceeded after the authorities told me in 1976 that there was no record of this railway being built, explaining: 'During the next three years, through local broadcasts and reunions I made contact with many who had worked on the railway. After I got a copy of the book *The Judy Story: The Dog with Six Lives*, I wrote to Hilton Stanton, who is named in the book. He worked with Frank Williams, Judy's keeper. I also made many journeys to Amsterdam to see Mr Hank Neumann, and others who had worked on the line. Hank gave me a copy of a letter written by the Japanese officer who had been in charge of the Sumatra Railway, pleading for his life, after being convicted of war crimes. He was hung in Medan Prison, Sumatra.'

I went on to tell him how, after submitting the evidence I had collected to the Imperial War Museum, everything was returned as there was no official record of the existence of this railway. 'Claude Thompson of Auckland had returned to Sumatra two years ago and suggested I contact the Caltex oil company in Jakarta, Java. He had not been able to find any evidence of the railway, apart from some derelict locomotives alongside the Siak River. It was this that made me decide to undertake this journey.' If my photographs taken along the route of the railway turned out well, they should prove beyond doubt that POWs built this railway.

That evening we spent at the local RSA club.[2] It would seem that few visitors were attracted to this small town, and one from 'home' was extremely rare. Everyone wanted to meet me. The bar closed at 10.00 pm, when the whole town seemed to die down, people making their way slowly home. No cars. No noise.

167

Eric was the warden of Kohitere Forest, a large area of hills above Levin. Early in the morning he invited me to accompany him to his hut on the highest point, from where he watched for signs of fire in the large area below us. Around midday, we ate our packed lunches and Eric phoned to report everything was in order. Later in the evening, after a good meal, we went again to the RSA club and met more of the friendly local people. The next morning, Eric drove me to the coach station for my return to Auckland. I thanked him and Betty for their kind hospitality and promised to keep in touch. As we said our goodbyes, Eric wished me every success in proving that the Sumatra Railway was built by prisoners of the Japs.

When the coach reached Palmerston there was an hour's wait before we continued on our journey. I took the opportunity to explore the town, which was reminiscent of quaint English seaside towns, with ornamental shop fronts and a pleasant, unhurried way of life. There were few vehicles. Back on the coach we passed through small villages and isolated farmsteads perched high on the hills. All these had water pumps driven by windmills, and sheep … lots of sheep! We had lunch at a small café – a full lamb roast and spotted dick and custard.

Claude and Margaret were waiting for me when we arrived in Auckland for my last night in New Zealand. I phoned my daughter Christine to give her my flight details. The next morning, Claude drove me to the airport and I found it hard to express my gratitude for their hospitality. 'Claude, if everything turns out well, I will send you copies of my films,' I promised, and then bade them farewell.

'Good luck, Geoff, all the best,' said Claude.

I boarded the British Airways jumbo jet for the long flight home. Soon we were taking off on the first leg to Melbourne, where the plane would refuel before heading for Bombay. On landing we were told we must stay on the aircraft as there had been a fire at the airport. This not only deprived us of a chance to stretch our legs, but also prevented the cleaning staff from coming on board. Now on the last lap, heading for home, I got a good view of the Alps as we crossed northern Italy. It seemed only a short time before the plane touched down at Heathrow. Soon I was passing through customs and there was Christine, Eddie, Darren and Dawn waiting to meet me.

'Hello, all of you, it's good to be back,' I said, giving the grandchildren a hug.

'I hope everything worked out, Dad. We were worried about you, knowing what you had undertaken, so it is good to see you arrive home again,' said Christine.

'I'll talk about it later. I'm all in now after twenty-six hours flying without sleep.'

'You need to put on something warmer. You're shivering.'

'Yes, I do feel cold, so would you get a pullover from my case, please? After weeks with the temperature 25°C plus, it is quite a contrast.'

We set off for home, but after what seemed just a matter of minutes to me, we drew into my drive. 'Here already?'

'Yes, it's taken just over three hours, stopping for a meal on the M1 motorway, and you never stopped talking all the way.'

After a cup of tea, I told them I must go to bed. 'I'll phone you at home tomorrow. Cheerio for now.'

Epilogue

Although I was anxious to see the results of my photography, I could not muster enough strength to take the films for processing for a few days. At last they were ready … now to see the results. Four rolls of one particular brand were completely blank – very disappointing as they covered Bali, Ambon, Haruku and part of Australia. Thankfully, there were few failures in the remainder and the most important being those of the railway, which turned out well considering the conditions under which they were taken. First of all, I had to have copies made from my negatives.

My most important task was to convince the Imperial War Museum that a railway nearly 200 miles long was built by prisoners of war through the jungle of Sumatra. I outlined my journey along the route of the railway, which the Caltex oil company had made possible. This I sent to the Imperial War Museum, together with photographs of locomotives and trucks deep in the jungle. I also included a photograph of the pillar marking the Equator, and a picture taken on 15 September by an Australian reporter showing No. 2 Camp Pakenbaru and another showing released prisoners under the wings of a DC-3 plane after it landed at Singapore on 20 September 1945. To complete the package I put in a copy of the report by Major Jacobs sent from Pakenbaru on 15 September 1945 and published in the South East Asia Command news-sheet, headed 'Living Dead Railway Slaves', plus the entry in the Pakenbaru newspaper recording my journey, after I met newsmen on 19 February 1990. Believing I had supplied sufficient evidence to warrant an entry being made into the war history, I waited for the result.

It came as a shock when, two weeks later, all the items were returned, together with a letter, stating: 'We have heard that some railway work was carried out in Sumatra by POWs but there is no record of a railway being built.' This seemed like the end of the line for me. I was devastated.

It was at the reunion of FEPOWS at the Festival Hall, London, that I met Mrs Jarvis again. Our last meeting was in Jakarta, Java, after she had been to Pakenbaru searching for evidence of the Sumatra Railway. She had been to the Imperial War Museum hoping to find out more about the railway but found nothing. She knew I had sent photographs and details of my journey along the route of the line to them as I had sent to her similar material. She failed to understand why it had again been rejected. I introduced her to others who had worked on the railway, hoping that someone might remember her cousin who died there just after the war ended.

Every year, I had spent a few days in Holland in order to attend a reunion in The Hague of former Sumatra Railway workers and to visit Mr Hank Neumann in Amsterdam, who wrote a book, *De Sumatra Spoorweg* (*The Sumatra Railway*), in which I am named as a contributor. It was in 1985 that Mr Neumann visited the Imperial War Museum and left a copy of his book with them. He had worked in Sumatra, which was part of the Dutch East Indies before the war, and had knowledge of the area. In 1992, he went along the various rivers to find remnants of the railway but had no means of travel between the rivers, along the jungle tracks, and I was able to fill in the gaps for him. A letter dated 30 July 1985, sent by Mr Phillip Reed, Deputy to the Keeper of the Department of Documents, told me of Mr Neumann's visit to the Imperial War Museum and that it appeared to be a definitive history of the Sumatra Railway. Five years after rejecting my evidence, the museum asked me to supply the photographs again. After another visit to the IWM in 1986, Mr Reed informed me that all the materials regarding the Sumatra Railway were now filed under my name.

In October 1986, I joined six other ex-RAF members for a journey to Java, and then on to Ambon and Haruku, where they had worked on the runway. This gave me the opportunity to take other photographs to replace the ones that had not turned out on my previous visit. We travelled on to Queensland to attend the reunion of FEPOWs, where I was able to meet other Australians who had worked on the Sumatra Railway.

In June 1988, a memorial was unveiled at Oosterbeek, Arnhem, Holland. This consisted of a pair of bogey wheels on a metre of rails spiked to three sleepers, which had been brought over from Sumatra. The plaque read: 'In memory of those who died building the Sumatra

Railway, between May 1944 and August 1945'. An estimated 10,000 natives also perished.

Finally, I was invited, along with several hundred members of the National Federation of Far Eastern Prisoners of War Clubs and Associations, to attend a reception at Guildhall, London, in the presence of Her Majesty Queen Elizabeth, The Queen Mother, on Tuesday, 9 December 1992, from 11.30 am to 2.00 pm.

Afterword
by Christine Bridges

My dad, Geoff Lee, what can I say? He came home from the war weighing 6 stone and no one believed that he'd been a prisoner of war building a railway in Sumatra, telling him instead he'd been in Burma. So he never talked about it again, until he spoke to my husband Eddie, in the 1970s. This fired up his determination to find other people he'd been with *where he had actually been*, and change history by providing the Imperial War Museum and Commonwealth War Graves Commission with proof.

During the 1980s and 1990s, Dad became Welfare Officer for the Nottingham and District FEPOW Association. He took his role seriously, providing support for veterans and family alike. He made many FEPOWS aware of the link between Strongyloides (a parasitic nematode worm that is common in tropical or subtropical climates) and digitalis (a drug obtained from the foxglove that is used to treat patients with heart disease as it strengthens contractions of the heart muscle). They are linked because the parasite stays in the body and if people who are infected with the parasite are then given digitalis, it causes a reaction that can lead to death. Once this was realised, anyone who had possibly been exposed to the parasite could have tests done over the course of a week in one of the hospitals for tropical diseases, in either London or Liverpool, and Dad arranged for many to have these done. Because of his work, he used to receive hundreds of Christmas cards every year, but never ever sent one to anyone … he didn't have time.

When in the late 1990s it was known that the National Memorial Arboretum at Alrewas in Staffordshire was being planned to honour the war dead and heroes, a friend of Dad's, Jack Plant, who had also survived the Sumatra Railway, wanted to erect a memorial to commemorate it. With input from my dad about the design, the memorial was based on a sketch by another FEPOW, Owen Greenwood, as well as on the Dutch Sumatra Railway memorial at Oosterbeek. Plans were drawn up between them and were approved by the NMA. Dad and Jack raised money for the construction from various ex-POW groups and they sourced materials from around the country, much of which were donated. It consists of a replica section of the Sumatra Railway, including wooden sleepers and railway track, set on an embankment, with a large pyramid-shaped memorial at one end of the track that has metal plaques inscribed with the details of the railway, and the names of those who built it and those who died in its construction (for more details, visit: iwm.org.uk/memorials/item/memorial/46466).

The memorial was unveiled on VJ Day, 15 August 2001, and was officially opened by Prince Charles and Countess Mountbatten on 14 May 2002, with Jack Plant in attendance, although Dad was too ill to attend on either occasion. Sadly, he never got to visit it and passed away in June 2002, but his name is included on one of the dedication plaques. His name is also in the list of FEPOWs involved in the building of the railway that is held by the Imperial War Museum in connection with the memorial. Defiant to the last, at his request the Cole Porter/Robert Fletcher song 'Don't Fence Me In' was played at his funeral.

Appendix I

Transcripts of the plaques on the pyramid-shaped memorial that was unveiled on 15 August 2001 at the National Memorial Arboretum at Alrewas, Staffordshire

Plaque 1

TRIBUTE

To Lady Edwina Mountbatten who flew into camp II at Pakanbaru unannounced, on 16th September 1945 to greet and comfort those P.O.W.s still awaiting repatriation. She made the journey at great risk to her own safety. The survivors salute a courageous lady.

ACKNOWLEDGEMENTS

We remaining British survivors acknowledge that this memorial would not have been possible without the support given by the following.

The National Memorial Arboretum Trustees and Staff.

The Severn Valley Railway PLC. Bewdley.

Railtrack, Euston House, London.

The Forestry Commission, West Midlands District.

Messrs. Ibstock Brick Ltd., Ibstock, Leicestershire.

Messrs. Trident Steel (Reinforcements), Hixon, Staffordshire.

Messrs. Hughes & Holmes, Willenhall, West Midlands.

Mr Stan Webb, Wood Craftsman, High St., Alrewas.

Mr Nadir Imamoglu, Architect, Long Lane, Essington.

And many others who contributed anonymously in various ways.

Presentation by Jack Plant and Geoff Lee (survivors) with acknowledgments to E. Van Witzen and H. Neumann (authors of 'The Sumatra Railway Documentation; 1982) and to D.W. Logchem of The Netherlands.

Plaques by: M.G.S. Signs of Willenhall, West Midlands.

Plaque 2

1944 THE SUMATRA RAILWAY – 1945

THE CONCEPT

During World War II, Sumatra, the largest island in Indonesia, fell to the Japanese. The island, 1,000 miles long, an asset to a warring nation by its geographical position and wealth of natural resources, was in fact quite wild territory having poor transport facilities; rivers had to be crossed by ferries; roads were few and far between; wild animals were in abundance. As the war progressed the threat of attack by the Allies from the west became imminent and the occupiers realised it was essential that facilities for moving troops and equipment from coast to coast quickly were improved. In fact a short length of rail-track from Padang, a port on the west coast, to Muaro about 40 miles inland, already existed. If that could be joined up with a port on the River Siak at Pakanbaru, then a quick route would be established east to west and vice versa. Such a rail link had been envisaged by the Dutch colonisers many years before but had not been acted upon because of the extremely difficult terrain. The Japanese occupiers having at their disposal a workforce of Allied POWs and native forced labourers (romushas) amounting to many thousands, determined to push ahead. Work began with parties working from each end in May 1944. The finishing date was to be 15th August 1945. The route would run through dense jungle, swamp and mountainous terrain; at halfway point it would straddle the equator.

THE PERSONNEL

To tackle the project the Japanese enlisted (1) the Japanese Railway Battalion 9th Regiment, some of whom arrived from Burma; (2) Guards from the Japanese 25th Army; (3) Korean conscripts to act as camp guards; (4) about 5,000 Allied POWs drawn from a variety of prison camps around Indonesia, and up to 30,000 romushas.

THE TOOLS

The heavy machinery of railtrack construction was imported from Burma, Malaya, Java and even from Japan. This included locomotives, steam and diesel powered; diesel trucks capable of running on rails or roads as necessary and open and closed wagons. Also imported were the engineering items such as rail-bending tackle and the track accessories; fishplates, some sleepers, spikes, gauges etc. and the hand tools like crowbars, sledgehammers, chunkels and what was commonly referred to as 'Chinese wheelbarrows', wicker baskets slung from bamboo poles. Also saws and axes from tree felling and making sleepers from jungle trees.

THE CAMPS

As work progressed laying the track, camps to accommodate POWs were set up in advance. To cover the 140 miles length, 14 camps were used, and discarded when no longer required. Camp I at Pakanbaru was the base camp for materials. The engineering workshops were here. Camp II was the base for personnel; the POW doctors had a sickbay here and the worst of the sick from up the line were brought back here for treatment. Camp VII at Lipat Kain was virtually on the Equator. Camp X was nearest the spot where the last spike was driven when parties working from either end met on 15th August 1945. The camp buildings were simple constructions in bamboo and rattan. Each billet accommodated about 50 prisoners on each side of a central gangway; each man had a space of about a half metre by a metre long, on a raised structure. Despite their simple construction the billets were reasonable shelters during heavy rain.

Each camp had a separate building set aside for cooking food.

All camps had 'tiger fires'; the threat from wild animals was real: evidence of their visits during the night was commonplace. The fires were maintained for 24 hours a day.

Round plaque mounted at one end of the replica railway section

SUMATRA RAILWAY
1944 – 1945
MEMORIAL
HIS ROYAL HIGHNESS
PRINCE CHARLES OF WALES
AND
COUNTESS PATRICIA MOUNTBATTEN
OF BURMA
VISITED THIS MEMORIAL
ON TUESDAY 14th MAY 2002
JACK PLANT
SURVIVOR IN ATTENDANCE

Appendix II

Poem written by Penry M. Rees MA, 239 Battery, 77th HAA (Heavy Anti-Aircraft Regiment) Royal Artillery, ex-POW Java and Sumatra

AT THE GOING DOWN OF THE SUN

To the south of Pakenbarue
    where the nightly tiger prowls,
And the Simians greet the morning
    with their ululating howls,
Through the Kampong Katabula
    and the district of Kuban
There runs a single railway track,
    a monument to man.

In a short and fretful period
    that was eighteen months of hell,
Through the tangle of the tropics
    and the oozing swamps as well,
Through the cuttings that they hollowed
    and embankments that they built,
They have laid a modern railway line
    on jungle trees and silt.

And in spite of tropic noonday
    and a host of wasting ills,
Ever southwards went the railway
    to Muara and the hills.

POW ON THE SUMATRA RAILWAY

Every sleeper claimed a body,
 every rail a dozen more,
'Twas the hand of fate that marked them
 as it tallied up the score.

Thirty times a score of prisoners
 fell asleep upon their back,
Thirty times a score of prisoners
 fell asleep beside the track,
Thirty times a score of times
 the sum of one immortal man,
Thirty times a score of ciphers
 in the councils of Japan.

On their ulcerated shoulders
 they transported rough-hewn wood,
With dying desperation
 carried more than humans should,
On their suppurating feet
 with beri-beri swollen tight,
From the rising of the sun
 until the welcome fall of night.

From the rising of the sun
 until setting of the same,
Theirs was just to grin and bear it
 and pretend it was a game,
Theirs was just to laugh and say
 they'd have a grill when it was done
And the cooling breath of ev'ning
 took the place of the scorching sun.

With the cooling breath of even
 came a leaven of repose,
And a narrow hard unyielding bed
 on which to rest their woes,
Just a width of rotten bedboard
 for a shrunken, rotten frame,

Where the bliss of sweet oblivion
    might eradicate the shame.

Yet the bliss of sleep's oblivion
    tarried long upon its way
While bedbugs left their havens
    for a drying, dying prey,
And the ants and the mosquitoes
    and the scorpions and the lice
Joined the rats and noisy chikchaks
    and the jungle's lesser mice.

So another day was over
    and another day was done,
So another day of misery
    was all too soon begun,
But the mighty Tenno Haika
    and the power of Japan
Can't recall a day that's done with
    -and Thank God there's no one can!

'Show a leg, my sleeping hearties!
    Oh, get up and rise and shine!
For the sky is blue and cloudless'-
    and they feared it would be fine.
There was breakfast for the hungry
    if their stomachs weren't too sour,
Made of boiling swampy water
    and of tapioca flour.

Back in England, paperhangers
    would refuse the mess,
But Japan must give them something
    and it couldn't give them less,
So they thought of those who loved them
    and with far, unseeing eyes
They consumed their mess of pottage,
    and the maggots and the flies.

There was someone trusting somewhere
    that a husband would return,
There were sweethearts praying softly,
    there were candle lights aburn,
There was God up in His Heaven
    and He knew about it all,
And He heard their falt'ring whispers
    and He listened to their call.

And they drew new strength from somewhere
    and they battled for their life,
Though the odds were overweighted
    in this too-unequal strife;
But they kept on carrying sleepers
    and they struggled with the rail,
And they still persisted hopeful
    when it seemed of no avail.

It was 'Kura!' and 'Canero!'-
    if you straighten up you shirk,
And the one excuse for living
    is a finished job of work.
'Twas the mercy of the Emperor
    that saved them from the gun,
There was nothing now to save them
    from the task they had begun.

There was nothing then to save them
    from the toiling and the sweat
But the saving grace of illness
    that was more exacting yet.
So they welcomed their malaria
    with its vomit and its ache,
So they welcomed their malaria
    for its semi-torpors sake.

There was dysentery, pellagra,
    and a host of sister ills,

Beri-beri and Bush Typhus,
    but no medicines or pills.
There was every cause for dying
    and but few for hanging on
When so many fell asleep and
    followed comrades who had gone.

It was tie them in a hurry
    in an old discarded sack,
With a plank of rough-cut timber
    to support them in the back.
It was lower them as gently
    as a withered muscle may,
And commend them to their Maker
    and remain a while to pray.

But for those they left behind them
    there were brutish things to bear
At the hands of brutish beings
    who were only well aware
Of the primitive upsurging
    of an animal delight
That enjoyed the thrills of torture
    and the quiverings of fright.

They could drag their aching bodies
    to their grass and timber huts,
They could rub the salt of impotence
    in open weals and cuts.
They could steel their will to conquer,
    to forget, perhaps to forgive,
But they found it mighty difficult
    to force themselves to live.

They had open huts of atap
    loosely tied to wooden poles,
And the roof and the partitions
    gaped and yawned in rotting holes.

Either side were filthy bedboards
    but a yard above the ground,
With a floor of earth and water
    and with refuse all around.

And to rest their weary bodies,
    overworked and underfed,
Sixty centis of this planking
    was their homestead and their bed.
Sixty centis night and morning,
    sixty centis well or ill,
Sixty centis for each body
    and it had to fill the bill.

Many talked of playing cricket:
    many said they played the game,
But they let the devil rider
    take the honest and the lame.
There are many will be tongue-tied
    when the trump of doom shall burst
On the ears of waiting sleepers,
    on the blessed and the cursed.

On the twenty-ninth of April
    there was nothing to be done.
On the birthday of the Emperor
    they rose to greet the sun,
And his Clemency Imperial
    made a fatherly decree
That the slaves might send a postcard
    to their wives across the sea.

When the Day at last arrived
    and when the rest of them were free
They devised a Union Jack
    and they displayed it on a tree,
And they thanked the God that made them
    that He let them live again,

POEM WRITTEN BY PENRY M. REES MA

And they prayed they might be better
  for the suffering and pain.

There they left their friends behind them
  thirty times a score or more,
Left them sleeping in the shadows
  on a distant tropic shore
And I pray to God Almighty,
  in the evenings of their lives,
Will be gentle to their parents
  and their children and their wives.

Pakenbarue, Sumatra 1944

* Penry M. Rees gave verbal permission for Geoff to reproduce this
  poem in his book. All efforts to contact Penry's living relatives to
  inform them of its inclusion here have been unsuccessful. Any reader
  who can provide details of how to contact them are invited to inform
  the editor (Christine Bridges) through the publisher.

Chapter Notes

Chapter 1: Farewell England

1. Correct modern-day spelling is Pekanbaru, the capital of the province of Riau in the eastern part of Sumatra Island, although Geoff spelt it Pakenbaru throughout his original manuscript and picture captions. It is spelt Paken Baroe in Geoff's pay book (although he had to fill this in himself, at a time when spelling would not have been the first thing on his mind). There are several other variants, including Pakan Baroe, Pakan Baru. On the memorial at the National Memorial Arboretum, Alrewas, it is spelt Pakanbaru.
2. RAF West Kirby at Larton, Wirral (although at that time in Cheshire), which was set up at the beginning of WW2 as a basic training camp for new RAF recruits. From 1940 to 1960, more than 150,000 young men passed through the camp, either en route to foreign parts in its early days or as recruits to be trained by the various drill instructors. (*see* rafwka.co.uk/id18.htm)
3. The coast of Sierra Leone was known as the White Man's Grave because of the high mortality rate amongst European missionaries and colonists who succumbed to malaria and other infections before the introduction of quinine in the 1850s.
4. Port Teufiq is Geoff's spelling of Port Tewfik (or Port Taufiq), now called Suez Port, which is to the west of the of the Suez Canal entrance.
5. This was in early January 1942. In his recollections of this meeting, Geoff recorded that the soldier was from the Royal Electrical and Mechanical Engineers, although the REME was not formed until October 1942 (from the Royal Engineers, the Royal Army Service Corps, the Royal Signals and Royal Army Ordnance Corps). Geoff didn't find out Jim was in the REME until he met him again after the

war so his assumption was incorrect about him being in the REME at this time and we now know that he was in the Royal Army Service Corps.
6. Giza.

Chapter 2: Where Now?

1. Krakatoa (also Krakatau).
2. This was Geoff's equivalent at the time of writing, which would have been in £/s/d in the 1940s.
3. Further research has shown that this information was not all correct and may have been broadcast for intelligence reasons.

Chapter 3: Java Journey

1. Kalidjati (usually Kalijati), Subang, West Java, where the Battle of Kalijati was fought from 1–3 March 1942 between the invading Japanese forces and the Dutch colonial forces over the control of the airfield.
2. Now Bandung.
3. Probolinggo, a city on the north coast of East Java province, Indonesia.
4. Geoff's pay book states that he was captured on 18 March 1942, perhaps reflecting that he may have been confused about the date at the time after three and a half years of captivity and torture.

Chapter 4: In the Bag

1. More commonly referred to nowadays as Yogyakarta.

Chapter 5: Garden of Eden

1. 6p is Geoff's estimate of the equivalent value of fifty cents at the time he wrote this part of the book; he would have been calculating in £/s/d, not decimal values, so we can assume he meant 6 old pence.

Chapter 9: Down But Not Out

1. An armed merchantman is a merchant ship equipped with guns for defensive purposes.
2. Although Geoff doesn't mention the name of the steamer here, it is almost certainly the *White Lady*, which is mentioned later in the text.

Chapter 12: Judy

1. We know there were three parties of POWs sent from Singapore to Pekanbaru/Pakan Baroe on the MS *Queen Elizabeth 2*, referred to as a ferry and known to Indonesians as *Kapul Putih*, or *White Ship*. The ship is believed to have vanished about 19/20 July 1944. It is unclear what date Geoff was on the ferry, but he also thought that the boiler had blown up while he was on it, although it could have been torpedoed.

Chapter 13: Is This the End?

1. Geoff's pay book records 43 Straits $ on 21 September 1945, although the Straits dollar was replaced by the Malayan dollar in 1939 (*see* https://en.wikipedia.org/wiki/Straits_dollar). We can only assume that the Straits dollar was still in use in some areas of commerce at the time or, perhaps, what was commonly known as the 'Straits dollar' was in fact the new Malayan dollar.
2. Geoff had no recollection of the sea journey back from Singapore; he zoned out on these sea journeys, as he explains in various parts of the book. It hasn't been possible to identify which ship he came back in as there are no passenger lists for them, although there is a list of the repatriation ships on a plaque at Liverpool Docks. It is thought he arrived in Liverpool on 16 December 1945, possibly in the *Atlantis*, although that is not listed on the plaque. There is a British Pathé film of this ship docking in Liverpool in December 1945, but when at the end of the film the soldiers are interviewed, they are repatriated from Europe, not the Far East. It is likely that the date is incorrect on the film as they would have returned much earlier in the year.

Chapter 16: Research

1. Varley, Edwin, *The Judy Story: The Dog with Six Lives*, Souvenir Press, 1973.
2. An unsuccessful initiative by the post-war British government to cultivate large tracts of its African trust territory with peanuts to supply margarine to Britain and to try to help this part of the British Empire to prosper.
3. Atjeh (Aceh) is on the northern tip of Sumatra, which had historically been a colony of the Netherlands. During WW2, the occupation by Japanese troops met resistance from the Acehnese, whose uprising in 1942 was considered a war crime by the Japanese, who, in retaliation, captured about 3,500 Dutch and native KNIL (Royal Netherlands East Indies Army) soldiers. Most of the natives were quickly released but some were interned in camp Lawe Sigalagala at Kutatjane, together with over a hundred Indo-European prisoners of war. The other POWs were concentrated outside Atjeh in April and May 1942, initially in the Uniekampong in Belawan, near Medan. The prisoners who stayed behind in Lawe Sigalagala were pressured in May 1942 to become heihos (auxiliary soldiers in the Japanese army). Most native former KNIL soldiers eventually agreed, but fifty-two of the Indo-European prisoners refused. The four leaders of this group were executed; the majority of the rest of them died from starvation in the prison of Kuala Simpang. Miyazaki Ryohei's letter implies that Maj Asami was being tried for Japanese war crimes committed against those who were captured during this incident.

Chapter 17: The Return Journey

1. Correct spelling is Kranji.

Chapter 18: The Railway

1. 1,400 rupiahs, equivalent to £1 at the time that Geoff was a POW.
2. As with some other place names, Geoff used the Dutch spelling Padang Pandjang, otherwise known as Padang Panjang.

3. Bukit Tinggi.
4. Correct spelling is Payakumbuh.

Chapter 19: Surprises

1. See plate section, page 1. The bottom photograph was taken by an Australian photographer at Singapore after Geoff's release from Sumatra on 20 September 1945. Geoff is sitting sideways with his malnourished body and bare back showing. The other photo was taken on his visit in 1980, when Geoff came across an old engine from the railway in Sumatra and then had his photo taken with local children.
2. It has not been possible to identify which organisation Geoff is referencing here.

Chapter 20: The Last Lap

1. In March 1942 the ship was scuttled by her crew at Tandjong Priok (port of Jakarta), as a blockade to stop the invading Japanese ships from entering the harbour. After the invasion the *Van Waerwijck* was refloated and then repaired by the Japanese and renamed as the *Harugiku (Harukiku) Maru*. The *Harugiku Maru* became one of the ships known as 'Hell Ships'.

   On 26 June 1944, the *Harugiku Maru* was transporting prisoners from Belawan (Medan) to Pekanbaru in convoy when she was hit by one of the two torpedoes fired by HMS *Truculent*. The ship then broke in two and sunk within minutes.

   The ship sunk around 100km south-east of Medan. It was carrying 1,190 POWs at the time of the sinking, with the loss of 198 lives. The survivors (including Judy, the POW dog) clung to debris and lifeboats for hours before being picked up by a passing tanker. The prisoners were transported to Singapore, staying there a month, before being transported to Pekanbaru, where they built the railway until the end of the war. (Taken from https://www.pekanbarudeathrailway.com/van-waerwijck, with thanks to Jamie Farrell.)
2. RSA club – one of many branches of the Royal New Zealand Returned Services Association.

Index